Russian Orthodoxy
under the Old Regime

Russian Orthodoxy under the Old Regime

Edited by
ROBERT L. NICHOLS
Associate Professor of History
Saint Olaf College

and

THEOFANIS GEORGE STAVROU
Professor of Modern Russian and Near Eastern History
University of Minnesota

UNIVERSITY OF MINNESOTA PRESS
MINNEAPOLIS

Printed at the North Central Publishing Company, St. Paul.
Published by the University of Minnesota Press,
2037 University Avenue Southeast, Minneapolis, Minnesota 55455,
and published in Canada by Burns & MacEachern Limited,
Don Mills, Ontario

Cover illustration:
Holy Trinity-St. Sergius Monastery. Western view.
A fragment from an eighteenth-century album.

Library of Congress Cataloging in Publication Data

Main entry under title:

Russian Orthodoxy under the old regime.

    Bibliography: p.
    Includes index.
    1. Orthodox Eastern Church, Russian — Russia — History —
Congresses. 2. Church and state in Russia — History —
Congresses. 3. Russia — Church history — Congresses.
I. Nichols, Robert Lewis 1942-   II. Stavrou,
Theofanis George, 1934-
BX491.R87   281.9'47   78-3196
ISBN 0-8166-0846-6
ISBN 0-8166-0847-4 pbk.

This volume is respectfully dedicated to
Father Georges Florovsky
in appreciation of his contribution to the
study of Russian Orthodoxy and culture.

Preface

Russian Orthodoxy during the two centuries before the Revolution could no longer claim to be completely integrated with Russian life. Peter the Great, of course, only bent the ties binding the church to its flock. Nevertheless, those years were a time of adjustment to the changes induced by Russian monarchs wishing to replace older traditions with a new outlook more in conformity with their design of Russia as a powerful national and European state. The attempt at imperial reconstruction of national life gives unity to this period in Russian Orthodoxy history by posing urgent questions which the church had to resolve. But beyond broad outlines, we still do not know much about the church's response.

American scholarship in this area is in its infancy, and much of the work currently being done is scattered and uncoordinated. In order to probe this neglected period, encourage further research, and bring a greater sense of purpose to the task, a conference on Russian Orthodoxy under the Old Regime was held at the University of Minnesota in April 1976, sponsored by the history departments of the University and Saint Olaf College. The essays in this volume derive from papers presented at that time. The participants were drawn from several disciplines, including history, philosophy, theology, and librarianship.

In addition to those taking a direct part in the program, a sizable number of invited scholars and students attended the two all-day sessions. The participation of the audience during the discussion period contributed substantially to a spirited symposium. It also demonstrated that interest in the study of Eastern Orthodoxy in general and Russian Orthodoxy in particular is much wider than is generally assumed.

This book presents the findings of some recent research on an important but neglected topic, offering for scholarly consideration some new interpretations of Russian Orthodoxy (at least of several of that subject's many facets) during the imperial era – interpretations often at variance with frequently encountered stereotypes. It arranges most of these interpretive studies under the umbrella of two broad essays on Orthodoxy in imperial Russia, in order that both students and the general public may gain some sense of the nature and significance of the whole topic. All of the essays also point out the rudimentary stage of development of our historical literature on Russian Orthodoxy.

No serious scholar doubts Orthodoxy's significance in Russian history and culture. Even Professor Richard Pipes in his most recently published work, *Russia under the Old Regime*, where he chooses to emphasize the negative aspects of the Orthodox church, devotes an entire chapter to the subject. In fact, there are signs that both in the Soviet Union and in the West Orthodox church history is now becoming an important area of inquiry. In the former, the work of N. N. Pokrovskii, *Antifeodal'nyi protest uralo-sibirskikh krest'ianstaro-obriadtsev v XVIII v.*, (Novosibirsk, 1974), deserves special attention because it is as enlightened about diocesan affairs and synodal-state politics as about the Old Believers. Pokrovskii has also directed a number of theses such as L. P. Shorokhov's "Tserkov' Sibiri v Kontse XVI-XVII vv." (Novosibirsk, 1971). In the West, too, interest is growing. Most of the authors in this volume have written doctoral dissertations on topics dealing with Russian Orthodox church history during the imperial era. These are good signs that scholarship on the subject under consideration merits and is beginning to receive respectable attention.

When the conference was in its planning stages, we did hope to include a third category that would have tried to put Russian Orthodoxy more directly in a world religious perspective. In other words, we had hoped that the church's relations with other religious groups, orthodox and nonorthodox, could be reexamined to give a better understanding of subjects such as missions and ecumenism as they relate to Russian Orthodoxy. In this context, the historic role of Russia and its relations with the Orthodox East could also be reexamined. For a number of reasons, chiefly economic, we had to postpone this topic until a future symposium, now being planned.

We should like to mention some dissertations completed or nearly completed at the University of Minnesota. This provides an opportunity to thank fellow scholars both in the United States and in the Soviet Union who have contributed to the training of these young people. These colleagues must know the extent of their contribution, but listing the dissertations may refresh their memories. If anything, this mention demonstrates the great need for professional and institutional cooperation for the adequate training of graduate students in this area of Russian history.

Most of these dissertations in the history department at the University developed out of the study of Russian-Near Eastern cultural relations or of the contacts of Russia with the Orthodox East. More specifically, they relate in one way or another to the question of Greek-Slavic cultural relations, which has received considerable attention at Minnesota. Most directly related to this field are the studies by Batalden of Eugenios Voulgaris in Russia and by Nelson of Konstantin Leontiev and the Orthodox East completed in 1975. Two years earlier, Peter Weisensel finished a dissertation in which he assessed the contributions of the traveler Norov to Russia's growing awareness of the Orthodox East. In the same year, James Cunningham wrote on reform in the Russian church, 1900-1906, a topic touched upon by Fr. Meyendorff in his essay in the present volume. In 1976, two studies dealt with the domestic and foreign concerns of the Russian church. The first, by Sawatsky on Alexander N. Golitsyn, concentrates on domestic changes, whereas Dyrud's on the Russian Question in Eastern Europe and in America examines, among other things, the question of ecclesiastical or cultural imperialism. The most recently completed study (1977), by Boerneke, deals with the response of the Russian church to ecumenical questions of the 1870s. Nearing completion are dissertations dealing exclusively with internal Russian affairs, such as the educational role of the Kiev Ecclesiastical Academy in the nineteenth century, and Orthodoxy and society in Tver province. Others go beyond the Russian frontier and are concerned with the Russian Missionary Society and Metropolitan Filaret's position with regard to the Eastern Question. The bibliography at the end of this volume includes detailed references to the completed dissertations. It is hoped that the essays in this book will contribute in some small way toward encouraging young scholars to devote more attention to the study of Russian church history.

In offering this volume to the public, we must acknowledge our indebtedness. Although his paper is not included among these essays, we should like to thank Professor George L. Kline for presenting to the conference his research on "Vladimir Solov'ev's Philosophical Theology: Orthodox or Heretical?" We also thank the other members who made the conference a success and initiated what Fr. Meyendorff subsequently hoped might become "a new beginning in the study of pre-Revolutionary Russia." Particular thanks go to our host, Professor Clarke Chambers, at that time Chairman of the History Department of the University of Minnesota, William Wright, then Director of the Office of International Programs at the University, and to President Sidney R. Rand, Dean William C. Nelsen, and Dr. Henry Fritz, Chairman of the History Department at Saint Olaf College. We are also happy to acknowledge the generous support and encouragement of Mr. Gordon Turner, Vice-President of the American Council of Learned Societies, and Dean Frank Sorauf of the University of Minnesota College of Liberal Arts. Additionally we thank the secretarial staffs of the history departments at the University of Minnesota and Saint Olaf College, especially Ms. Gretchen Asmussen and Mrs. Maryann LoGuidice, without whose enthusiastic and patient efforts this task would have been harder, longer, and less adequately performed. In addition to performing many other chores connected with the conference, Mrs. LoGuidice also typed the

entire manuscript. Special thanks are due to Urve Daigle for her artistic contributions. Finally, our thanks go to Ms. Susan Williams for
her various contributions to the organization of the conference and
its smooth operation.

Robert L. Nichols
Saint Olaf College
Theofanis George Stavrou
University of Minnesota

Contents

Preface vii

Introduction. 3
    Robert L. Nichols, *Saint Olaf College*
    Theofanis George Stavrou, *University of Minnesota*

Part I Church, Society, and Culture

Russian Orthodoxy and Society 21
    Donald W. Treadgold, *University of Washington*

Feofan Prokopovich and the Kiev Academy 44
    James Cracraft, *University of Illinois at Chicago Circle*

Orthodoxy and Russia's Enlightenment, 1762-1825. 67
    Robert L. Nichols, *Saint Olaf College*

Revolt from Below: A Priest's Manifesto on the Crisis in Russian
Orthodoxy (1858-59). 90
    Gregory L. Freeze, *Brandeis University*

Part II Church and State

Church and State in Imperial Russia 127
    Marc Szeftel, *University of Washington, Emeritus*

The Inquisitorial Network of Peter the Great 142
    Alexander V. Muller, *State University of California, Northridge*

The System of Nicholas I in Church-State Relations. 154
  David W. Edwards, *University of Arkansas*

Russian Bishops and Church Reform in 1905 170
  Father John Meyendorff, *St. Vladimir's Orthodox
  Theological Seminary*

The Idea of a Council in Russian Orthodoxy in 1905 183
  Paul R. Valliere, *Columbia University*

Sources and Archives

A Bibliographical Essay on the Documentation of Russian
Orthodoxy during the Imperial Era. 205
  Edward Kasinec, *Harvard Ukrainian Research Center*

Guide to Further Reading in Western European Languages 229

List of Contributors. 241

Index 247

List of Illustrations *(following page 114)*

1. View of the *Skit* Honoring the Beheading of St. John
   the Baptist at the Optina Monastery in Kaluga Province
2. Interior of Bethany Monastery, built by Metropolitan Platon
3. The Holy Synodal Typography in St. Petersburg
   at the end of the 1840s
4. Gethsemane *Skit* near the Holy Trinity-St. Sergius Monastery
5. Interior of Gethsemane *Skit*
6. Archbishop Feofan Prokopovich of Pskov
7. Metropolitan Filaret (Drozdov) of Moscow
8. Two generations of professors and rectors of Moscow
   Ecclesiastical Academy
9. A parish priest in modern times
10. Khar'kov pilgrims on a journey to Kiev's famous
    Monastery of the Caves
11. Members of the National Council of the Russian
    Orthodox Church in 1917-18
12. Easter celebration on St. Nicholas Day, May 1918
13. His Holiness Tikhon, Patriarch of Moscow and All Russia
14. Professor Nikolai N. Glubokovskii

Russian Orthodoxy
under the Old Regime

Introduction

Robert L. Nichols
Theofanis George Stavrou

It has been frequently asserted (or assumed) that the close identification of Russian Orthodoxy with the imperial government determined the church's status and future. Or, as John Curtiss put it, the church "would stand or fall with the power of the Tsar."[1] Yet the collapse of the Russian monarchy did not result in the destruction of Russian Orthodoxy, which apparently had other more durable supports that served it well despite the persecution it faced during the interwar years. Stalin's antireligious campaign brought the church to its knees by 1939; nearly half its parishes had ceased to function. Many hierarchs fell in the Great Purges. Numerous priests were arrested. As Bossuet said during another age of religious suffering, the church "experienced a great punishment." Still, the Communists and many western observers might have misjudged how deeply rooted Russian Orthodoxy was, as the religious revival in the USSR in recent years attests. The Soviet writer Vladimir Maximov, in his novel *The Seven Days of Creation*, has the Communist Andrei declare:

More than twenty years of Soviet power and their [the peasants'] heads are still full of incense. You hammer it into them over and over again— "There isn't any God, you're your own master." And still they stick to their old ideas. How long can you go on hammering? It's time people like them came to their senses.[2]

3

An important reason for this underestimation of the church's power derives from the investigators rather than their subject, for Russian ecclesiastical history is often regarded as something existing in isolation from the forces which generally shape society. When historians and others think about Orthodoxy as though separable from secular history, they acknowledge, however unconsciously, that they are studying an artifact, a curious survival of some earlier age which has no important place in the transformation of Russian society.

The identification of Russian Orthodoxy with every side of Russian life distinguished the church's history before the imperial era. In an illuminating passage in the seventeenth-century account of his life, the Archpriest Avvakum writes that

by the gift of God among us there is autocracy; till the time of Nikon, the apostate, in our Russia under our pious princes and tsars the Orthodox faith was pure and undefiled, and in the church was no sedition.[3]

For Avvakum church, autocracy, and society were one, and none could be changed without the others also undergoing alteration. He saw this plainly, feared western innovations when they came ("It was as if winter was of a mind to come; our hearts froze, our limbs shook"), and struggled against the new currents. "'How long, archpriest, are these sufferings to last?' asked his wife. 'And I said, 'Markovna! till our death.' And she, with a sigh, answered, 'So be it, Petrovich; let us be getting on our way.'"[4] In the end, Avvakum and others like him failed to stem the tide of change which overflowed into Russia from the West. From his day onward, the church found itself in a new social and political environment unlike that known in the Muscovite past, and was challenged to find new ways to survive and adapt. In this respect, Orthodoxy shared a fate with all other Russian organizations: its ideals received the same shocks administered to other institutions.

Two centuries of imperial rule posed new and unprecedented problems for the church: the loss of its patriarch, incorporation into the state administration, westernization of its clergy, and secularization of the social life in which it existed. The church suffered from severe deficiencies throughout this period, and in many ways it proved inept at dealing with the new challenges to doctrine and discipline. Like other churches at different times, it occasionally resorted to coercion to pro-

mote its ends. Yet the Orthodox church was more than a source of coercive power or a depository for outworn ideas and rules. For its members it was the ark of the covenant, and, despite all the inroads of secular life and a growing inability to provide "warmth" to its believers, Orthodoxy still gave most men and women an intelligible purpose and
place in God's universe. To this it added the gift of salvation—the ultimate and exclusive possession of its members.

Much of the existing knowledge of Orthodoxy in this period
amounts to no more than a survey of outward forms and constitutes
only a preliminary step toward an understanding of the inner energies
of its organizations. Even in the essays included in this volume, the individuals, institutions, and offices dealt with are the most articulate or
most prominent ones. If we descend to the lower levels of parish and
monastery, we encounter a large mass of Orthodox Christians whose
thoughts and experiences are at present largely unknown. In many
respects we are more fully informed about the Russian sects existing on the fringes of the church. Much still remains to be done in examining and classifying the records of Russia's Orthodox religious life
during the imperial era; yet only when Orthodoxy is studied as an aspect of secular history can we begin to understand the church's limits
and strengths and the ways in which it may be said to be continuous
with the present-day church or separated from modern Soviet life by
the great divide of the Revolution.

The essays that follow are arranged in two parts, one examining Orthodoxy's role in Russian social and cultural life during the imperial
era, the other dealing with the church's relationship to the tsarist regime. An effort has been made to introduce the reader first to a general
survey of each of these broad topics. Thus, Professors Treadgold and
Szeftel inquire into the reasons why the church occupied the position
it did in Russian history before 1917 and into its strengths, shortcomings, and prospects during that period. The papers that follow these introductory essays and constitute the bulk of the volume raise specific
analytical questions: How did Peter I approach church reform, with a
preconceived program or experimentally? By what precise steps did
Nicholas I attempt to reduce the church to a bureaucratic department
of state? What was the outlook of an educated Orthodox bishop at the

outset of the eighteenth century and how was it formed? Which elements proved to be the formative ones in the attempt to refurbish and strengthen the clergy during the era of the Great Reforms? What contributions did the church make to education and the development of Russia's national life?

Lenin considered the priest one of the two essential elements needed by an exploiting class to maintain its dominance, the other being the executioner. Yet Orthodoxy as a religious, social, and cultural force during the imperial era appears to have been something other than an instrument of class exploitation. The uncongenial environment provided by Peter's "reform" of the church, of course, seriously hampered its capacity to discharge its educational, pastoral, sacramental, and theological duties. How well the church performed these major social functions is the subject of Professor Treadgold's historical survey of "Russian Orthodoxy and Society."

As an educator, the church achieved only modest success. One is compelled, however, to agree with Professor Treadgold that, modest though it may have been, it was much greater than is generally assumed. During the imperial period, the church's primary efforts in education were devoted to the development of the clergy. Numerous examples can be cited to show that only a small portion of them received adequate instruction and that the village *pop* (priest) was often ignorant and disinterested in theology. Moreover, serious obstacles lay in the path of an Orthodox education suited to a Russian pastor working in Russian society. For much of the eighteenth century and part of the nineteenth, Protestant scholasticism and the Latin language formed the core of a curriculum which gave many clergymen a westernized outlook quite distinct from that of their parishioners; not until the 1830s was Russian adopted as the language of instruction. The quality of church schools apparently improved throughout the nineteenth century, despite the fact that, in Professor Treadgold's words, "the level of knowledge of many seminarians remained abysmally low." Yet, on the eve of the Great War, the Orthodox theological academies—the highest ecclesiastical schools, "located at the gateway to Asia and led by people conscious of both universality and locality"—did achieve standards "comparable to those anywhere in Europe." Moreover, as late as 1905, church schools constituted nearly half (46%) of those devoted to primary Russian education.

By the early 1900s, thoughtful Orthodox observers began to recognize that the church was losing its attraction for many Russians. Sheer paperwork crushed the efforts by bishops to overcome separation from their flocks. The parish priest was often better situated in this regard, but grinding poverty, semiofficial status, and narrow education handicapped his effectiveness. Pastorally, the Orthodox church began to fail from what V. Sokolov described as the lack of "autonomous" (*samodeiatel'naia*) life. Professor Treadgold aptly quotes Vladimir Solov'ev's remark that the church "slumbered under the canopy of state tutelage." One is tempted to speculate that the visible signs of peasant loss of identity with the church were in some way related to the withdrawal of peasant loyalty from the crown. However, in the years just before the Revolution, Orthodoxy experienced a number of popular religious movements such as those led by Father John of Kronstadt and Ivan Churikov which indicate that it still possessed a vitality and importance in the lives of peasants greater than that which sustained popular allegiance to the tsar. In any case, the church, like the peasantry itself, endured the Revolution, whereas the monarchy did not. Also, perhaps these manifestations of Orthodox vitality encouraged some of the westernized intelligentsia (e.g., Merezhkovskii) to see the church as a possible bridge across the gulf separating educated society from the peasantry.

The church found greater reward in performing its sacramental functions. Professor Treadgold reminds us that the ordinary parishioners attending the liturgy "felt that it brought them close to the divine," and adds that the Orthodox liturgy has a beauty which does not escape even the most secular visitors to a Russian Orthodox church. In this regard, one is further reminded of Mary Matossian's description of the role played by the village church:

The Russian peasants acted out the drama of life in a world whose central focus was the church in the *selo*. The church was the meeting place for heaven, earth, and the world underground. From heaven to the altar and down into the crypt; this was the peasant's *axis mundi*.[5]

Instances of the Orthodox church engaged in issues involving theological principles are provided by events during the late imperial period: anti-Semitism, enforced conversions to Orthodoxy, and relations with the state. Professor Treadgold rightly contends that the church had no actual policy of anti-Semitism, and although examples can be found of individual hierarchs supporting such reactionary groups as the Union of the Russian People, it is easy to find examples of hierarchs who opposed pogroms. Parish priests, as well, "often appeared not to take either side." As for toleration, non-Orthodox religions professed by non-Russians and non-Ukrainians frequently received equal or better treatment within the empire than did the Orthodox church. Generally speaking, the church reacted sharply to other faiths only when the Orthodox converted to them. Professor Treadgold points out, however, that the Orthodox authorities made perhaps their most egregious error when they connived at or accepted the state's use of compulsion to break the organizational link of the Uniats with Rome. Professor Treadgold's discussion of theology helps to clarify the church's relationship to the state. While remaining under state control throughout the imperial era, the church adhered to the basic Christian position of acknowledging the claims of existing civil authority without exempting the state from the roster of those human institutions standing under divine judgment. Moreover, after the Duma was established, clergymen could be found among the Kadets and revolutionaries as well as among the parties of the right, which indicates that the picture is more complex than a simple identification of the church with the Old Regime. Thus, the church's balance sheet on theologically related issues reveals pluses and minuses which as yet invite no final conclusions about its performance during the last two centuries before the Revolution.

Whatever its actual record in discharging its theological functions, during the reign of Nicholas II the church witnessed the passage of Russia's foremost intellectuals from Marxism through "idealism" to Orthodoxy: a journey interrupted by the Revolution but renewed in our times by such Christian writers as Akhmatova, Mandelshtam, Pasternak, Tarsis, and Solzhenitsyn. Professor Treadgold voices the thoughts of many when he concludes, "In 1977 there is, in the view of many, only one major religious prophet alive: Alexander Solzhenitsyn. . . . He comes directly out of the traditions formed in the Orthodox church during the imperial period, especially its later portion. That fact ought to say something about the desirability of studying and understanding the topic more fully."

An essential step in understanding Orthodoxy during the imperial era is an examination of its contributions to "high culture." Many have denied that such contributions were made, least of all during the eighteenth and nineteenth centuries. Chaadaev's famous dismissal of the Russian church in his first "Philosophical Letter" has often served as a manifesto for those taking this view. Of course, the church—that is, its educated clergy—did lose many of its ties with both Muscovite traditions and the Greek churches. Instead, its cultural orientation steadily shifted westward. As Professor Cracraft's essay in this volume so well indicates, the transformation in the outlook of Russian bishops goes back at least to the formative years of Russian Orthodoxy's modern history. Professor Cracraft focuses his attention on Feofan Prokopovich, Peter's close collaborator in church reform; yet his research has a significance beyond the purely biographical facts it adduces about Feofan. The biography of a Russian bishop provides a particularly advantageous, if restricted, point for observing the split between the educated clergy and the rest of the Russian Orthodox churchmen and believers. Moreover, a look at Feofan's "early years" gives some insight into the world which shaped his life and outlook and suggests why Peter I found a man of his caliber and temperament suitable for enlistment in his reform program.

Feofan received his education during the golden age of the Kiev academy in the Polonized Ukraine and then in Rome at the College of St. Athanasius. He became intimately familiar with Roman Catholic scholasticism, Latin, classical literature, Italian sixteenth-century classicism, as well as being exposed to the artistry and scientific learning of Europe's most cosmopolitan city. Thus by the age of twenty-one, Feofan could be described as a formally well-educated cosmopolitan with a love of learning, not only for itself, but for what it could obtain and for its capacity to improve individuals and institutions. These qualities, among others, made him the ideal reformer of Russian Orthodoxy along Peter's westernizing lines. Moreover, this sort of background enabled a number of similarly educated Orthodox hierarchs to redirect the outlook of the church toward a new western goal. As a teacher and rector of the Kiev academy (1705-16), Feofan, the "Russian Cicero," used his knowledge of classicism to create a new and lasting tradition of poetry at the academy. His earlier attention to science in Rome enabled him to draw more widely from advanced scientific thinkers (Galileo, Descartes, Boyle, and Johann Zahn) than his predecessors. But most importantly, Professor Cracraft observes, Feofan brought to his teaching a "freedom of inquiry" which above all gave his theological lectures a radical quality. Hence, this study of Feofan implies what Fr. Meyendorff observes elsewhere in this volume, that outside its "cultic" functions, the clergy (high and low alike) found in education and culture the greatest areas for social participation.

Certainly by Catherine's reign educated churchmen and church schools had become a significant force, even if that force has not always been recognized. In his essay "Orthodoxy and Russia's Enlightenment, 1762-1825," Professor Nichols maintains that, contrary to the widely held belief that it acted during the imperial period as an anti-intellectual force, the Russian Orthodox church played a profoundly important role in Russia's national development. The church schools formed in the eighteenth century contributed greatly, both directly and indirectly, to the growth of Russian law, medicine, and the learned professions by providing many students and teachers for Russia's professional schools and by furnishing the bulk of the necessary secondary and preparatory educational institutions.

Moreover, Professor Nichols contends that during this period, in education and outlook, educated Orthodox clergy existed in a world not radically different from that of educated Russian nobles. Drawing on the examples of two outstanding clergymen—metropolitans Platon (Levshin) and Filaret (Drozdov)—he attempts to demonstrate that their interests and views had many points in common with the western-educated gentry. Furthermore, monastery seminaries and noble "boarding schools" had more than a passing resemblance to one another. Far f om being isolated from the West of freemasonry, deism, sentimentalism, pietism, and idealism, to which the gentry was attuned, educated churchmen faced in the very same direction and for a brief time even anticipated the gentry's interest in philosophical idealism. Thus it was not the church's anti-intellectualism or isolation from the thought of the West and western-educated nobles which constituted its greatest danger. "As a consequence of the wholly western education which the clergy received, and in light of the ideals it inspired in the church's representatives, there was a real danger that the church might become simply a western institution." Nevertheless, some Orthodox hierarchs, particularly Metropolitan Filaret, recognized this problem and attempted to recover the "true face of Orthodoxy." By this attempt, the church schools took their first tentative step toward providing an education that could advance not only western but Russian thought as well. Thus, the greatest contribution of the church and its schools may lie not only in the number of professors, lawyers, and doctors the church and its schools helped to provide and train, but also in the schools' recovery and nourishment of Orthodox tradition, which ultimately served as an inspiration for such thinkers as Dostoevsky and Vladimir Solov'ev who "believed that Russia could discover something of universal value within itself only by proceeding from the soil of Orthodoxy."

These accomplishments, however, should not be allowed to obscure the fact that by the mid-nineteenth century Orthodoxy faced grave problems. Professor Freeze, on the basis of new archival research in the USSR, examines the celebrated case of a provincial priest, I.S. Belliustin (1819-90), who endeavored to awaken the public to one such problem: the impoverished life of the parish clergy. Although historians have given little attention to the "Belliustin affair," it was a sensational case at the time, marking in Professor Freeze's view the birth of "clerical liberalism" and "a sharp dividing line between the Nikolaevan epoch and the new era of ecclesiastical Great Reforms." The controversy began with the appearance of Belliustin's exposé, *A Description of the Rural Clergy (Opisanie sel'skogo dukhovenstva)*, published anonymously in Leipzig in 1858. Among other things, the book constituted an attack on the monastic hierarchy at at time when it was seeking to recover lost privileges and the state was edging toward ecclesiastical reform. Church distrust of Belliustin and possible state-imposed uncanonical changes led to his disgrace; reform was postponed. Professor Freeze's richly detailed study of the ecclesiastical politics surrounding the Belliustin affair helps to show why this major institution alone remained unaltered during an era of "Great Reforms." It also makes clear how important was the state's conditioning influence on the relationship between church and society. Indeed, all the essays in the first part of this volume assume the dominant role of the state in church life as an essential part of the background for their subjects. Historians of Orthodoxy omit its relationship with the state at their peril. However, that relationship was more complex than is suggested by the frequently encountered description of the church as simply the "handmaiden of the state."

Therefore, it is useful to ponder the long history of church-state relations as outlined by Professor Szeftel, who emphasizes two enduring and shaping elements: the Byzantine-Muscovite legacy and a Protestant-inspired but essentially secular pattern. The Byzantine, and especially Muscovite, legacy proved more durable than one might suppose, for the emphasis on the religious and mystical aspects of the tsar's power "continued to resonate strongly in the popular mind, not only after 1721 but until the Revolution in 1917." Moreover, before 1721 the authority of the church and that of the tsar had blended to create a popular impression of diarchy, thereby laying a religious foundation for church-state relations. Subsequently this Muscovite legacy gave the church "the possibility to construe its subjection to the state not as subordination to lay authorities, but to the divine right monarch."

After 1721, the Petrine reform produced a new relationship between the tsar and the church, based on the Protestant model of state administration of the church through the Holy Synod (which replaced the patriarchate) and its lay representative, the overprocurator. From the moment of the Synod's creation, the church steadily lost its independence. By 1817, the overprocurator had become the sole intermediary between the Synod and the emperor; by 1835, he had achieved the status of cabinet member. From 1842, even the permanent ecclesiastical members of the Holy Synod were sometimes not summoned to its meetings. Despite the efforts of some churchmen, the legal reforms of 1864 left this increased juridical dependence of the church unaltered.

From the church's point of view, the constitutional changes adopted in 1906 created a confused and potentially dangerous situation. By insisting on the religious foundation of church-state relations, the tsar attempted to prevent the newly created Duma from interfering in church administration. Nevertheless, through its budgetary powers, the Duma steadily succeeded in asserting itself. Faced with these actions, many in the church and in the Duma called for the summoning of a national synod or council (*sobor*), that is, an autonomous religious body which could legislate for the church and which would enable it to recoup its lost liberty. Professor Szeftel's conclusions deserve particular attention: despite all difficulties, on the eve of the Revolution, the recovery of independence was possible and "some light at the end of the tunnel could be seen for the Russian church during the last years of the empire."

The remaining papers in this section explore in greater detail some features of church-state relations during the imperial era. Professor Muller examines Peter I's introduction of "inquisitors," or churchmen charged with the supervision of church administration at the intermediate and lower levels. These inquisitors had their parallel and prototype in the secular fiscals who carried out administrative and judicial supervision on behalf of the Ruling Senate. By Muller's focusing on this relatively neglected aspect of the Petrine experiment in church administration, Peter's intentions and his experimental approach toward church reform become clearer. Although the inquisitorial network ultimately proved a failure, it provides an instructive example of Peter's efforts to fix *raison d'état* as the "principle of highest public priority" and illustrates his attempts to modify the church's administration in order to achieve affinity with the organs of state administration.

After roughly a century, the process of assimilation had gone quite far, as Professor Edwards shows in his study of church and state under Nicholas I. He contends that Nicholas intended to integrate the church fully into his general system of imperial government and stresses that Nicholas wanted more than tidiness in church administration; he wanted complete unanimity: "not . . . intellect and interpretation, but . . . the precise meaning of the dogma," as the emperor put it. After a period of trial and error, Nicholas found in Count Protasov an able overprocurator who could translate this conception into practice. By concentrating on legal codification, Nicholas attempted to hedge in

the church by elaborate state laws. Through bureaucratic reorganization, his assistant Protasov in effect tried to transform the Synod into
a ministry. Finally, various methods, including police denunciations,
were employed to undermine ranking hierarchs. Such tactics cul-
minated in a tragic clash in the Synod in 1842. When the metropolitans
Filaret of Moscow and Filaret of Kiev failed to shield the Russian translation of the Bible from sharp criticism, Protasov, the "Patriarch in a
soldier's uniform," ordered both men from the Synod. After that,
Professor Edwards contends, the Russian Orthodox church became
fully incorporated in a centralized, bureaucratic, lay-dominated administration.

State domination of the church had serious consequences for its
vitality and led many churchmen and laymen to ponder its problems
and future. Since the church's formal structure remained largely untouched by the Great Reforms, its problems continued to grow larger
and more insoluble. Thus, it is not surprising that by 1905-6 great excitement should have surrounded the question of church reform, an excitement which burst into the open with the revolutionary agitation of
those years. "Two months ago we neither expected nor intended anything of this sort – and not only we poor mortals but even the very
people standing in the forefront of the reform," exclaimed V. Skvortsov, the editor of *Missionary Survey (Missionerskoe obozrenie)*, in
January 1905. In that year the Russian hierarchy began to review systematically many of the difficulties and possibilities to which Professor Treadgold alluded in his introductory essay. Fr. Meyendorff provides a more detailed picture of how in 1905 the Russian episcopate,
armed with a complete awareness of Russian Orthodoxy's many shortcomings, attempted to take a comprehensive view of the church and its
dependent relationship to the state. Overprocurator Pobedonostsev provided the occasion when he requested that the Russian bishops be asked
if they desired reform. Apparently he hoped they would reply with a
resounding no, but when the *Replies (Otzyvy)* came back, it was clear
that the bishops had some ideas of their own on church administration. Paramount among their thoughts were the composition, procedures, and agenda for a future council (*sobor*) of the entire Russian

church. But the elaboration of these questions required a discussion of such matters as decentralization of church administration (actually the bishops seemed to be grappling with the ways in which the church might acquire an adequate ecclesiastical structure, including a patriarchate), divorce, relations of the clergy with the life of society, and so on. Fr. Meyendorff briefly indicates how these problems were posed in the *Replies*. Throughout their commentaries the bishops repeatedly emphasized that all aspects of church life needed to be brought into conformity with canon law and church traditions. For example, the issue underlying decentralization of church administration was the uncanonical dependence of the church on the state. At one point several bishops invoked apostolic canon 30 invalidating episcopal appointments made "by worldy rulers." However, any rigid adherence to that canon could not be realistically countenanced. A literal interpretation of it "would actually mean that *all* the episcopal appointments since Peter were invalid!" Thus came the recognition that canonical "norms" rather than their literal application should be the church's objective.

The solutions to the problems suggested in these *Replies* show the church hierarchy groping for new answers amid the changing currents of Russian life. How could the clergy participate more meaningfully in society both in their clerical duties and as citizens? Should a priest or a bishop seek elective office or participate in "politics" at all? Fr. Meyendorff comments that "the bishops were aware of the difficulty of precisely demarcating those 'politics' forbidden to the clergy from those 'social responsibilities' which are an unavoidable part of the church's functions. Clearly, but understandably, they lacked practical experience in such matters."

Fr. Meyendorff in conclusion notes a possible criticism that all the proposed reforms could not yield lasting solutions until common ecclesiological presuppositions were agreed upon. Still, the *Replies* provide a cross section of the church both in the capitals and in the dioceses—in the major theological academies as well as among the provincial clergy. They also give us a glimpse of several men who became the leading personalities of Russian church history during and after the 1917 Revolution. Finally, the *Replies* make clear that the frequently encountered stereotype of a hierarchy happily content with the "privileged" position of state church and oblivious to its inadequacies or dependence on the state can no longer be maintained.

Unlike the other essays in this volume, which approach the subject of church and state from a legal, political, or social standpoint, Professor Valliere takes his point of departure from theology. Studying the same events as Fr. Meyendorff, he argues that by concentrating on the "idea of a council," or *sobor*, we have an opportunity to explicate "the mind of the Russian Orthodox majority on one of the leading problems of the period." Professor Valliere stresses that several reasons make the idea of a council a good starting point for discussion. First, the idea of a council raised the question of the distribution of power; one of the main foci was the problem of church and state. But this question was not primarily one of politics but rather of the proper structure of the church. At stake were "the proper form of authority and even Orthodox communal identity." Thus, the idea of a council not only posed a question of power, but it demanded a theological answer. Second, the idea of a council became a powerful social symbol: the council possessed the "mystique of *sobornost*," which might in one sense be defined as an "assent to Orthodoxy." The *sobor* as social symbol has a special relevance, for it was part of the social change provided by "modernity." Conceptions of it varied from emphasis on a "liberal historic" view to a "spiritualizing-ideal" approach, and at the center of these interpretations was the question of the proper role to be assigned to the bishops. However different the approaches to reforms may have been among the various groups (and they should not be minimized or exaggerated), in the face of the "unprecedented religious situation imposed by modernity" these divisions did not prove irreconcilable. As it turned out, however, such deliberations did not result in any reform under the Old Regime, but they did help prepare the way for the All-Russian Council of 1917-18.

An important purpose of the present volume is to encourage the study of Russian Orthodoxy. In this regard, Professor Kasinec's bibliographical essay performs a much-needed service by surveying the basic Russian literature and bibliography on the church. Perhaps his most important conclusion is that bibliographical classification thus far has shaped the direction of research on the subject; every investigator needs to be conscious of this fact; otherwise preestablished categories rather than the researcher command the sources. Professor Kasinec's presentation, together with the bibliography at the end of this volume, should serve as a suitable starting point for further research.

The ten essays contained in this book constitute a report on the status of current research more than they represent fully integrated studies of all the important elements of Orthodox history in imperial Russia. It is hoped that they will illuminate some aspects of the history of Russian Orthodoxy as well as bring the church into the mainstream of research. In one way or another, the church united all Orthodox Russians of every social class. Orthodoxy was always an integral part of Russia's national heritage; from very early times it entered into the culture, the speech, the daily life of the people. Despite changing governments and social orders, Orthodoxy endured. Yet neither its survival nor its contributions to Russian life are as widely known and appreciated as they deserve to be.

NOTES

1. John Shelton Curtiss, *Church and State in Russia: The Last Years of the Empire, 1900-1917*, New York, 1940, reprinted 1965, 32.

2. New York, 1975, 114.

3. Serge A. Zenkovsky, ed., *Medieval Russia's Epics, Chronicles, and Tales*, New York, 1963, 363.

4. *Ibid.*, 329, 342.

5. Mary Matossian, "The Peasant Way of Life," in Wayne S. Vucinich, ed., *The Peasant in Nineteenth-Century Russia*, Stanford, 1968, 39.

PART I: CHURCH, SOCIETY, AND CULTURE

Russian Orthodoxy and Society

Donald W. Treadgold

It has long been assumed that Alexander Sergeevich Pushkin and St. Serafim of Sarov were mutually ignorant of each other's existence throughout their lives. (By the nature of things the proposition cannot be proved right, though it is theoretically possible for it one day to be proved wrong.) If Pushkin, the greatest of Russian writers, and St. Serafim, the greatest of modern Russian saints, lived in two mutually impermeable worlds, then the Russian Orthodox church must have been foreign indeed to the realm of high culture, and the area of cultural creativity must have been oblivious to the life of the church. The generation in question was perhaps the one which of all generations in Russian history experienced the maximum extent of estrangement between the westernized intellectuals of the cities and the Russian culture of the unlettered *narod*. And yet it is a striking illustration of the cultural gulf that was so significant to the determination of the fate of the Russian people during the Revolution. I should not wish to leave this example, however, without noting that in the reign of Nicholas I the intellectuals were even more cut off from old Russian culture than was the Russian church from the West that inspired the intellectuals; indeed, the impress of western ideas on the church, in the eighteenth and early nineteenth centuries in particular, remains little understood

21

despite the modest efforts some of us have made to restore perspective to this question.

The separation of the westernized intellectuals from Russian culture and from the Orthodox church was only one of the consequences of Russia's intensified contact with the West. Such contacts had occurred sporadically for centuries; they became a good deal more significant than before in the seventeenth century, partly in connection with the complex developments attending the schism of 1667 and following it. But it is still true, as long and widely thought, that Peter I's ecclesiastical "reforms" had a pervasive and profound effect on the Orthodox church and on its relation to society (using the term in our sense rather than *obshchestvo* in the meaning it had acquired by the nineteenth century).

Those "reforms" had a substantial effect on Russian intellectual and cultural history. My subject here, however, is the manner in which the relations between the Orthodox church and society changed from 1717 to 1917, a matter of social rather than cultural history, though the latter is not unrelated and cannot be entirely omitted from a study focusing on the former. The Petrine "reforms" established an institutional dependence of the church on the state, a dependence that determined how the church should operate in a variety of ways. During the subsequent two centuries, there were repeated attempts to discharge the ecclesiastical functions of the church as the church thought proper, though not until the twentieth century was there a perceptible movement directed toward recovering the church's legal and institutional autonomy. The functions under consideration may be classified under four general headings: (1) educational, (2) pastoral, (3) sacramental, and (4) theological.

The exercise of all four functions was dependent on the monarchy from the time of Peter I's ecclesiastical reform (or, perhaps, "revolution"). This reform was carried out from 1717, the date to which the ascendancy of Feofan Prokopovich as Peter's chief adviser for cultural affairs may be assigned, culminating in the *Ecclesiastical Regulation* of 1720 and the creation in 1721 of the body which became the Holy Synod. It was charged with a series of responsibilities: the preservation of the uncorrupted doctrine of Orthodox Christianity and proper norms for the conduct of church services, the combating of heresy and schism, the verification of reports concerning miracles and saints, the extirpation of superstition, the supervision of preaching, the choice of worthy hierarchs (bishops, archbishops, and metropolitans), the supervision of ecclesiastical schools, the censorship of ecclesiastical books, and several others.[1] As one might have expected, more time and effort was devoted to certain of these tasks than others. Other specified problems, formerly handled by clergymen, were taken out of clerical hands and assigned to civil courts—for example, inheritances or marriages contested for one reason or other. More significant was the question of the sense in which the Holy Synod's legal responsibilities may be said to have been exercised by the church. The Synod was made up of clerics, but it was itself subjected to state control and its individual members at a given moment may have reached their ecclesiastical positions by state action. From the creation of the Synod until 1742 the Moscow diocese, for example, lacked even its own bishop and was directly administered by the Synod. The Synod was not a body of the church but of the state; it was a kind of Lutheran consistory, "an administrative body of clerical and lay officers appointed by civil authority to administer ecclesiastical affairs" (Webster's dictionary definition).

As monarchs changed frequently in the eighteenth century, so did the name and character of the Synod. First called the Ecclesiastical College (using the terminology of Peter I for other governmental agencies he created), within a few months it was renamed Most Holy Governing Synod. The Monasterial Prikaz was transferred from control of the Senate to that of the Synod, and renamed Kamer-kontora in 1724. In 1726 the Synod was divided into two bodies. One was an Ecclesiastical Synod, composed only of clergymen, concerning itself with the ecclesiastical affairs; the other, called College of Economy of the Synodal Administration, consisted of secular persons and occupied itself with the financial affairs of the church. In 1738 the latter body was placed under the supervision of the Senate. Under Elizabeth, who became empress in 1741, the Synod was once again dubbed "Governing," and the College of Economy was taken back into it under the name Synodal Chancellery of the Economic Administration. Under

Catherine II the chancellery was abolished, at about the same time that ecclesiastical lands were "secularized." All these changes reflected changes in rulers and their advisers, not the initiative of the church; what is more, it is unclear which of them were real and which remained on paper.

In the early years the overprocurator (*oberprokuror*) of the Synod had little significance. The very first, Col. I.V. Boltin, was arrested at the instance of Feofan Prokopovich, Peter I's trusted adviser for religious and cultural affairs after 1717. Only after Elizabeth named Prince I.P. Shakhovskoi to the position at the end of 1741 did the position acquire lasting importance. Catherine II appointed one overprocurator, Prince A.S. Kozlovsky, whose main accomplishment was the confiscation or "secularization" of ecclesiastical lands. He was followed by two men who were overtly anticlerical, and at least the second was a self-proclaimed atheist: I.I. Melissino and P.P. Chebyshev. In 1805 Prince A.N. Golitsyn became overprocurator; he had been a deist but had undergone a pietist conversion. In neither incarnation did he have any perceptible commitment to Russian Orthodox traditions, and in the second — in particular as head of the "combined ministry" of cults and education from 1817 to 1824 — he did a good deal to undermine them. During much of Nicholas I's reign two men held the office: S.D. Nechaev, like Chebyshev a Mason, and Count N.A. Protasov, who was surrounded by men formerly concerned with the Uniat college at Polotsk.

The first two overprocurators of Alexander II's reign were insignificant, but in 1865 came one of two important figures who were to hold the office for fifteen and twenty-five years respectively: Count D. A. Tolstoi (1865-80) and K. P. Pobedonostsev (1880-1905), whose term thus spanned the reigns of three emperors. During the last twelve years of Nicholas II's reign there were eight overprocurators, none of whom was particularly noteworthy.

Thus during much of the eighteenth century the Synod itself was in a state of turmoil not unrelated to the procession of coups d'état and consequent demotion and promotion, exile and recall, of high governmental and also ecclesiastical personages. Seldom was the overprocurator influential, and when he was influential he might be unfriendly or downright hostile to anything distinctively Russian Orthodox. Many clergy felt the church to be under attack, and many high clergymen were in fact attacked, dismissed, and punished for various reasons. Leading clerics welcomed the accession of the Empress Elizabeth following the bleak reign of Anna Ivanovna and the German ascendancy (followed in turn by the fleeting, nominal emperorship of Ivan VI). Two archbishops mustered sufficient hope and courage to petition Elizabeth to restore the patriarchate, or at least to give the Synod a president and to abolish the overprocuratorship and the College of Economy. But the empress was in fact and by choice of image the daughter of Peter the Great, who had abolished the patriarchate and created the Synod, so the only gesture she made in response to the petitioners was to place the College of Economy under the Synod.

Neither restoration of the patriarchate nor even the holding of a national council could be looked for as a result of governmental action. In the reign of Alexander III there were congresses of bishops in Kiev, St. Petersburg, Kazan, and Irkutsk, a nationwide congress of missionaries in Moscow, and a congress in Kiev of teachers in parish schools.[2] On the parish level, the Synod in 1905 enacted a procedure by which councils elected by all parishioners and presided over by the local priest could be established; yet four years later it appeared that some councils had been created in Orël province, but nowhere else.[3] The church had to deal with lay officials not only in the central government but in the dioceses; if the Synod was itself a kind of consistory, bodies called by that very name, beginning in 1744, came to exist in the dioceses. Even at this level the lay secretaries of the consistories had substantial powers, and when an attempt was made to "reform" the institutions as late as 1910 those powers were strengthened, allowing them to appoint officials of the diocesan chancery and act in a range of different situations so as to threaten the prerogatives of the bishops themselves.[4]

Demands for genuine reform of the church, beginning with alteration of the basic relation between church and state, were advanced in the nineteenth century. Finally, after the retirement of Pobedonostsev as overprocurator, first one meeting and then another were permitted by way of preparation for the national church council which many clergy and laity desired as the proper vehicle for thoroughgoing reform. The preconciliar meetings of 1906 (*predsobornoe prisutstvie*) and 1912 (*predsobornoe soveshchanie*) accumulated much information and made possible the exchange of many opinions. However, they were unable to effect any institutional changes, and the convening of a national council had to await the period following the overthrow of the imperial government. It met only in August 1917, and the exigencies of the Bolshevik Revolution outstripped its capacities to inaugurate change of the sort desired by the leaders of the church.

The church suffered from too much governmental control, and also from too little ecclesiastical structure (which in turn made it easier for the lay officials at the diocesan level to exert their influence). In 1700 there were only 22 dioceses in the whole of the empire. By 1764 there were 3 metropolitanates (bishoprics of the first class), 8 archdioceses (bishoprics of the second class), and 15 ordinary dioceses, a total of 26, plus 3 Ukrainian dioceses. In 1917 there were 63, and in addition 4 in Georgia and 1 in the Aleutians and North America.[5] The diocese of Kiev, with four million Christians, was only one example of an ecclesiastical unit far too large and populous for any bishop to visit effectively or systematically, let alone manage properly.[6]

There were thus formidable obstacles to the discharge of any of the four functions earlier mentioned. The educational function was twofold, educating the clergy in their profession and seeking to provide the rudiments of education for the ordinary parishioner under the auspices of the church, with the inclusion of religious instruction in the curriculum.

The education of the Russian clergy was a supplementary task assumed in a more or less unforeseen and unplanned manner by the Roman Catholic Jesuit schools of Poland in the late sixteenth and seventeenth centuries and by the Orthodox schools of the Polish-ruled Ukraine in the seventeenth century until the Muscovite annexation of Kiev and other areas. Under the impact of such intellectual competition a single "Helleno-Greek" Academy was founded in 1685.[7] But Russia was given nothing like a system of higher education until after the *Ecclesiastical Regulation* of 1720. By 1727 there were forty-six ecclesiastical schools, whose language of instruction was

Latin and much of whose thrust came to be based on the models of Protestant scholasticism. A reform was inaugurated in 1808-14 which tried to strengthen both the financial and educational foundations of the system. Only in the late 1830s, however, was Latin replaced by Russian as the language of instruction. Still another reform was introduced in 1867-69. However, despite all these efforts the level of knowledge of many seminarians remained abysmally low.[8]

In the education which reached the parish level, much depended on the local priest, often justifiably criticized, sometimes unfairly maligned. The parish priest, wrote Kudriavtsev in 1906, had to be a teacher, notary, agronomist, first-aid man, and much else, indeed a jack-of-all-trades in relation to his parish, and also had to fulfill governmental demands of various kinds.[9] In his teaching he might be subjected to the most unexpected dangers; the archbishop of Kherson, for example, "rained down thunder and lightning" on a priest of his jurisdiction because his parish-school library contained Ushinskii's *Rodnoe Slovo.* The same archbishop, Nikanor, reported with chagrin, however, that a famed preacher who came from the area, Innokentii of Kherson, was threatened with exile from St. Petersburg in twenty-four hours because of some sermon which he had prepared but which remained unknown to the public. The example of a candidate who was forbidden to write a dissertation on the theme "The Relation of Seneca to Christianity" was by no means unique.

In 1914 there were 4 academies, 57 seminaries, and 185 schools in the Russian Orthodox church.[10] In the eighteenth century the seminaries and academies had become the exclusive preserve of the clergy, or the "clerical class" (*dukhovnoe soslovie*). A law of 1867 had permitted enrollment of the sons of other classes in ecclesiastical schools, but it was not a success. Subsequently, if not as a result of the law, the total number of students enrolled fell by more than 3,000.[11] At the same time, it was enacted that men from any class could be ordained if qualified; nevertheless, clergymen were still drawn almost entirely from the same class as before. In 1884 the schools were reorganized and once again the same objective was sought: both seminarists and pupils of secular schools were permitted to take the entrance examinations to the academies. Again in 1902 new rules were issued, and the nonseminarists were excluded. In assessing the whole course of ecclesiastical education in the reign of Alexander III and the early part of that of Nicholas II, Kudriavtsev concluded that the church as a cultural-historical factor did not depend on the support of the state, and quite unmistakably implied that state aid had been on balance deleterious in its effect in the educational and cultural realm. His purpose was to contrast the happier days of Alexander II with the more affluent and yet less successful period, from the standpoint of the church and its educational role, that followed, and he had some justification for so doing.

One of the four academies was that of Kazan, whose journal *Pravoslavnyi sobesednik* permits one to follow to some extent the activities of these institutions. The year 1912-13 was one in which there was a change of rector. Archimandrite Anatolii was chosen to replace Anastasii, who had been ordered by the Synod to become bishop of Iamburg. Anatolii simultaneously became bishop of Chistopol and vicar of the Kazan diocese. In his inaugural address he declared, "elevation to the episcopate is the death of all personal desires, the end of all doubts and hesitations. A bishop must exclusively concentrate on living an intense inner religious life and on the life of his flock."[12] Whether he took his episcopal and rectoral duties that seriously in fact, we cannot easily determine, but his intentions seem clear.

Among the events of the academic year were the following. In March an Old Believer leader of the Riabinovskii sect, S.I. Kondrashev, a peasant of Elantov village of the Chistopol'skii *uezd*, was received into the Orthodox church after a period of contacts with the staff of the academy lasting some ten years. The transfer was solemnized through chrismation (*miropomazanie*) administered by Rector-Bishop Anastasii.[13] In April a similar conversion of a Muslim was reported.[14] In May came the defense of his dissertation for the degree of master of theology by N.V. Nikolskii, described as a teacher of courses in mission work at the academy. The dissertation was entitled "Khristianstvo sredi Chuvash Sredniago Povolzh'ia v XVI-XVII vekakh." Nikolskii himself was a Chuvash, a member of one of the few Turkic peoples substantially Christianized under Russian rule, and the son of a peasant of Iadrinskii *uezd* of Kazan province. A substantial list of his published writings and the text of his lecture accompanied this report.[15] There is no basis in the chronicle of events from which these items are extracted for any solid conclusions, let alone any general evaluation of the state of intellectual and spiritual health of the academies. It is enough to say that a picture emerges of an institution, located at the gateway to Asia and led by people conscious of both universality and locality, whose standards were comparable to those anywhere in Europe.

From the standpoint of pastoral functions, to be sure, the church was suffering from severe disabilities. V. Sokolov, addressing a meeting of Octobrists[16] in the spring of 1906, stressed the problems the church faced on the eve of the council he imminently expected. Despite or perhaps because of the Religio-Philosophical Assemblies of 1901-3, according to V.A. Ternavtsev, "the gulf has become more pronounced between the intelligentsia and the Church."[17] Some *intelligenty* were indifferent, others deeply interested in ecclesiastical problems but not brought at all closer to the church by such interest—D.V. Filosofov was given as an example. Still others were passionately concerned with religious questions rather than eccleasiastical ones: an unidentified speaker at the assemblies had declared, "we are not believers, but we are tormented by a mortal (*smertel'naia*) thirst for God and love."

Obviously men like Sokolov had been driven by the experience of the assemblies, in which the clergy and the intelligentsia had met in a structured and continuing manner for the first time since there had come into being a difference between the two groups, to think about the problems of the Orthodox church in a new light. The church was failing to meet the religious needs of a substantial segment of the people of Russia. Not only did it fall short in satisfying the intelligentsia, or those among the group who were open to religious issues, but it could not hold many simple people, who found the attraction of the Old Believers and sectarians, especially the Stundists, great and often strong enough to lure them away.

Sokolov interpreted the problem as one of pastoral failure. The tie between the shepherd and his flock had become tenuous. Today's bishop, he wrote, was a person who was restricted to two functions— the solemn conduct of religious services and the discharge of official and administrative duties. He had to supervise seminaries and parish schools, the diocesan consistory, monasteries, a candle factory, banking and insurance operations, and much else. He was deluged with reports and petitions. The paperwork was crushing in its weight. One bishop reported receiving 8,000 items annually directed to him personally, 20-30,000 for the action of the consistory. The cause of the bishop's separation from his flock was not his own preference, but the distractions from which he could not escape. The parish priest, reported Sokolov, was better off. (Already here we face somewhat unexpected testimony, given the frequent tendency to assume that the Orthodox parish priest was apt to be capable of little more than occasionally sobering up to bring God into His house for the temporary edification of the peasants present.) A priest could visit everyone in a small parish, and he was called upon to answer all sorts of questions, moral and theological. Yet he was severely handicapped by three facts: that he had been compulsorily converted into a quasi-official and defender of the state, a status weakening his moral authority; that he had been trained in a narrow kind of school, which did not prepare him to answer his parishioners' questions; and his poverty, which preoccupied him. (Of course the priest had a family, often a large one, which he had to care for, and therefore one could not simply remind him that he ought to fix his attention on higher things.)

Sokolov approvingly quoted the writer V.V. Rozanov, who said simply that the Orthodox church was "cold" and therefore people ran to the sects where it was "warmer."[18]

Sokolov traced the pastoral difficulties of the church, however, not to its financial problems or even to its administrative responsibilities, except insofar as they were state-imposed. The root of the problem he found in the lack of authentic, "autonomous" (*samodeiatel'naia*) church life. The church was not a united, organized, and cohesive body. Except for the small part of the clergy engaged in teaching or administration, it was merely a mob. All important parish questions were decided not by the parish or even the diocese but by the Synod. The only clerical meetings were diocesan gatherings concerned with financial affairs, if even those were held. No effective links among dioceses existed. In the words of Vladimir Solov'ev, the church "slumbered under the canopy of state tutelage." All of this indeed was calculated to serve as an argument for the speedy convocation of a council and for action by church and state to end the fatal tie — as Sokolov saw it — between them. However, much of what he says is persuasive enough independent of his didactic purpose.

Of the sacramental functions of the church we need say little. Most of the church's critics are prepared to acknowledge that the liturgy, conducted by the least educated and morally least estimable village *pop*, had several continuing results. Amidst the artistic fruits of centuries of Christian culture in Russia in both painting and architecture, the liturgy, with its marvelous music and its mellifluous Slavonic texts, brought literature and the fine arts to the regular attention of a large share of the Russian people. (It is not necessary here to debate whether the people understood any large fraction of the Slavonic, or whether the substitution of Russian would automatically have produced a great increase in understanding; the Catholic peasantries of Ireland, Spain, and Italy were at any rate still worse off in that respect.) If choral singing was apparently a relatively late development in the Russian church and yet did not come to include the whole congregation, it is still the case that the congregation was not merely passive, as in many Protestant churches. Its members had to stand, for longer periods than many non-Russian visitors could easily manage, and thus could not fall asleep; the parishioners frequently crossed themselves and knelt, even if not always at the same times, and lit candles before icons and kissed them, if not necessarily at the most appropriate moments during the services. (An Orthodox friend once complained to me about the American congregations which, during the liturgy of the catechumens, at the injunction "Bow your heads, ye catechumens" do indeed bow their heads, though most or all are *not* catechumens.) If mental concentration or spiritual contemplation was not an invariable accompaniment of attendance at the liturgy, physical effort was certainly required. Ordinary parishioners felt that their part in what was happening was of some significance, and that it brought them close to the divine. The Orthodox liturgy has a beauty that does not escape the most secular visitors or even (despite allergic reactions to any message other than verbal directed to the senses) the most anticeremonial of Protestant religious observers. It is for this reason that such people as Lev Aleksandrovich Zander, for a

time general secretary of the Russian Student Christian Movement in
exile, established in 1933 as an ecumenical activity in Western Europe
concerts of the church music by Russian theological students which
continued for several years.[19] (To be sure, that meant extracting one
element, even if a significant one, from the liturgy and the general ecclesiastical setting.)

Whatever the strengths and weaknesses of the liturgy as performed
by the village priest, there were efforts in the reign of the last tsar to
improve it. As a result of the Synod's well-known session of March
1905, when in the chance absence of Pobedonostsev the synodical
bishops mutinied, so to speak, and demanded a council, the bishops of
the church were consulted and their answers collected in four volumes
(published in St. Petersburg in 1906). Some of the answers reflected
previous and continuing discussions among clergy and laity rather than
only the bishops' private opinions. In them appeared proposals for introducing congregational singing, printing services to make it easier for
parishioners to follow them, instituting something analogous to a teen-
ager confirmation service (since chrismation was still conducted immediately subsequent to baptism and therefore was administered to in-
fants), restorating the diaconate for women, holding frequent communion, and much else.[20] In most cases the proposals probably were
not implemented, but they indicated a direction pursued after the
Revolution by certain branches of Orthodoxy if not, as it appears, in
the Orthodox church in the USSR.

There remain to be considered the theological functions of the
church. In a sense, of course, a Christian and in particular an Orthodox
Christian may wish to argue that the church has no theological functions, or at any rate that its only such functions are to teach the unchanging theology of the universal church and to correct errors when
they appear in such teaching. Since the Seventh Ecumenical Council
(787), the Eastern Orthodox church, not only its branch in Russia, has
proclaimed or approved no new doctrinal formulations. To be sure,
the Eastern church has been less ready to condemn new theological ex-
plorations as error or to call anyone to task for risking heterodoxy than
the Roman Catholic church or a few other Western Christian groups—

notably the Missouri Synod Lutherans. Perhaps the only noteworthy exception during the last years of the empire was the so-called excommunication — technically not quite that — of Count Leo Tolstoy. (Here there was no serious question about his not being orthodox in his beliefs; he himself did not claim to be. The question was whether taking public action against a man as personally saintly as Tolstoy, whose teachings did not threaten the church, ought to be the item of highest priority on any defensible ecclesiastical agenda.)

As the nineteenth century wore on, the Orthodox church was required to pronounce on a series of political and social issues about which its high clergy were reluctant to say anything. An example is the case of the composition of the Emancipation Proclamation of 1861 by Metropolitan Filaret of Moscow, one of the outstanding clergymen of the whole imperial period and the person who in many ways was more responsible than any other for the spiritual renewal and revival occurring in the church in the later nineteenth and early twentieth centuries. Many secular historians took a rather puzzled account of his authorship of this document, if they noted the fact at all.[21]

At the time the manifesto was not a success. Turgenev, not knowing that Filaret had drafted it, wrote to Herzen that it "was evidently written in French and translated into awkward Russian by some German or other."[22] In fact, Filaret was as reluctant to perform the task as Chief Justice Warren was to investigate the Kennedy assassination, partly because he regarded it as not the affair of the church and partly because he feared the consequences of "the unclear understanding of freedom and the irrationally exaggerated hopes" that emancipation might provide.[23] He apparently would have preferred another kind of solution, one reached through amicable agreement in partriarchal fashion, one unaccompanied by the tortuous operation of redemption payments and therefore landless, but not risking the multiplication of beggars or the sale of peasant property for nonpayment of dues. Other clergymen, such as Archimandrite Iosif, were willing to speak more unequivocally: "neither birth, nor social necessity, nor civil law can legitimize slavery (*rabstvo*)."[24] It is not necessary here to try to decide whose position was the most Christian, but it may be worthy of note that Filaret's "moral authority and influence" in Russian society, such as none of his predecessors had enjoyed since the abolition of the patriarchate, were obviously significant in his being chosen for the task in question.[25]

During the latter part of the imperial period a number of issues using theological principles as a basis of discussion came to the fore. Here three might warrant brief mention. The first was anti-Semitism. As with other problems involving Russian Orthodoxy and society, this one should be related to the historical context. The record of the whole Christian church was variable for the long period in which Christianity became dominant and Judaism represented only a tiny minority of the population of Europe. (For the earliest decades of the church, when the differences between Christians and Jews were just being defined and their strength was roughly equal, in Palestine and other nearby areas, neither group can claim consistent toleration of the other.) There was, on the one hand, liturgical and theological reference to alleged Jewish guilt for the death of Christ and anti-Semitic measures and actions taken by Christian rulers, and, on the other, Christian prelates intervening repeatedly to protect Jews from violence or oppression; and we should remember that during much of the Middle Ages the safest place for Jews was the Papal States. If there were anti-Semitic political groups in Western Europe in the nineteenth and twentieth centuries in which clerics sometimes took part, before the rise of the Nazis the so-called Black Hundreds probably had the dubious distinction of engaging in or encouraging anti-Semitic action to a greater extent than any other group on the continent. The Union of the Russian People, the Union of the Archangel Michael, and other groups and parties included some clerics and were supported by others. Probably a more careful effort is necessary than has been usual to avoid simply equating anti-Semitism and political reaction, and to note that there might be grounds for opposing revolutionary parties and their actions other than religious or ethnic prejudice against Jews.[26] There is no doubt that it is easy to find statements made by highly placed clerics in the early twentieth century who support the Union of Russian People.[27] However, it is also easy to find statements and actions by high clergy who opposed the pogroms. Bishop Platon, a vicar of the Kievan diocese, risked his life to protect Jews. Bishop Innokentii of Tambov told the believers of his diocese that appeals in favor of pogroms were sinful. Bishop Simeon of Ekaterinoslav opposed the Union of Russian People and disapproved participation of the diocesan clergy in its activities, arousing the provincial governor's displeasure.[28] More difficult to assess is the attitude of the parish clergy and ordinary monks. Curtiss writes, "while many of the higher clergy were strongly conservative, it appears that the bulk of the parish clergy did not follow their lead."[29] (This is another instance of simply equating anti-Semitism, which has been the topic of several preceding pages of his book, with opposition to revolution.) Curtiss is convincing when he speaks of the opposing pressures to which many lower clergy were subjected. The gentry might urge support of the Black Hundreds while the peasantry might demand opposition to them—and to the extent the peasants opposed such groups common assumptions of the universality of anti-Semitism among the Russian masses may need reassessment. Urging might be accompanied by threats in both directions. Partly as a result, the parish priests often appeared not to take either side.

The second issue involving theology is the pressure or compulsion used on non-Orthodox Christians to join the Orthodox church or else have disabilities imposed on them. Islam in general fared far from badly at the hands of the imperial regime, though it was treated more gently in Central Asia than in the Caucasus. Perhaps a case can even be made that the position of Islam under the empire was stronger than that of Orthodoxy. Somewhat the same thing may be said of Buddhism. The lot of Roman Catholics and of Protestants varied, sometimes being equal treatment or better, sometimes becoming quite unenviable. All these faiths were associated with non-Russians. The regime and the church hierarchy may well have agreed on one point at any rate: the value of the homogeneous religious community, and the tendency to identify Russians and Ukrainians with Orthodoxy. That did not necessarily mean that the position of Old Believers and sectarians, who were mainly Russian and Ukrainian, was intolerable or the worst of all; it did mean that conversions of Orthodox to either provoked sharper reactions from church hierarchs and state officials than did individual conversions to other faiths. Perhaps the most egregious, and even unnecessary, mistake of this sort was made in compelling the Uniats to

break their organizational tie with Rome and affiliate with the Orthodox church. Such action was taken for the Ukraine and Belorussia in
1839, for the former Kingdom of Poland in 1875. It was ill-considered,
hasty, and counterproductive. By 1899 a category of "determined re-
sisters ' had come to be recognized and was for the predominantly
Polish provinces alone estimated at 81,000.[30] Measures of fluctuating
severity were taken in relation to Stundists and Baptists, to be sure, but
they probably yielded those groups net benefit from the manner in
which they bore with dignity the charges and penalties in question. But
the compulsory end of the Unia within the empire was a self-defeating
act of the civil authorities in which the Orthodox church authorities
connived or which they accepted only at the risk of compromising their
own Christian beliefs.

The third issue under the heading of practical implications of theology involves the state. Here care is needed, as with the problem of anti-
Semitism. The basic Christian position, beginning with Jesus' distinction between the domain of Caesar and that of God, has been to acknowledge the claims of existing civil authority and to submit to it
whereas at the same time it does not exempt the state in general, or any
government in particular, from the roster of human institutions that
stand under divine judgment and may merit human criticism. To be
sure, the church was under state control. However, it is obviously un-
true to say that all or most of the clergy identified themselves with the
state or the government, either before or after 1905-6, when some possibility of legal political life and activity was created.

In the First Duma all six of the Orthodox priests elected deputies
were critics to some degree of the existing order or past deeds of the
autocracy, and denounced the death penalty, pogroms, and much else.
In the Second Duma two bishops and eleven priests appeared; among
the priests were three Kadets and four revolutionaries. In the Third
Duma the forty-five clergy were apportioned as follows:[31]

Progressists	4 priests
Octobrists	9 priests
Moderate Right	13 priests and 1 bishop
Nationalists	2 priests
Right	15 priests and 1 bishop

In the Fourth Duma there were forty-six clergy:

Progressists	2 priests
Octobrists	2 priests
Center	2 priests
Moderate Right and Nationalists	19 priests
Right	19 priests and 2 bishops

There was a clear effort by the government to use the clergy in the elections to the Fourth Duma, held in 1912, which excited much criticism on the floor of the Duma (leading to an interpellation), in the press (including such conservative newspapers as *Novoe vremia*), and within the church itself.

In general, during the period of the Duma, that is, the single period of imperial history when there existed the possibility of identification with political parties, the clergy was far from indicating that it had been converted into a tool of the imperial regime, the monarch, or the ministry of the moment. Probably, confusion on the Left regarding the compatibility of Christianity with socialist dogma or revolutionary violence was quite as widespread as confusion on the Right about what Christianity required concerning anti-Semitism or "true Russian men" or the autocracy. The subsequent history of the Living Church would suggest as much.

Doubtless many priests, including those supposed to know better, were unable to wrestle with any kind of theological issue or make any assessments of historical or political kind that required education and discrimination. (As an example, consider the exchange between Prince Sergei Trubetskoi and Father Butkevich in 1890-91, in which the latter's total misunderstanding of Trubetskoi's *Metafizika v drevnei Gretsii* was shown by the maligned author through the use of parallel columns.)[32]

Yet, there were a sizable number of clergymen and church people who were distinguished scholars or theologians. Let us mention only a few from among the bishops of the last three reigns: Metropolitan of Moscow Makarii (Bulgakov), the son of a village priest, a theologian and historian, and member of the Academy of Sciences and most archaeological and historical societies, who donated 120,000 rubles of royalties from his books to the academy for scholarly prizes (and made other, smaller donations in other directions); Metropolitan of St. Petersburg Grigorii (Postnikov), who was responsible for founding *Khristianskoe chtenie* and *Dukhovnaia beseda* in St. Petersburg and *Pravoslavnyi sobesednik* in Kazan and was himself a doctor of theology; Metropolitan of Kiev Flavian (Gorodetskii), not from the clerical class, a former teacher on the law faculty of Moscow University; Metropolitan of St. Petersburg Antonii (Vadkovskii), former editor of *Pravoslavnyi sobesednik* and Professor at the Kazan Academy, who was a representative of the Orthodox church at the 1897 jubilee of Queen Victoria; and the first two candidates for the office of patriarch chosen by the council in 1917 — Antonii (Khrapovitskii), a doctor of theology and later head of the Russian Church Abroad, and Arsenii (Stadnitskii), a doctor of church history, rector of the Moscow Academy for a time and an archaeologist.[33] (It will be remembered, incidentally, that it was the third candidate, Metropolitan Tikhon, formerly having held the see of North America, who was actually chosen, by lot, to be the first patriarch since 1700. Perhaps if he had been better prepared theologically, his sad and difficult tenure of office might have gone a trifle differently, though no one should overestimate what could have been done.)

We should also mention a few of the saintly men and women among clergy and laity who graced the church by their lives reflecting a practical theology of one sort or another. On the one hand there were contemplative persons, notably the *startsy* of such monasteries as Optina Pustyn, Bethany near Zagorsk, and Zossima northwest of Moscow: during the last three reigns they included Varnava of Bethany, Aleksei of Zossima, spiritual adviser to many groups and persons, and others. There were pious lay people: Vasilii Arseniev, two of whose sons became priests; Pavel Mansurov, director of the Moscow archives of the Foreign Office and an expert on the history of the Byzantine church, whose son Sergei was a noted scholar and priest. A number of these were women: Princess Trubetskaia née Lopukhina, mother of Sergei and Evgenii; Princess Varvara Nikolaevna Repnina, who devoted her life as a single woman to the poor; the Grand Duchess Elizaveta Fedorovna, widow of the Grand Duke Sergei, who after her husband's assassination by terrorists founded or patronized homes for the poor, orphans, and aged. We have already mentioned the Abbess Ekaterina of Lesna (see n. 20), who worked for revival of the perpetual diaconate for women; also noteworthy was the Abbess Magdalena (formerly the Countess Orlova-Davydova), who lived on into the period of Bolshevik rule to the age of ninety-two, dying blind and lame in a small hut, and was a patroness of charitable institutions, many of which she financed herself.[34]

Many of these people deserve to be better known. Thus far interest in them seems to have been largely confined to devout émigrés, clerics, and laymen outside the community of scholars.

During the reign of Nicholas II there were indications that some of the best intellectuals were finding their way back to the church. A number had been Marxists, indeed the leading members of the generation of Marxist leaders of the 1890s, when it first became significant in Russia whether one was a "Marxist" within the previously undifferentiated socialist camp or not. Struve, Berdiaev, Bulgakov, and others made their own individual passage from Marxism to "idealism" (that is, philosophical idealism) and then to Russian Orthodoxy. The milestones of this passage are well known: *Problemy idealizma*, 1902; *Vekhi*, 1909; *Iz glubiny*, 1921. This is not the place to describe and analyze this literature, although the task of doing so may well be regarded as still incomplete. Let us note merely that this was a historic development which did not, like the Romanov monarchy, come irretrievably to an end. The same current has been resumed in our time, partly as a result of the work of a series of outstanding Christian writers of the Soviet period: Akhmatova, Mandelshtam, Pasternak, Tarsis, Solzhenitsyn. (In fact the list may be lengthened.) Solzhenitsyn and some of his friends have in the last few years consciously resumed the development of the tradition in question in *Iz pod glyb*, explicitly invoking echoes of *Iz glubiny* in the title they chose for the book (in English, *From under the Rubble*) and discussing *Vekhi* at length.

One particular observation deriving from this story of the reconciliation of intellectuals with Russian Orthodoxy may be made. Of the brief listing of Soviet Christian writers I have offered, two were Jewish converts: Mandelshtam and Pasternak. Other converted Jewish intellectuals have been significant in the story: S. L. Frank, the philosopher, Ilia Bunakov-Fundaminskii, coeditor of *Novyi grad* in the 1930s, and others. Can we account for this phenomenon?[35] Did Vladimir Solov'ev's interest in Judaism and his forthright repudiation of anti-Semitism have an effect on the environment in which such feelings were possible? Did Jews who converted to Christianity play a comparable part in the cultural life of any other country in recent times? Once again we see that topics of real interest remain to be studied within the framework of Russian Orthodoxy's relation to the society of Russia.

The reconciliation of certain leading Russian intellectuals with the Orthodox church was not mainly an effort to produce a theology of history and politics replacing the Marxism many of them had once embraced and then abandoned. Perhaps it should best be described as a considered attempt to prevent any kind of political ideology from obstructing the perceptions of the human intelligence or from being used as a weapon of inhuman and oppressive state authority. Orthodox Christianity, like the rest of the Christian church and faith, offers no neat blueprints for the future, no unambiguous or inescapable principles of hermeneutics for use in the political or economic realm, no ready-made program of action for Christians who face the painful dilemmas of human life, whether or not complicated by the weight of oppression they suffer in the USSR or other totalitarian or authoritarian countries. The leaders of the church of the later imperial period labored under these handicaps, suffering from state control, if not oppression, in a variety of ways. Solzhenitsyn has suggested that if the church had performed its duties adequately, if it had been in fit condition, the Revolution might not have occurred. That may be true, or it may not. Some saw what might lie ahead: Filaret of Moscow, two months before his death in 1867, told his suffragan bishop Leonid that he perceived "a terrible thunder stormcloud that draws towards us from the West." Two generations later Vladimir Solov'ev experienced similar forebodings. One could mention other examples.

My conclusion is that the Orthodox church during the imperial era was caught up in problems its past had ill fitted it to cope with; that even considering those undoubted inherited handicaps, it did not do all it could—when does any of us ever do all that one can? And yet its record is not as unrelievedly bleak and unsuccessful as it has been made out; moreover, much of the story has yet to be told and understood.[36] In 1977 there is, in the view of many, only one major religious prophet alive: Alexander Solzhenitsyn. (That is perhaps true despite the fact that some of us may not accept all his political recommendations and may feel concerned lest he be used by political forces and leaders in various countries who care nothing for the church.) He comes directly out of the traditions formed in the Orthodox church during the imperial period, especially its later portion. That fact ought to say something about the desirability of studying and understanding the topic more fully.

NOTES

1. Summarized in Filaret Gumilevskii, *Istoriia russkoi tserkvi*, 5th ed., Moscow, 1888, V, 9-10.

2. N. Tal'berg, *Istoriia russkoi tserkvi*, Jordanville, N.Y., 1959, 749.

3. John Shelton Curtiss, *Church and State in Russia: The Last Years of the Empire, 1900-1917*, New York, 1940, reprinted 1965, 302.

4. *Ibid.*, 293-94.

5. Igor Smolitsch, *Geschichte der russischen Kirche 1700-1917*, I, Leiden, 1964, 359-60, 706.

6. Nicolas Zernov, *The Russian Religious Renaissance of the Twentieth Century*, New York, 1963, 41.

7. It bore the title "Slavo-Latin" from 1700 to 1775. A few other schools of the kind were created by bishops: see Smolitsch, *Geschichte*, 540.

8. *Ibid.*, 688, gives some depressing reports from the period 1906-13.

9. P. Kudriavtsev, "Po voprosam tserkovno-obshchestvennoi zhizni," *Trudy Kievskoi dukhovnoi akademii*, June 1906, 337.

10. Smolitsch, *Geschichte*, 711.

11. *Ibid.*, 340.

12. "Rech' rektora Imperatorskoi Kazanskoi Dukhovnoi Akademii, Arkhimandrita Anatoliia pri narechenii ego vo episkopa Chistopol'skago, vikariia Kazanskoi eparkhii," *Pravoslavnyi sobesednik*, July-August 1913, 5.

13. *Ibid.*, 212-14.

14. *Ibid.*, 230-31.

15. *Ibid.*, 233-52.

16. At this point formally merely the "Union of October 17"; later a political party.

17. V. Sokolov, "Predstoiashchii Vserossiiskii tserkovnyi Sobor; ego sostav i zadachi," *Bogoslovskii vestnik*, May 1906, 36.

18. *Ibid.*, 44.

19. Zernov, *Russian Religious Renaissance*, 278-79, 351-52.

20. *Ibid.*, 79-80. The revival of the diaconate for women was advocated not only by bishops but by Professor S. Troitskii and the Abbess Ekaterina of Lesna (1850-1925), described by Zernov in *The Russians and Their Church*, London, 1964, 151, as the "ablest Russian woman theologian of her time."

21. Michael T. Florinsky describes it as "an insincere and pretentious manifesto written by the Metropolitan Philaret, another enemy of emancipation." *Russia: A History and an Interpretation*, New York, 1953, II, 888. One might be grateful for even this reference. Some years ago at a session of the American Historical Association devoted to Russian history an esteemed colleague challenged those present to name a single Russian clergyman from the whole nineteenth century—perhaps stopping at 1900 to prevent anyone from replying, "Father Gapon." I believe no one did reply. To be sure, much has been published on the history of the Orthodox church since that time.

22. Quoted by S. Mel'gunov, "Mitropolit Filaret, deiatel' krest'ianskoi reformy," in A. K. Dzhivegelov et al., eds., *Velikaia reforma*, Moscow, 1911, V, 162.

23. *Ibid.*

24. *Ibid.*, 159.

25. *Ibid.*, 160. Mel'gunov contends that such influence (the phrase is quoted from Sukhomlinov's article in *Istoricheskii vestnik*, 1885) was *not* the reason for the choice but rather the fact that Filaret was experienced in "knowing how to get out of the most delicate situation." Mel'gunov's article is a direct attack on Filaret, and the phrase cited in the preceding sentence is not persuasive because of the obvious animus that lies behind it. A more concrete glimpse of the impact of Filaret's personality on those about him is provided by the poet F. I. Tiutchev, who saw Filaret at his fiftieth anniversary jubilee in 1867, a few weeks before he died: "Short, frail, reduced to the simplest expression of his physical being, but with eyes full of life and wit, with incomparable strength he [Filaret] dominated everything taking place around him." Quoted in N. Tal'berg, *Istoriia*, 741.

26. Curtiss, *Church and State*, 268 and elsewhere, sometimes makes the necessary distinction and sometimes not. On 272 he mistakenly refers to the reactionary Union of the Archangel Michael, mentioned in the Duma debate from which he quotes, as the "Union of the Archangel Gabriel [sic] ."

27. None of the statements of the sort that Curtiss quotes, however, mentions Jews at all; *Church and State*, 267-72.

28. *Ibid.*, 271.

29. *Ibid.*, 275.

30. *Ibid.*, 179.

31. *Ibid.*, 202-04, 341-43.

32. Trubetskoi, "Mnimoe iazychestvo ili lozhnoe khristianstvo? Otvet O. Butkevichu," *Pravoslavnoe obozrenie*, Moscow, March 1891, 1-27.

33. Tal'berg, *Istoriia*, 741-57, refers to these and many others.

34. Nicholas Arseniev, *Holy Moscow*, London, 1940, devotes his Chapter 9 to such people.

35. Certain aspects of the problem have been recently touched upon by Mikhail Agurskii in "Evrei-khristiane v russkoi pravoslavnoi Tserkvi," *Vestnik Russkogo Khristianskogo Dvizheniia* (Paris), CXIV, 1974, 52-72, and CXIV, 1975, 117-38.

36. The writer is aware of the extensive research that still needs to be done on the relations between the Orthodox church and Russian society, especially at the diocesan and parish levels in the various regions of the country, before anyone can confidently generalize about the subject.

Feofan Prokopovich
and the Kiev Academy

James Cracraft

Any list of the outstanding figures of "Russian Orthodoxy under the Old Regime" would have to include the name of Feofan Prokopovich.[1] An ecclesiastic virtually the whole of his life, he rose to the highest ranks of the Russian church, where it was his fate to be the author, in the literal sense, of the reform of that church undertaken by Peter the Great; and in this capacity he helped set the pattern of Russian church-state relations which was to last, with some modifications, until 1917 and even, in a sense, until our own day. He was also a theologian or, more generally, a religious writer of the first importance in imperial Russia, one of whose works in this vein, a defense of the relics of the Kiev Monastery of the Caves, was reprinted as late as 1905.[2] In addition, he was for a long time closely associated with a distinguished ecclesiastical institution, the celebrated Kiev academy, whose importance in the early modern cultural history of the Eastern Slavs has become something of a truism. His was perhaps the longest and closest such personal association on record, and it coincided, moreover, with what has rightly been called the academy's golden age.

The purpose of this paper is to discuss briefly the earlier part of Prokopovich's life and particularly his association with the Kiev academy. Such a profile may help to illuminate both the major historical figure that Prokopovich was to become and the somewhat tenebrous world in which the man was formed. That the Prokopovich of history remains a controversial figure, the subject of spirited attacks by, among others, church historians, encourages our efforts to understand the earlier, formative, and comparatively neglected years of his life.[3]

Prokopovich was born in 1681 in Kiev. According to his first biographers, friends, and admirers of his later years, he was of "respectable" family, his parents having been "citizens" of the city, his father a merchant or trader—*mercator*, in Latin, is how one writer has put it.[4] By birth he belonged to the Kievan *meshchanstvo* or burgher class, which traditionally had supported the patriotic Orthodox-Ukrainian Brotherhood movement in whose local establishment, the Kiev Brotherhood monastery, the academy was located (until 1701 it was, strictly speaking, still a "college").[5] The shops and residences of the *meshchanstvo* were concentrated in *podol* (or *podil*), the lower, riverside part of Kiev where the academy and its supporting monastery were also to be found. In the 1680s this class still retained certain corporate rights and privileges and so possessed, we may assume, a certain corporate identity whereby its members distinguished themselves from, say, the Russian governor and his officials and garrison encamped up in the old city, from the landed and martial cossacks, many of whom kept houses in Kiev, or from the numerous countryfolk and pilgrims who periodically came to town and/or temporarily settled in its outskirts.[6] Prokopovich's origins in this class, in other words, might be the source of that pride in Kiev and of that Orthodox-Ukrainian (or "Russian") patriotism which are features of his earliest writings, as we shall see. They might be invoked to explain, as well, a certain resentment of aristocratic privilege that he was also to exhibit, for instance in 1706, in the earliest of his surviving speeches, where he praised Peter the Great for promoting the meritorious among his subjects regardless of their background.[7] In any case, his social origins and Ukrainian birth require more attention in an attempt to understand him than they have so far been accorded in the scholarly literature.

Similarly, it is of more than passing interest that when Prokopovich lost both parents at a tender age he was taken under the wing of his uncle Feofan, a learned churchman with excellent connections in Kiev.

Feofan Prokopovich I, as we might call him, had taught for at least ten years at the Kiev academy, where he had risen to the position of professor of philosophy, then the highest subject taught in the school. In 1685 he had actually been elected rector and head of the Brotherhood monastery but had declined these honors owing, it was said, to his humility. He was also known to his contemporaries as a "sweet-spoken" orator, as a "skilled preacher of God's word."[8] It was because of him that our Prokopovich began to learn Latin as well as Slavonic. Although he died in either 1689 or 1692, when his nephew would have been only eight or at most ten or eleven years old, he had undoubtedly made a profound impression on the child. We cannot help noting that later in life our Prokopovich was to distinguish himself similarly as a scholar and preacher, and that when it came time for him to profess monastic vows, he took the name Feofan (his baptismal name was Elisei). So we may conclude that in his uncle the child had found a model, his "ego ideal," and that in this most fortunate relationship lie the seeds of Prokopovich the churchman, educator, and orator of history. We might only wish that there were space to dwell on the implications of this relationship—and of other facts we have of Prokopovich's youth. For it is hard to avoid the suspicion that in his early circumstances were rooted certain settled beliefs of the mature man: his belief in the universal necessity of a strict and God-fearing upbringing, for example; his belief in the curative (or restorative) power of education, for another; or his belief in the necessity of a strong authority, including especially monarchial authority, which he would tend to view in paternalistic terms.[9]

However, the main lines of Prokopovich's future career were definitely set at the Kiev academy, where he spent the rest of his childhood and his adolescence. One of his first biographers (Bayer) records that even as a schoolboy he possessed an "acute mind and tenacious memory," that he "never surrendered himself to dicing and other foolish things," and that in addition to making rapid progress in his studies he was "richly endowed with an amiable and graceful nature." From this and other evidence we can readily imagine an intellectually gifted, industrious, and attractive boy whose efforts to repay the favor of his patrons — they soon included the distinguished metropolitan of Kiev himself, Varlaam Iasynskii — were appropriately rewarded. He was apparently one of that minority of poorer students at the academy who was on full scholarship, and so did not have to sing for his supper in the parishes of Kiev or to join the student beggars and thieves in the streets of the city. In due course he became what we should call a teaching assistant and precentor of the school choir. From the poetics class he progressed to the rhetoric form, thence to philosophy and, finally, to theology, which had only recently been introduced into the academy's curriculum. It should be noted that to be advanced to the philosophy and theology forms at Kiev was to be separated from one's less dedicated and perhaps less able student contemporaries. Moreover as things then stood at the academy advancement to the theology form implied a decision by the student in question — or by his superiors — that he was to pursue a career in the church. Prokopovich was at this point twelve or thirteen years old, and we may justifiably wonder about the degree of latitude he himself had had in this decision. Probably it was very little, which we should bear in mind when reflecting that he was never to earn a reputation for piety and was perhaps never able to perceive, in Fr. Florovsky's words, the "mystical reality of the church."[10]

But a more intriguing point to be made about Prokopovich's theological studies at Kiev concerns the identity of his teacher, who was, almost certainly, none other than Stefan Iavorskii. The later hostile rivalry of the two men, in which theology, politics, and even their personalities came to be interfused (and in which, it is not too much to say, the fate of the Russian church was at stake), has been the subject of considerable scholarly inquiry.[11] Here we might add only that this fateful antagonism may have originated in Iavorskii's theology classes, where Prokopovich may have first learned the distrust of Jesuit scholasticism which was to figure prominently in his own works. For Iavorskii was, in the jargon of the times, an ardent "Latinizer." Himself a product of the Kiev academy, he had gone on to study philosophy and theology at the Jesuit colleges of Lwów and Lublin, and at those of Vilnius and Poznań; and after his return to Kiev he eventually taught, from 1693 to 1698, a full course in theology, being only the second person in the academy's history to do so (the rector of the time, Ioasaf Kro-

kovskii, was the first). From what is known of Iavorskii's lectures and
of his later theological writings, it is clear that he followed the general
scheme of Thomas Aquinas as it had been digested by certain Jesuit
schoolmen, only pausing from time to time to indicate, still in scholastic language, those points of dogma on which the traditions of the
Orthodox East were considered to differ from the teachings of the
Roman church: such polemics, it seems, occupied especially the fifth
and last year of his course, which was devoted to the question of the
Trinity (the procession of the Holy Spirit) and to the nature of the
church (the claims of the papacy).[12] Iavorskii's "Latin" teaching here,
from which his students learned "much that is not Orthodox," was
criticized thus by Patriarch Dositheus of Jerusalem, a leading contemporary exponent of Orthodox doctrine[13] — criticism that was probably
echoed much closer to home. But his theology course might more
sympathetically be viewed as reflecting the general Orthodox dilemma
of the age, when the church of the East was caught intellectually unprepared by the controversies of the western Reformations and felt
constrained to adopt, in an effort to clarify its own position, the
weapons — the language and even the concepts — of its adversaries.
The dilemma was perhaps especially acute in Polonized Ukraine, where
the "Latin learning," as represented indeed by Iavorskii's theology, was
establishing its hold on the mind of the church. And the risky nature of
Iavorskii's enterprise, the inherent ambiguities of such a position, may
well have dawned on his eager, sharp-witted student. It is a fact that
Prokopovich's own theological lectures at Kiev were to be characterized
by the priority he gave to polemics with the Latins, by his effort to
liberate himself from scholastic terminology, and by his search for an
authentic — scriptural, patristic, and Byzantine — Orthodox tradition.

Yet clearly, the more decisive experience in his gradual alienation
from the theological (and literary) conventions of Kiev was the time he
spent in Rome, which he reached after traveling through Poland and the
Austrian dominions, having stopped at various colleges and other
Catholic establishments along the way. On completing the theology
course at Kiev he had been encouraged by his superiors to pursue his
studies abroad. And here again we might register the proof this fact
offers of Prokopovich's outstanding abilities and of his patrons' high re-

gard for him: only a handful of his fellow Kievan graduates — Iavorskii was one, Metropolitan Varlaam Iasynskii another — had gone on to study abroad; and fewer still — we know of only one in his immediate world, Ioasaf Krokovskii, the rector of the academy — had made their way to Rome. Moreover, Prokopovich's departure for Rome implies, as his friend Bayer also implies, that in Kiev he had reached the end of his tether; that at about the age of seventeen he was dissatisfied with what he had learned and needed something more.

In Rome he became, for three years, a student of philosophy and theology at the Greek College of St. Athanasius, where he seems to have found something less than the answer to his prayers.[14] The Greek College was sustained by papal subsidies officially for the purpose of training Greeks and Slavs to work for the union of the Eastern and Western churches or for the conversion of the infidels; and to study there Prokopovich had been obliged to become, like all his fellow Orthodox, a Uniat, and so to conceal his true loyalties. Bayer reports that on hearing the annual public reading of the bull "In Coena Domini," which consisted of fulminations against schismatics and heretics, Prokopovich suppressed a smile, and later in life would avail himself of opportunities to pronounce his own anathemas "in retaliation" (we are reminded of the difficulties, if not precariousness, of the contemporary Orthodox situation). Bayer further reports that Prokopovich particularly disapproved of the lectures he heard on moral theology, that is, on casuistry or "cases of conscience," which were designed to instruct the students in the Catholic theory of confession. We can also sense in the sources a provincial and somewhat prudish resentment of, or embarrassment at, Baroque Catholic opulence and worldliness. Indeed Bayer once heard his friend declare that nowhere was the truth of Christianity so much in doubt as in Italy. And in Prokopovich's later writings, as suggested above, we can frequently find sometimes quite lengthy asides denouncing the "papist spirit," Catholic "idolatry" and "superstition," or the alleged evils of the Jesuits.

But these are only negative effects on him of his Roman "stage." There were decidely positive results as well, which even Prokopovich, anti-Catholic that he became, would willingly have admitted. In Rome he mastered Latin, learned Italian, and thoroughly acquainted himself with Aristotelian thought (the records of the Greek College show that he "publicly defended the whole of philosophy *cum laude*"). In his free time he read widely in the classical authors, all of them, Bayer emphasizes, in unexpurgated editions: Demosthenes, Cicero, Quintilian, Virgil, Ovid, Juvenal, Horace, Catullus, Martial, Livy, Suetonius, Sallust, Tacitus, as well as certain "moderns" – mostly Italian classicists of the sixteenth century – are mentioned by name, and references to most of these as well as to other classical or classicist authors are frequent in Prokopovich's own works. Dissatisfied, as he appears to have been, with the theology course at the Greek College, he delved into the writings of both the Greek and Latin fathers, and into church history, finding there, as his friend puts it, an "antidote" to the "vain science" of Jesuit scholasticism. And of course there was, for the wide-eyed young Ukrainian to devour, the Eternal City itself, the artistic capital of Europe, a center still of science and learning, not the largest but as yet the most cosmopolitan of European cities.

Were we to summarize the effects on Prokopovich of his education, in Kiev as well as in Rome, both formal and informal, it would be to stress, apart from the particular achievements already mentioned, three or four general points. By the age of twenty-one, when he left Rome for the return journey home, he had acquired what proved to be a lasting love of learning for its own sake: as he himself wrote, much later, "an educated man, in spite of his formal education, is never satisfied with what he has learned and will never desist from studying, though he live for as long as Methuselah."[15] Second, Prokopovich had acquired a more practical sense of the value of learning – of its value both for the individual, as the means for securing the pleasures of a civilized life, and for society, as the means of eradicating various evils. Thus in a poem of 1705 he portrays monasticism – he meant the academic life – as a "sylvan grove of peace and shade," as a refuge for philosophers and poets from the "wretched" world of "distress and cares" outside inhabited by "fools, the vile rabble, and stinking cooks[!] ."[16] And elsewhere he would write (one of many such instances which could be adduced) that "when the light of learning is lacking it is impossible that the church should be well run, that it should not be disorderly and subject to numerous ridiculous superstitions as well as dissensions and the most absurd heresies."[17]

Third, by the age of twenty-one Prokopovich had acquired, for someone of his background, a quite remarkable breadth of culture, whose outstanding features, perhaps, were a certain cosmopolitanism and a devotion to classical antiquity. Bayer would recall, in the dedication to Prokopovich in one of his books, how the latter "had only to begin speaking and it seemed to me that I was in Greece, in the schools of the ancient poets, rhetoricians, and philosophers. . . . Again, you as it were led me by the hand to Rome or to some other city of Italy famed for its sacred or secular monuments. . . . How pleasurable it was for me to hear you describe the antiquities you had seen!"[18] or as Prokopovich himself was to declare, in a speech of 1717:

In traveling we not only observe the remains of antiquity, we see for ourselves the affairs and activities of nations, their projects and concerns, their councils and their courts, their manners and forms of government. There [abroad] the reasonable man sees oft-changing fortune at play, and learns forbearance; sees the causes of felicity, and learns the maxim; perceives misfortune, and learns to defend himself; sees also in foreign nations, as in a mirror, himself and his own people, their strengths and weaknesses.

"Foreign travel [*peregrinatsiia ili stranstvovanie*]," Prokopovich concluded here, "makes a man much the wiser in a few years than does advanced old age."[19]

Lastly, it might be noted how Prokopovich's exceptional abilities and experiences, his breadth of culture and love of learning, would almost inevitably have combined to make him, when he returned to Kiev, not just a man apart but something of a rebel. By twenty-one he had begun to outgrow that peculiar, largely derivative Baroque culture in which he was initially formed; and his criticisms of this or that aspect of it, usually implicit but sometimes explicit, would figure prominently in the lectures of the Kiev academy teacher it seems he had always been destined to become.

Between 1705 and 1716 Prokopovich taught successively poetics, rhetoric, philosophy, and theology at the academy, where he also became prefect and then rector, posts which he owed in part, according to the Kievan system, to his progress as a teacher. Here there is room only to comment briefly on the lectures, perhaps half of which remain in manuscript and are just beginning to be studied, leaving any consideration of his administration of the school.

The outstanding characteristics of Prokopovich's poetics course include the high regard, indeed the passion he displayed for the "most noble art" of poetry;[20] the thoroughness, in the rules and examples he put forth, of his classicism; and the degree to which, within the Kievan context, he was innovative. In his poetics course he in effect broke with the local tradition of uncritical acceptance of certain Polish or Jesuit masters and encouraged instead the study of the classical authors themselves or of such modern (Renaissance) poets as Tasso and Jan Kochanowski; in so doing he set precedents that were to be followed by various of his successors in the poetics chair at Kiev.[21] Nor was it a case simply of citing or quoting the poetry of others. In his discussion of the hexameter for instance Prokopovich is thought to have made an original contribution to the theory of that verse form and to have hastened its appearance in Russian;[22] although his treatment of the epigram, which included ten examples of his own composition, surpassed in its thoroughness any to be found in the works of his likely modern mentors. Moreover, in his poetics course he furnished four substantial examples of his own verse (in Latin, as are the lectures themselves), where both in their more purely classical form and in their largely secular content he again broke with certain Baroque conventions of the Kiev academy. Prokopovich was to write poetry, in Latin and in what he called the "vernacular idiom," for the rest of his life, his most ambitious such effort being his five-act tragicomedy in verse *Vladimir*, which also dates from his Kievan days. But the play, like most of his verse, awaits thorough linguistic as well as content analysis.

Enthusiasm, classicism, a strong innovative streak: these are also features of Prokopovich's rhetoric lectures,[23] a subject which he defined to include, in a mainly conventional way, the art of "eloquentia" itself, historiography, the writing of letters and epitaphs, the actual techniques of public speaking, and the principles of "sacred eloquence," or homiletics as it came to be called. But although in general he seems to have followed here the established Kievan pattern (or to have based himself, more exactly, on some of the standard textbooks), Prokopovich's course is remarkable for the vigorous attack it contains on what he termed the "Polish eloquence" and especially on the published sermons of the Polish Jesuit Thomas Młodzianowski.

The most common disease of our time [Prokopovich begins the attack] is that which we call, not without reason, the curious style; for among other means of acquiring scholarly renown certain learned blusterers have in particular adopted a manner of speaking which employs the astonishing, the unusual, the unexpected. Thus they invent odd yet thoroughly flaccid and ridiculous ways of reasoning. They ask [such questions as] : why in the name of the Most Holy Virgin [Maria] , or in that of Jesus, are there five letters? Why did God say such and such through the prophet and not something else? . . . And having detained the poor audience a fair while with such mindless delays, these orators at last straighten up, go into raptures, become agitated, and, sustained by the attention of the ignorant crowd, begin with affected gravity and sunken cheeks to pronounce the most absurd nonsense.

The worthy Father Młodzianowski knows none but this sort of eloquence, and so the entirety [of his work] consists of such nonsense . . . two great volumes. . . . Tell me where there is anything serious and sensible in this scribbler of idle chatter? Is there even a shadow here of oratorical skill? Where is the art conceived and passed on by its most learned exponents, ancient and modern? Where the sound arguments, the sincere gestures, the necessary perorations? Where is the rhythmical structure? Where the adornment, brilliance, wit, power, gravity, felicity? Where the vigor, the weightiness of thought and expression, the unity of parts?

I would not mention this orator [Młodzianowski] were his example, if not beneficial, at least not harmful to others. But when I see that many approve of and greatly praise him, and that young students of eloquence take only him for a model, and thus diverge from the true art into a fatal path—then I count it my duty briefly to set forth what I think about him. It does not trouble me that my thoughts will be displeasing to a great many, only that I should speak the truth. And I firmly believe that anyone at all familiar with the art of oratory will approve my views.

These passages are perhaps sufficient to illustrate both Prokopovich's own conception of the true art of oratory and the nature of the currents against which he was swimming. In condemning Młodzianowski and one or two other Polish Jesuits whom he named, in condemning indeed the whole of "Polish oratory," he was condemning the models and practices of "many," as he says, of his fellow Kievans (features of the "curious style" can be found for example in the sermons of Stefan Iavorskii, as in his use of what Prokopovich considered "tasteless" dialogues and rhetorical questions). But noteworthy too is the specifically anti-Polish aspect of Prokopovich's attack, an aspect which appears elsewhere in the rhetoric lectures—anti-Polish, it should be stressed, rather than simply anti-Catholic or anti-Jesuit (Prokopovich cites with approval various of the established Spanish, Italian, and French Jesuit rhetoricians of the sixteenth and early seventeenth centuries, who he says would agree with him in condeming the "Polish eloquence"). And this anti-Polish aspect is probably attributable to more than a neo-Renaissance or protoclassicist distaste for what was by now the decadent Polish Baroque: there was it seems something robustly nativist, something Ukrainian, at work here too. In any case, manuscript copies of Prokopovich's rhetoric course were to circulate among specialists not only in Kiev but later in Moscow, where such luminaries as Lomonosov, Novikov, and Sumarokov would eventually acclaim him, the "Russian Cicero," as their teacher.[24]

As for his philosophy lectures, here too Prokopovich would introduce bold if less immediately consequential innovations. The first of these was to devote the whole of one year to mathematics.[25] Although in this respect his course corresponded with the standard western textbooks of the day, it was unusually detailed and thorough; and in his "Geometria" he provided what has been judged a masterly introduction to the best of Renaissance thought on the subject—the first such course in his homeland to be "erected on a scientific basis," being in this regard superior in particular to Magnitskii's *Arifmetika* of 1703, which remained for half a century the basic textbook of mathematics in Russia.[26] Next came his lectures on logic, of which only fragments survive.[27] But from them it is clear that it was not in his emphasis on the importance of logic or on the usefulness of disputation that Prokopovich differed from his Kievan predecessors. This distinction was, rather, in his more frequent reference to Aristotle himself, in his concern for the strict conduct of disputation, and in his overall method, where a most unscholastic effort appears to have been made to avoid subtleties and unnecessary speculation, to be as concrete and practical as possible, and to make sure, by repetition and frequent questioning, that his students understood him.

In his lectures on physics, as Prokopovich himself says, "a primo loco sit autoritas Aristotelis."[28] And apart from his very conception and organization of the course, whole sections of his physical lectures amount to digests of the corresponding parts of Aristotle. In this once again Prokopovich resembled his predecessors at the Kiev academy. Moreover, like them, his mentors and theirs, he was willing in these lectures to engage in questions which properly belonged to Christian apologetics, if not to theology, or to assert, as he did at one point, that science cannot contradict Scripture. Yet Prokopovich seems to have drawn more often than his mentors and predecessors directly on Aristotle's works themselves as distinct from scholastic textbooks and commentaries. His range of secondary authorities was considerably wider, too: on certain points he cites some of the most advanced thinkers of the age—Galileo (whom he also defended in a poem against the pope);[29] Descartes, Boyle, Brahe, Borelli, and Johann Zahn. He could depart from the Master and from the scholastic tradition enough to raise, as an interesting hypothesis, the Copernican view of the earth's position and movements. Or rather than speculate, in scholastic fashion, on when exactly the world was created, he simply presented to his students a "Hexaemeron" of Greek patristic views.

But it was perhaps in what his friend Bayer called his "new method" that Prokopovich differed most from both his predecessors and immediate successors in the teaching of physics at the Kiev academy. For him it was not only a matter of using the best authorities, of being a master of one's subject, and of constantly striving to make things clear; both by precept and by example he advocated a kind of freedom of inquiry. His ideal, as he says in one place, was a "scientia tranquilla, libera, nullo alio negotio occupata, nedum oppressa mente." There was even room in his view of physics for careful personal observation and for a little scientific experimentation. He was to retain, so far as his other activities permitted, a lifelong interest in mathematics and physics (a Danish scholar who met him in the last year of his life was struck by his "deep knowledge of mathematics and extraordinary fondness for that art");[30] and this was one of the qualities which would endear him to Peter the Great.

The remainder of Prokopovich's philosophy course was devoted to lectures on metaphysics and ethics. Nothing of the former survives, and very little of the latter.[31] The loss of the ethical lectures is particularly unfortunate. For Prokopovich appears to have been the first and for a century almost the only professor of philosophy at Kiev to teach the subject, and we might have learned from his lectures why this was so. Was it simply another instance, as with mathematics, of Kiev's lacking the fullness of scholastic tradition—where "natural" ethics, like metaphysics, occupied in any case a subordinate position in philosophy, no doubt because they both impinged on the realm of the sacred? Or was it that, somewhat analogously, Prokopovich's predecessors and most of his successors had chosen to avoid the subject lest they become imbued—being ignorant or afraid of Aristotle himself—with Roman Catholic or Jesuit doctrine? Was it a religious prejudice, in other words, that kept the study of ethics out of the Kiev curriculum, with all that this might imply for the development of ethical thought among the East Slavs? And by introducing the subject, therefore, did Prokopovich exhibit a typically Renaissance (or humanist) bent for moral philosophy? His ethical lectures could well have provided further evidence of an independent, critical, open, and, given his time and place, original mind.

Finally, regarding Prokopovich's theological lectures,[32] which he never completed, we must confine ourselves to mentioning, or repeating, only two of their more notable characteristics. The first is the critical spirit in which he approached all but the most central of the classical Christian dogmas; and the second is the degree to which he attempted to base himself on Scripture and on the works of the fathers, especially those of the eastern church. That is to say, Prokopovich's theological lectures at Kiev strove to embody the principles which he himself laid down in his *Ecclesiastical Regulation* of 1720, where he wrote:

He who would teach theology must be learned in holy Scripture and able to expound correctly its true essence and to corroborate all the dogmas with Scriptural evidence. And for help in this he should diligently search the writings of the holy fathers. . . . And while a teacher may seek assistance from modern authors of other faiths, he must not imitate them and give credence to their expositions but only accept their guidance in the arguments they employ from Scripture and the ancient teachers, particularly as regards those dogmas wherein other faiths agree with us. However their arguments are not to be credited lightly, but rather examined to see whether such and such a quotation is to be found in Scripture or in the patristic writings and whether it has there the sense in which they use it. . . . Thus a teacher of theology must not teach according to foreign expositions, but according to his own understanding.[33]

Later in the eighteenth century, and in the early nineteenth, editions of Prokopovich's theological lectures were to be printed and used in the ecclesiastical academies of Kiev, St. Petersburg, and Moscow.[34] Yet in his own time they aroused the hostility of his colleagues, some of whom, led by Stefan Iavorskii, would denounce his teaching as "innovative and opposed to our holy apostolic church," as being in effect un-Orthodox, even Protestant,[35] charges which have been repeated by later writers.[36] And to the learned "Latinizers" of the Kiev academy and their (apparently few) Muscovite followers (Prokopovich's disputes with the Muscovite traditionalists or with the Old Believers are separate problems, concerned with other than high theological matters), his "critical-historical" approach to theology must indeed have seemed radical, as a comparison of his lectures with what was perhaps the finest flower of Kievan scholasticism, Iavorskii's *Rock of Faith*, would indicate.[37] Indeed one authority has observed, perhaps a little closer to the mark, that at some points Prokopovich's theological lectures have a philosophical character comparable to the reflections on God of Bacon, Descartes, Spinoza, or Leibnitz,[38] some of whose works we know he had read. But in any historical assessment of Prokopovich's theology it would seem that several points ought to be borne in mind: the theological impoverishment, by comparison with the contemporary West or its subsequent history, of the eastern and especially the Russian church of Prokopovich's time;[39] the criticism of Iavorskii's own theology by a principal Orthodox spokesman of the day, as mentioned above; the fact that in their theologies both Prokopovich and Iavorskii, in their different ways, were responding to the challenge of western theology (Iavorskii being more concerned with the Protestant menace, Prokopovich with the Catholic);[40] and the necessity of distinguishing Prokopovich's theology proper, which was entirely the product of his years as professor at Kiev, from the works—especially the more or less overtly political works—of his later, St. Petersburg period, where indeed clear traces of "Protestant" (rationalist, secularist, early Enlightenment) thought can be found. Prokopovich was neither the first nor the last Orthodox churchman to hold in effect that his theology was one thing, his views on church administration, or his politics, another. And if we are to criticize him as a churchman, it will not be perhaps for the un-Orthodox nature of his theology as it were retroactively defined, but for his excessive involvement, as it came to be, in worldly affairs.

Prokopovich did not complete his theology course according to plan because late in 1715 he was summoned to St. Petersburg by the tsar, whose commands, as Iavorskii and other Kievans had discovered, were not to be resisted. But unlike Iavorskii, who in Russia remained preeminently a churchman of unchanging views and grew steadily apart from the tsar, Prokopovich broadened his horizons, and soon became Peter's church reformer and leading apologist. This brings up the last topic to be briefly discussed here, namely the emergence, still during his period of association with the Kiev academy, of Prokopovich the *homo politicus*.

Expressions of patriotism are to be found in most of Prokopovich's earliest surviving works, those dating from before 1709 or so, a group which includes the lectures on poetics and rhetoric, the tragicomedy *Vladimir*, a few shorter poems, and two sermons. Among the poems is one celebrating the Dnieper, toward the end of which there is a reference to the river's "greatest monument," namely "Urbs hac ipsa [Kiev itself], decus patriae, materque potentis / Imperii . . .," a city which the river nourished and protected and whence in times past armed ships descended to the Black Sea itself,[41] which, of course, in Prokopovich's time was largely under Turkish control. Similarly, various passages of *Vladimir* and of the two sermons in question reveal a pride in

Kiev as a city with a glorious past, which was then undergoing a cultural renaissance and, beyond that, a general Orthodox-Slavic or "Russian" consciousness.[42] Prokopovich's attack on the "Polish eloquence" has been mentioned. There, in his rhetoric lectures, he also insisted that Młodzianowski and the "Polish eloquence" did "great harm . . . to the state and religion." He warned his students that "our enemies" both openly and insidiously fostered·a hostile, falsifying, and reproachful view of "our fatherland and faith"; and doubtless he had Polish Jesuits in mind here and the growing encroachment of the Uniat church, which even the Brotherhood of Lwów, the major city and cultural center of western Ukraine, shortly was to join. Elsewhere in his rhetoric course Prokopovich denounced the "papist deceivers" for distorting church history and for "despoiling" the writings of the fathers: indeed history, he argued, could be a powerful weapon in exposing the "Latins" and in reviving the glorious past of one's own country—in creating a new national consciousness, he might have said. This attitude no doubt influenced his choice of subject in *Vladimir*, whose central theme, in the words of the play's prologue, was "none other than the story of the conversion to Christ of our prince equal-to-the-apostles, Vladimir."

But the question arises of what Prokopovich meant by such terms as "Russia [*Rossiia*]," the "All-Russian realm," "all the Russian lands," the "Russian folk [*narod*]," the "Slavonic-Russian lands," or the "Slavonic-Russian people [*rod*]": in short, whether he was, on the evidence of these works, at this time a Ukrainian nationalist.[43] My own view[44] is that since we do not know for certain what Ukrainian writers of the period generally meant by the term *Rossiia* (or *Rosiia*) and by any adjectives formed from it (as distinct from such terms as *Rus'*, *Malorossiia*, *Ruthenia*, or *Ukraina* and any adjectives formed from them); and that since, in the works in question, Prokopovich consistently identified his country by the term *Rossiia* (though even here we must be careful, since none of these works is known from an original manuscript or even from a closely contemporary copy): that in view of these considerations we simply cannot say that Prokopovich meant to restrict the term to what was, or is, called "Ukraine"—that he meant, in particular, to exclude Orthodox Muscovy from his patriotic or national purview.

Nor can we be any more certain, on the evidence available, whether Prokopovich felt that his ultimate political loyalty in the years before 1709 was owed to the hetman or to the tsar, though the references to the two in *Vladimir*, and his speech of 5 July 1706,[45] strongly suggest that it was to the tsar. The speech, whose enthusiastic and quite specific praises of Peter seem to go well beyond contemporary panegyrical conventions, was delivered to Peter himself in the Trinity church of the Monastery of the Caves on the occasion of the tsar's first visit to Kiev, whose fortifications he had come to strengthen against the common enemies. It was their first meeting (the church is so small that they would have stood no more than a few feet apart); and knowing Peter's partiality for a good speech, as well as what Prokopovich actually said, we might well conclude that the basis of their future collaboration was laid there and then, in Kiev in 1706.

The point is of some importance in understanding Prokopovich's political evolution because another class of his critics has said or implied that before 1708 or 1709 he was primarily loyal to the hetman and thus a Ukrainian nationalist in an exclusivist sense, with aspirations for Ukrainian independence whether from Poland or from Muscovy.[46] In this view, Prokopovich then opportunistically championed Peter's cause when in 1708-9 Hetman Mazepa abandoned his allegiance to the tsar and went on to lose the battle of Poltava in company with his new-found allies, the kings of Sweden and Poland. After Poltava Prokopovich did indeed clearly enunciate the strongly pro-Peter, monarchical, and pan-"Russian" views from which he was never thereafter to waver; and until the final summons to St. Petersburg he did in his remaining years in Kiev accept various imperial commissions. But apart from the considerations already mentioned, it must be emphasized that from what can be known for certain of Prokopovich's political views—if such they can be called—before Poltava his behavior afterwards was neither necessarily inconsistent nor particularly opportunistic. Indeed before Poltava his attitudes in this regard, as expressed in the works we have discussed, were undeniably two things, and only two: first, staunchly anti-Catholic, anti-Uniat, and especially anti-Polish Catholic; and second, just as staunchly pro-Kievan, the latter amounting to a kind of civic patriotism in which local traditions—Kiev as "the second Jerusalem"—and classical or Renaissance ideals were thoroughly mixed.

But in conclusion it should be remembered that only for the origins of the *homo politicus*, of the future church reformer and spokesman of enlightened absolutism, can we look in the records of Prokopovich's Kiev period. The works of these years are overwhelmingly academic in character: even *Vladimir* and the shorter poems were composed as academic exercises, and the two speeches or sermons that we have referred to were given by Prokopovich in his capacity as professor of rhetoric. Indeed, had he never gone to St. Petersburg, had he died, rather, in 1715, he would still be accounted the most distinguished member of the Kiev academy during its golden age. And for that reason alone, it might be urged, his works of this period deserve to be carefully studied.

NOTES

1. To be consistent with previously published work on Prokopovich in English, or with accepted English usage, the transliteration of certain Ukrainian names follows Russian rather than Ukrainian spellings: thus Prokopovich or Iavorskii, not Prokopovyč or Javors'kyj; Kiev, not Kyjiv.

2. *Razsuzhdenie o netlenii moshchei sviatykh ugodnikov bozhiikh v Kievskikh peshcherakh, netlenno pochivaiushchikh*, Moscow, 1786, 1799; Kiev, 1823, 1852, 1875, 1890, 1905. The work was originally written in Latin and first published in Prokopovich, *Miscellanea sacra. . .* , Breslau, 1744, 65-122.

3. The basic scholarly biography is still I. Chistovich, *Feofan Prokopovich i ego vremia*, St. Petersburg, 1868. Only a few of its more than 700 pages are devoted to the first half of Prokopovich's life most of which was spent in Kiev. For details of the growing body of scholarly literature on Prokopovich, and for a comprehensive list of his surviving works (including MSS), see James Cracraft, "Feofan Prokopovich: A Bibliography of his Works," *Oxford Slavonic Papers*, n.s. VIII, 1975, 1-36: hereafter cited as "Bibliography."

4. "Vita Theophanis Procopovitsch," in J.B. Sherer, ed., *Nordische Nebenstudien*, I, Frankfurt and Leipzig, 1776: the "Vita" was probably written soon after Prokopovich's death by G.S. Bayer, a German scholar and original member of the St. Petersburg Academy of Sciences who knew Prokopovich during the last ten years of his life; "Vita Auctoris," in Prokopovich, *Tractatus de Processione Spiritus Sancti*, Gotha, 1772 (see "Bibliography," no. 144): the author of this "Vita" as well as editor of this work was probably Dmitrii (later Damaskin) Semenov-Rudnev (or Semenovich Rudnev), who was prefect and rector of the

Moscow ecclesiastical academy (1775-82) and may once have been Prokopovich's pupil in St. Petersburg; and the biographical note written about four years after Prokopovich's death by his friend and protege Antiokh Kantemir, in Kantemir's *Satiry i drugiia stikhotvorcheskiia sochineniia*, St. Petersburg, 1762, 39: reprinted in Z.I. Gershkovich, ed., *Antiokh Kantemir: Sobranie stikhotvorenii*, Leningrad, 1956, 100-101.

5. On the Kiev academy at this time, see N. Petrov, *Kievskaia akademiia vo vtoroi polovine XVII veka*, Kiev, 1895; S. Golubev, *Kievskaia akademiia v kontse XVII i nachale XVIII stoletii*, Kiev, 1901; D. Vishnevskii, *Kievskaia akademiia v pervoi polovine XVIII stoletiia*, Kiev, 1903; and Z.I. Xyžnjak, *Kyjevo-Mohyljans'ka akademija*, Kiev, 1970. For details, see also V. Askochenskii, *Kiev s drevneishim ego uchilishchem akademieiu*, 2 vols., Kiev, 1856; N. Mukhin, *Kievo-Bratskii uchilishchnyi monastyr': Istoricheskii ocherk*, Kiev, 1893; and Mukhin, *Kievo-Bratskii uchilishchnyi monastyr': Istoriko-arkheologicheskii ocherk*, Kiev, 1895. A useful introduction in English is A. Sydorenko, "The Kievan Academy in the 17th Century," Ph.D. Diss., University of Illinois, Urbana-Champaign, 1974.

On the Brotherhood movement and its schools, see K.V. Kharlampovich, *Zapadnorusskie pravoslavnyeshkoly XVI-nachala XVII veka*, Kazan, 1898; E.N. Medynskii, *Bratskie shkoly Ukrainy i Belorussii v XVI-XVII vv. i ikh rol' v vossoedinenii Ukrainy s Rossiei*, Moscow, 1954; and Ja. D. Isajevych, *Bratstva ta jix rol' v rozvytku ukrajins'koji kul'tury XVI-XVII st.*, Kiev. 1966.

6. On Kiev at this time, see the relevant parts of Askochenskii, *Kiev s drevneishim ego; Opisanie Kieva*, 2 vols., Moscow, 1868; V.B. Antonovich and F.A. Ternovskii, eds., *Sbornik materialov dlia istoricheskoi topografii Kieva i ego okrestnostei*, Kiev, 1874; and V.E. Dement'eva *et al.*, eds., *Istoriia Kieva*, 2 vols., Kiev, 1963: original Ukrainian ed., Kiev. 1960.

7. "Slovo privetstvitel'noe na prishestvie v Kiev Ego Tsarskago Presvetlago Velichestva," in Prokopovich, *Slova i rechi . . .* , ed. S.F. Nakoval'nim, I, St. Petersburg, 1760, 1-11.

8. *Sochineniia sv. Dimitriia, mitropolita Rostovskago*, Kiev, 1824, I, 326; Petrov, *Kievskaia akademiia*, 40, 133.

9. For a clear expression of these beliefs, see Prokopovich's *Pervoe uchenie otrokom. . . . Kratkoe tolkovanie zakonnago desiatosloviia, Molitvyi Gospodni, simvola very, i desiati blazhenstv*, St. Petersburg, 1720 ("Bibliography," no. 123); translated excerpts quoted in James Cracraft, *The Church Reform of Peter the Great*, Stanford, 1971, 281-85.

10. G. Florovsky, *Puti russkago bogosloviia*, Paris, 1937, 92.

11. See Iu. Samarin, *Stefan Iavorskii i Feofan Prokopovich* (=vol. 5 of Samarin's *Sochineniia*, Moscow, 1880); J. Šerech, "Stefan Yavorsky and the Conflict of Ideologies in the Age of Peter I," *Slavonic and East European Review*, XXX, no. 74, December 1951, 40-62; or Cracraft, *Church Reform*, esp. 45-49 and 133-35, with further references.

12. For Iavorskii's career, see Cracraft, *Church Reform*, esp. 122-64, with further references. For his theology in particular, see Samarin, *Stefan Iavorskii*; I. Morev, ed., *"Kamen' very" Mitropolita Stefana Iavorskago*, St. Petersburg, 1904; and Petrov, *Kievskaia akademiia*, 49-50, 53-56, 115ff.

13. Cracraft, *Church Reform*, 124-26.

14. For information on Prokopovich's Roman "stage," see, in addition to Bayer's "Vita," R. Stupperich, "Feofan Prokopovič in Rom," *Zeitschrift für osteurop'äische Geschichte*, V, 1931, 327-39, which is based on the records of the Greek College.

15. In the *Ecclesiastical Regulation* of 1720: see the critical ed. by P.V. Verkhovskoi in his *Uchrezhdenie Dukhovnoi kollegii i Dukhovnyi reglament*, Rostov-on-Don, 1916, II, 53.

16. "Elegia ascetica filii ad parentum, a vita monastica ad civilem se sollicitantem," in Prokopovich, *Miscellanea sacra*, 159-60; also I.P. Eremin, ed., *Feofan Prokopovich: Sochineniia*, Moscow and Leningrad, 1961, 262-63.

17. *Dukhovnyi reglament*, ed. Verkhovskoi, II, 51.

18. G.S. Bayer, *Museum sinicum*, I, St. Petersburg, 1730, dedication, 4ff.

19. "Slovo v nedeliu osmuiunadesiat' . . . ," in Eremin, *Feofan Prokopovich*, 60ff.

20. *De arte poetica libri III, ad usum et institutionem studiosae juventutis roxolanae dictati Kioviae in Orthodoxa Academia Mohyleana a. d. 1705*, ed. G. Konisskii, Mogilev, 1786; reprinted (without app.) in Eremin, *Feofan Prokopovich*, 229ff: see "Bibliography," no. 167.

21. Vishnevskii, *Kievskaia akademiia*, 132-33, 143-46; N. Petrov. *Ocherki iz istorii ukrainskoi literatury XVIII veka: Kievskaia iskustvennaia literatura*, Kiev, 1880, 13ff; M. Dovhalevs'kyj. *Poetica*, trans. V.P. Masljuka, Kiev, 1973; R. Luzhnyi, "'Poetica' Feofana Prokopovicha i teoriia poezii v Kievo-Mogilianskoi akademii," in D.S. Likhachev *et al.*, eds., *Rol' i znachenie literatury XVIII veka v istorii russkoi kul'tury*, Moscow and Leningrad, 1965, 47-53.

22. Eremin, *Feofan Prokopovich*, translator's note, 496f.

23. *De arte rhetorica libri decem: A Theophano Prokopovicz, olim ex variis authoribus, collecti*: a mid-eighteenth-century MS at the Lenin Library, Moscow (fond 354, no. 221, 178ff.); cf. "Bibliography," no. 168.

24. See N.D. Kochetkova, "Oratorskaia proza Feofana Prokopovicha i puti formirovaniia literatury klassitsizma," *XVIII vek: sbornik 9*, Leningrad, 1974, 50-80.

25, "Duo primi et uberrimi rerum mathematicarum fontes: Arithmetica et Geometria; in gratiam studiosae roxolanae juventutis in Academia Kijovomohyleana explicatae. A.D. 1707 et 1708": an eighteenth-century MS at the Library of the Ukrainian Academy of Sciences, Kiev (fond Dukhov. akad. p. 43, ff. 257-335).

26. O.A. Sichkar, "Feofan Prokopovich kak matematik," *Voprosy istorii estestvoznaniia i tekhniki*, XIV, 1968, 44-46.

27. "De legibus et regulis rectae disputationis cum aliis institutionis," in N. Bantysh-Kaminskii, ed., *F.C. Baumeister et Elementa philosophiae recentioris . . . usibus juventutis Rossicae adornata*, I, Moscow, 1777, app., 108-25; I have so far not been able to inspect the relevant MS at the Library of the Ukrainian Academy of Sciences.

28. "Physica. . .": an eighteenth-century MS at the Library of the Ukrainian Academy of Sciences (fond Dukhov. akad. p. 485, ff. 1-102).

29. "Cur naturae agilem, vexas, papa impie, mystam?", in *Trudy Kievskoi dukhovnoi akademii*, no 3, 1869, 385-86.

30. Peder von Haven, *Reise in Russland . . .,* Copenhagen, 1744, 19.

31. R. Stupperich, "F. Prokopovič und seine akademische Wirksamkeit in Kiev," *Zeitschrift für slavische Philologie,* XVII, 1941, 96-99; based on an MS then to be found in the State Public Library, Kiev.

32. *Christianae orthodoxa theologiae in Academia Kiowiensi a Theophane Prokopowicz . . . adornatae et propositae,* 3 vols., Leipzig, 1782-84; contents of vol. 3 not by Prokopovich (see "Bibliography," no. 138).

33. *Dukhovnyi reglament,* ed. Verkhovskoi, II, 55.

34. See "Bibliography," nos. 110, 132, 136, 137, 138, 139, 141, 143, 144.

35. See Cracraft, *Church Reform,* 134.

36. Samarin, *Stefan Iavorskii;* G. Kowalyk, *Ecclesiologia Theophanis Prokopovycz: influxus protestantismi,* Rome, 1947; A.V. Kartashev, *Ocherki po istorii russkoi tserkvi,* II, Paris, 1959, 336ff; and Kartashev, "Byl li pravoslavnym Feofan Prokopovich?", in *Sbornik v chest' D.F. Kobenko,* St. Petersburg, 1913; Florovsky, *Puti russkago bogosloviia,* 89-97; or R. Stupperich, "F. Prokopovičs theologische Bestrebungen," *Kyrios,* IV, 1936, 350-62. Some of these charges have recently been countered by H.-J. Härtel, *Byzantinisches Erbe und Orthodoxie bei Feofan Prokopovič,* Würzburg, 1970.

37. See Morev, *"Kamen' very" Iavorskago.*

38. F. Tikhomirov, *Traktaty Feofana Prokopovicha o Boge edinom po sushchestvu i troichnom v Litsakh,* St. Petersburg, 1884, 65.

39. Cf. T. Ware, *The Orthodox Church,* London, 1963, 109: "Looking back [on the seventeenth and early eighteenth centuries] . . . one is struck by the limitations of [Orthodox] theology in this period: one does not find the Orthodox tradition in its *fullness.*"

40. As Father Florovsky says, "The historical fate of Russian theology in the eighteenth century was to be decided in the course of a struggle between the epigones of post-Reformation Roman and Protestant scholasticism" (*Puti russkago bogosloviia,* 97)—a remark which can be taken to mean that by later and better informed standards neither Prokopovich nor his critics were properly Orthodox.

41. "Laudatio Borysthenis," in Eremin, *Feofan Prokopovich,* 265-66.

42. The critical edition of *Vladimir* is in Eremin, *Feofan Prokopovich,* 149ff. For the two sermons, see n. 6 above, and the "Slovo v den' Sviatago ravnoapostolnago i velikago kniazia Vladimira," also in Prokopovich, *Slova i rechi,* III, St. Petersburg, 1765, 335-49.

43. As suggested by J. Šerech, "On Teofan Prokopovič as Writer and Preacher in his Kiev Period," *Harvard Slavic Studies,* II, 1954, 211-23; reprinted 1971.

44. For some critical discussion of which see the *Minutes of the Seminar in Ukrainian Studies held at Harvard University,* no. 5, 1974-75, 60-62.

45. As cited above, n. 7.

46. See works cited in nn. 43 and 44 above.

Orthodoxy and Russia's Enlightenment, 1762-1825

Robert L. Nichols

The study of education has always been important in
Western thought, attracting the interest of the greatest
intellects in every age. Yet after several thousand years of
close attention a precise definition, particularly of the more
normative and ideational aspects of education, still eludes
us. We do have the very strong implicit feeling that
education is concerned with the maintenance of a social
and cultural consciousness, with the transmission of an
informed tradition that sustains civilization. Today,
however, more than ever before, the study of education is
of crucial significance since we expect not only the
sustaining of our cultural traditions but also their critical
revision and development. We demand of education that it
provide a means to ever greater cultural vitality. And this,
moreover, is often made without any clear realization that
the demand itself is the result of historical processes.

James Bowen, *A History of
Western Education*, II

Many western writers on Russian learning and education assert that historically the Russian Orthodox church either has been anti-intellectual
or its contributions to education have been negligible. In the more

specialized writings on Russian education, one notices a conspicuous absence of attention to the church schools of the eighteenth or nineteenth century. W.H.E. Johnson's *Russia's Educational Heritage* depicts Russia's heritage in exclusively secular colors and leaves the impression that practically the only education Russians received came in state or private schools. With the exception of a few passing paragraphs on seventeenth-century church schools, his focus is entirely on state-sponsored education.[1]

Nicholas Hans similarly neglects the church schools of the eighteenth and nineteenth centuries. After briefly noting that "these clerical schools for the whole [eighteenth] century remained the chief source of students for all Russian higher education," Hans simply avoids them in his discussion of education for those years.[2]

One final example may suffice to illustrate how little attention to the ecclesiastical schools monographs on Russian education pay. In his single chapter relating to the period from 1700 to 1855, Patrick Alston devotes only a few lines on three scattered pages to the role of the church in education, although he mentions that for the most of the eighteenth century the church "was responsible for providing what limited [educational] opportunity there was for the general population."[3] Thus, despite any such passing recognition, the general impression is that the church actually played a minor role and that its contributions were unimportant and not worth investigating.

Fortunately, the church schools have quite recently received much better treatment from western historians of eighteenth-century Russia. Max J. Okenfuss, for example, argues that the invariable description of the church schools as "religious" obscures that they were in reality "classical colleges," for they were not narrowly religious, exclusively theological schools, or even confined to the clerical estate. By recognizing the essentially classical and multiclass character of Russia's church schools, the biographies of such men as Speranskii, Lomonosov, Levitskii, Bantysh-Kamenskii, and other prominent secular figures educated in these schools become more comprehensible. Also, the origins of the "democratic intelligentsia" can be accounted for, and the tendency of Russian book printers to concentrate on technical and classical studies is more easily understandable. Seen in this light, the schools undoubtedly were successful as centers to prepare Russians for secular as well as ecclesiastical positions. Such was the hope of Peter I for Russian education. "What more could Peter ask?"[4]

These remarks must be commended as long overdue. If anything, they do not go far enough in insisting on the importance of these classical and "humanitarian" schools. Moreover, such remarks should be extended beyond the period in which the schools preserved a multi-estate character to encompass the later eighteenth century and much of the nineteenth, when the seminaries served as schools exclusively for the clergy. My purpose is to do that by summarizing some information about the ecclesiastical schools during the period 1762-1825, and thus to correct some prevailing judgments about those schools and the church which cared for them. Essentially the task is twofold: first, to emphasize that the Russian church played a profoundly important role in Russia's educational and professional growth; second, to stress the very close relationship between these schools and their students on the one hand and the broad intellectual and cultural currents in Russia on the other. This brief survey may begin laying to rest the widely held belief among western (and many Russian) writers that Orthodoxy maintained an age-old indifference to thought, that it was incapable of any significant educational labor, and that the church and the clergy therefore remained isolated from the winds of change blowing over Russia from Peter's day onward. It is time to abandon the view that the church, possessing little or nothing of higher value historically, and acquiring nothing from the West, stood apart and untouched by the influences transforming the country during the imperial era.

A casual glance at the growth of Russian education during the reign of Catherine II reveals the church vigorously, if somewhat reluctantly, at work on behalf of her ambitious schemes for Russia's enlightenment.[5] The so-called popular schools (*narodnye shkoly*) figured prominently among her educational projects, and any success which these schools achieved during the last decades of the century resulted very substantially from the church's support. Impressed by Joseph II's description of the Austrian school system, Catherine decided to form a commission in 1782 for creating a similar system in Russia. Count P.V. Zavadovskii, a graduate of the Kiev academy (and thus a fitting representative of the church's contribution to these schools), took charge of the commission. A triple tier of primary, secondary, and normal schools soon extended over twenty-five provinces of the Russian Empire, and in 1783 the commission created a special Teachers Seminary to train the teachers needed to staff them.

Since the secular schools had nothing like enough teacher candidates nor even the teachers to prepare them, Zavadovskii's commission turned naturally and repeatedly to the church schools for draftees. Initially, the commission, armed with an imperial directive, ordered the Alexander Nevskii Seminary to send twenty of its best students to teach in the hastily opened primary schools—the lowest tier and the first to open. A similar directive the following year ordered the seminaries in Moscow, Kazan, Smolensk, and Tver to provide a total of fifty teachers.

Such temporary and expedient measures accompanied the commission's longer-range efforts to produce qualified teachers at its own Teachers Seminary. Here, too, the existing seminaries supplied the needed student body, and the first entering class at the new seminary consisted of 165 students drawn from various ecclesiastical schools. In fact, the commission attempted to find nonseminary candidates by prevailing upon Moscow University and the Gymnasium attached to it to send students, but the task proved impossible. The Gymnasium could provide none, while the four sent by the university all returned there the next year. Volunteers, too, were accepted, and twelve such students enrolled at the seminary—but all twelve turned out to be seminarians. Not surprisingly, then, of the approximately 400 teachers trained by the seminary between 1782 and 1801, well over 300 came from the Orthodox clergy.[6] Given these data, it is time to discard the view sustained in the detailed studies and popularized by textbooks that such "popular schools" had to be established "not because the authorities had any prejudice against the participation of the Church in education but because the Church simply could not produce sufficient priests capable of teaching."[7]

A picture similar to that of general education emerges from a study of Russia's higher education, professional schools, and learned societies.

On the same day in January 1803 that the Ministry of Education (Catherine's old commission reorganized, renamed, and once more headed by Zavadovskii) received guidelines for public higher education, the imperial government decreed that "diocesan bishops be instructed to release that number of seminarians [to enroll in the universities] deemed necessary by the Ministry of Education."[8] As a result, Khar'kov University opened that year with fifty-four students, of whom forty had come from Kursk Seminary and Khar'kov Collegium. Moreover, the university's medical lectures went unattended until the church permitted seminarians to hear them.

The story is identical at Kazan University, and, even in Moscow, throughout the first decades of the nineteenth century, Russia's oldest university continued to request of the Holy Synod indirectly through the Ministry of Education that students be sent to it from the seminaries. According to the *Biographical Dictionary* (*Biograficheskii slovar'*) of Moscow University professors, until the end of the eighteenth century the university had sixty-four teachers: thirty-three foreigners, twenty-two who had received their training in Orthodox seminaries, and eleven who were educated elsewhere.[9] The practice of seminarians to study and then become professors at Moscow University lasted well into the nineteenth century, as is demonstrated by the career of Russia's greatest historian, V.O. Kliuchevskii. Beginning his education as a poor "bursak" at the Penza ecclesiastical school, Kliuchevskii subsequently entered the Penza Seminary (1856) and Moscow University (1861). Eventually he succeeded to the chair of his former teacher S.M. Solov'ev (who, like Kliuchevskii, came from a clerical family).

The Teachers Seminary, reorganized in 1804, renamed the Pedagogical Institute, and attached as a separate division to the projected University of St. Petersburg, opened only because Zavadovskii's influence enabled a student body to be acquired from the Alexander Nevskii Seminary. In fact, only a third of the first three graduating classes (totaling 330 new teachers) had previously attended state schools. Later, in 1828, when the Pedagogical Institute was once more reconstituted as a separate school called the Central Pedagogical Institute, seminary students comprised the entire enrollment. This situation continued for the next two years, but subsequently the proportion of seminary students slowly dropped.[10]

The role of Russian Orthodoxy as an agent for popular and higher education is essentially repeated in the professions. Church schools made notable contributions to the growth of both medicine and law.

Most of the eighteenth century witnessed a barely perceptible growth in Russia's medical profession, restricted by a combination of the low social esteem for Russian medical practitioners and the lack of adequate secular secondary education. Medical authorities under Empress Elizabeth tried to ease this problem by opening the medical academies and Moscow University to children of the clergy.[11] But at the century's end, the number of physicians remained small, increasing from twenty-one in 1760 to thirty-eight in 1800 for a population approaching 35 million.[12] During the 1790s the government expanded its efforts to establish a functioning medical profession and increase the number of people with even rudimentary medical knowledge. For the latter purpose, the seminaries began to teach medicine along with the other subjects considered necessary, so that "from [the seminaries] might come doctors of both the body and soul."[13] For example, at Trinity Seminary medicine was expounded according to William Buchan's *Domestic medicine, or a treatise on the prevention and cure of diseases by regimen and simple medicines* (translated into Russian from a French edition). One can only speculate about the value of such training. In a letter to his father, Metropolitan Filaret expressed the hope that "neither you nor mother will ever need [Buchan's] medicines."[14]

In any case, following a decree issued in 1797, the Moscow Medico-Chirurgical Academy and the imperial Medico-Chirurgical Academy (as the St. Petersburg academy was renamed in 1790) began to acquire many more students. The seminaries were now required to supply annually fifty students for medical training. In 1803 the government reaffirmed that decree, but removed any upper limit on the number that might be sent, hoping that still more could be drawn into the study of medicine.[15] The results were impressive. Between 1808 and 1822 the Imperial Medico-Chirurgical Academy produced 654 physicians and

108 veterinarians. From 1824 to 1838 the academy graduated 677 medical trainees of all types.[16] Although these statistics do not indicate the number of seminarians among the graduates, in light of earlier decrees and later information we have about many individual graduates it is reasonable to assume that a good many of these new doctors had earlier received secondary training in church schools.

The increased number of seminarians entering the medical schools after the turn of the century not only expanded the pool of medical personnel, it also ensured that Russian medicine would make the transition from dependence on foreign sources to being a national profession. In this way the Orthodox schools directly contributed to the development of Russia's human resources and to the growth of a profession, a growth that was vital if Russia was to benefit from its national talent. Of course the seminaries were only a part of the process of creating a national medical base (which indeed remained far too small to meet Russia's needs), but their contribution is undeniable.

In turn, many of the medical students supplied by the seminaries became professors in the St. Petersburg and Moscow medical schools. Between 1830 and 1860, with the leadership provided by such "seminary" medical professors as Evstafii Bogdanovskii (1833-88) and Mikhail Rudnev (1837-78), Russian medicine began to reach the level of that in the German schools as well as take hold as a national force capable of contributing to the empire's well-being.[17] Moreover, those seminarians who received medical training, often in German universities, did not always confine their activities to practical medicine. Some, notably Daniil Vellanskii (a pseudonym for D.M. Kavunnik), turned to *Naturphilosophie*. A contemporary described Vellanskii as the "Russian Schelling," and his influence was great among university students in the 1820s and 1830s.[18]

The law also benefited from the aid given by church schools. As with medical training, every university acquired seminarians in its law classes. But the government also took steps to promote special legal training by enlisting seminary students in the state-sponsored programs. Hence in 1828 it began sending seminarians to the so-called "Professional Institute" at Dorpat University, at that time considered one of the best schools for teacher training: in 1828 it had been designated an institute for the preparation of teachers for the Russian universities.[19] Special schools for legal training in Russia such as the Iaroslavl Juridical Lyceum, or lycée Demidov, enrolled substantial numbers of seminarians. In fact, as late as 1876 the *Yearbook* (*Vremmenik*) of the lycée Demidov shows that of the 483 students who entered after the reform of education during the reign of Alexander II, more than four-fifths were former seminarians.[20] Thus, as in medicine, seminarians constituted an important base for Russia's nascent legal profession.

That same year, 1828, the Second Section of His Majesty's Own Chancellery passed a measure stipulating that six of the best students from the St. Petersburg and Moscow ecclesiastical academies travel to Berlin for study with Friedrich Carl von Savigny. Six more students were sent the following year. This program was a part of Speranskii's renewed work on the collection of the Russian laws, and he hoped to prepare learned jurists for assisting in codifying the laws as well as to raise the level of Russian legal training for subsequent generations of lawyers.

The students sent to Germany justified Speranskii's confidence. Beginning in 1835, with the return of the first group from Savigny's lectures in Berlin, they began occupying the chairs of jurisprudence in Russian universities. Nikita Krylov (1807-79), for example, became a professor of law at Moscow in 1835. He gained wide popularity as one of the university's outstanding lecturers, and like the other Russian disciples of Savigny began to push Russian jurisprudence beyond natural law toward the historical school. In this connection K. A. Nevolin (1806-55) was perhaps even more important. Becoming professor of law at the University of St. Vladimir in 1835, he proceeded to compile a textbook of law on historical principles (*Entsiklopediia zakonovedeniia*, 1839-40). His work came to fruition in his *History of Russian Civil Law* (*Istoriia rossiiskikh grazhdanskikh zakonov*, 1851), based on the sources published at that time by the Archaeographic Commission. The Ministry of War invited Nevolin to help reform the military-criminal laws beginning in 1852. A final example is provided by the career of V.N. Leshkov (1810-81), who also studied with Savigny in Germany and attended the lectures of Ranke. He returned to Russia to pioneer the study of criminal law, which, interestingly, he interpreted as social law. A vigorous man (a model of "the old Moscow professor"), he endeavored to unite Russia's lawyers and jurists by organizing the first congress of Russian jurists in 1875. He also became a leader in the Moscow provincial *zemstvo*.[21]

In sum, as for medicine, the seminaries served as catalysts for drawing out the nation's resources and the seminarians formed a small base for creating a national legal profession. Without them, the task of acquiring European law for state administration, the judicial system, and the general strengthening of Russia's legal foundations would have been much more difficult. How long might the Great Reforms have been delayed?

Finally, Russian learned societies derived much of their strength from the church and its schools. When Princess Dashkova sponsored the creation of the Russian Academy in 1783, its membership included a high proportion of Orthodox clergy. Of the seventy members belonging to the academy from 1783 until 1796, nearly a quarter came from the monastic and parish clergy.[22] Metropolitan Gavriil (Petrov, 1730-1801), the academy's most eminent member, directed the compilation of its famous *Dictionary* (1789-94), that "rich and copious dictionary" which Princess Dashkova intended to be the garland of the Russian language. Moreover, later during the reign of Nicholas I, when the Russian Academy lost its independence by becoming part of the Academy of Sciences and was reorganized in divisions, the Division of Russian Language and Literature still had many members of clerical origins. The division's journal, the *Miscellany* (*Sbornik*), is filled with the writings of learned members of the clergy and professors from the ecclesiastical academies.[23]

Quite similar remarks can be made about the Society of History and Russian Antiquities founded at Moscow University and long served as secretary by professors O.M. Bodianskii (1846-48; 1858-77) and I.D. Beliaev (1849-57), both of whom had received their secondary education in ecclesiastical schools. The *Proceedings* (*Chteniia*) of the society contain many scholarly articles by and about the Orthodox clergy; and many valuable manuscripts on early Russian history, including Giles Fletcher's account of Muscovy, graced its pages under the editorship of the two professors.

This brief review of contributions by the church and its schools only sketches part of a broader outline. But the connections between the church, clergy, and schools on the one side and popular and higher education, the legal and medical professions, and assorted learned societies on the other does perhaps sufficiently indicate that such judgments as the following stand in need of considerable modification:

The Orthodox church never found a common language with the educated because its conservative outlook made it pronouncedly anti-intellectual. Following the medieval precept, "all evil comes from opinions," it showed little interest even in its own theology to which it resorted mainly when compelled to defend itself from heretics or foreigners. It met all attempts to revitalize it with instinctive suspicion which turned into hostility, sometimes accompanied by denunciations to the authorities and excommunication, whenever it felt independent judgment was being brought to bear on its dogmas or practices. One by one, it pushed away from itself the country's finest religious minds: the Slavophiles, Vladimir Soloviev, Leo Tolstoy and the laymen gathered in the early 1900's around the Religious Philosophical Society. It also showed little interest in educating its flock. The Russian Orthodox church first began to involve itself in elementary schooling on any scale only in the 1860's, and then on orders of the state which was becoming alarmed over the influences of the intellectuals on the masses. . . . The clergy now became very much isolated from society, especially from the well-to-do and educated.[24]

In addition to serving as pillars of educated Russian society, these schools also testified to the close identification of educated churchmen with the major trends in Russian thought. In fact, the seminaries and academies did more than mirror the intellectual searchings of the gentry (or rather that minority which interested itself with religious, social, or political questions), for on occasion they anticipated the direction of thought among gentry intellectuals. That the Orthodox schools played this role throughout the period 1762-1825 has not been sufficiently emphasized. And the often noted high incidence of seminarians in the "to the people" movement of the 1870s suggests that the seminaries were not immune to western influence even long after the death of Alexander I. Space does not permit any exhaustive demonstration of these points, but it may be worthwhile to examine briefly the careers of two prominent Orthodox metropolitans, Platon Levshin (1749-

1812) and Filaret Drozdov (1782-1867), in order to relate the elements shaping their views as the "climate of opinion" in Russia changed. These two men cannot be regarded as "typical" of the entire clergy or even all educated clergymen, yet since they served as authoritative voices in the church and as powerful influences on Orthodox intellectual life, they illustrate well the best the Russian clergy was capable of producing in the eighteenth and nineteenth centuries.

Metropolitan Platon, the son of a minor church servitor, attended the Slavonic-Greek-Latin Academy in Moscow, where he studied Latin, poetics, rhetoric, philosophy, and theology. Outside class he discovered "there was no more pleasant exercise . . . than reading both world history and that of the Fatherland" and taught himself Greek, a relatively rare accomplishment in mid-eighteenth-century Russia, even in an academy with "Greek" in its name.[25] St. Paul, St. John Chrysostom, and St. Augustine worked powerfully upon him. He knew the *Reading Menaea* and *Prologue* in Church Slavonic, and he also studied Stefan Iavorskii's *Rock of Faith* (*Kamen' very*) in Russian, but he gave his true allegiance to the classical and Latin works of Cicero and Caesar Baronius. "No one was so pleasing to his [Platon's] taste" as Quintus Curtius Rufus.[26] Platon combined his love of classics with the scholastic theology derived from a schooling differing little from that of Lomonosov's generation.

However, like other educated men whose outlooks were shaped during the reigns of Elizabeth, Peter III, and Catherine II, Platon felt the full force of pietism and sentimentalism (which approximated pietism in several respects), and for him these movements proved enduring. His popular catechetical lectures delivered at the Slavonic-Greek-Latin Academy in 1757-58 sought to explain the Nicene Creed in the language of the pietists, and indirectly those lectures evoke the image of Jacob Böhme (1575-1624), the influential German theosophist. But most important, Platon shared Rousseau's religious temperament, respect for the Bible, awe of the cosmos, and love of solitary meditation. In the same vein, he practiced Rousseau's commandment to cultivate man's best traits — kindness, generosity, honesty, and sympathetic understanding. He may have held a more favorable opinion than Rousseau about the positive qualities of education. He told Catherine he had become a monk "because of a special love of learning."[27] But the author of *Émile* would have appreciated that for Platon the monastery was a "school of piety," providing a "withdrawal from the world" of "excessive worldly vanity, the impious examples of others, harmful associations with bad people, every weakness and obstruction to good works and the pious life." Here, surrounded by solitude and peace, nestled in the bosom of true fraternity, he could contemplate "the beautiful works of a wise creator."[28] Platon, like Rousseau, studiously appreciated Nature.

Whatever Platon's accomplishments may have been as an administrator, bishop, or preacher (he was an outstanding preacher: "Father Platon does as he likes with us; if he wishes us to cry, then we cry," Catherine once said), as an educator he was engaged in intellectual searchings quite similar to those of the gentry.[29] He aimed to modify the military-penal character of the rules governing seminary education outlined in Peter I's *Ecclesiastical Regulation*, a document which candidly confessed that the regime it laid down for the church schools might seem "irksome and similar to imprisonment."[30] Unlike the author of the *Regulation*, Platon believed that prayer and study, ardent attention to the Bible and manners, and honorable conduct and reverence could and would lead to the cultivation of the whole man and to a "community and friendship . . . founded on fraternal love."[31]

Platon shared this outlook with many prominent secular figures of Catherine's reign. His ideal of a new humanity reared behind protective monastery walls is a part of the same ideal which inspired I.I. Betskoi and others in their quest to discover the appropriate education suited to a new nobility, a "new breed of man," on the model of Western Europe. Betskoi's famous schools for women, the Smolnyi Institute in St. Petersburg (1764) and the Novodevichy Institute in Moscow (1765) were located in and formed integral parts of monasteries. And if it is true, as Marc Raeff suggests, that the "major concern [of Betskoi and others] was to mold the 'entire man'—particularly his heart and spirit—thereby endowing each nobleman with a new dignity and worth," then perhaps it is not too much to suggest that Platon hoped to endow each seminarian with a similar appreciation of himself.[32] If educators of the nobility were thoroughly convinced that the "entire man" could be realized only in "boarding schools" which isolated students from the outside world and particularly from a "family milieu that had not yet acquired a Western polish and outlook," then it is not suprising that some churchmen could believe monastery "boarding schools" (and the seminaries *were* boarding academies by Catherine's day) might be suitable instruments for providing a western polish and outlook to children of clergymen. At the least, one can suggest that in organization and subject matter the schools for the nobility and Platon's schools in Moscow bore a remarkable resemblance to each other. Those similarities, as well as the philosophies underlying them, derived from the shared belief that the true curriculum for the schools could be found only in the West. Even the complaining seminarian in Radishchev's *Journey* makes clear the western content in the education supplied by the church schools (both as that education existed and as he hoped it might become).

There is still such a deficiency in our manner of education. . . . The knowledge of Latin alone cannot satisfy the mind thirsting for knowledge. I know Virgil, Horace, Titus Livius, and even Tacitus almost by heart. But when I compare the knowledge of the seminarians with that which I have had a fortunate opportunity to become acquainted, then I must conclude that our schools belong to the preceding century. We know all the classical authors. . . . We are taught philosophy from logic through metaphysics and ethics to theology, but in the words of Kuteikin in *The Minor* [*Nedorosol'*] , we reach the end of philosophy study only to start all over again. Is it any wonder? Aristotle and the scholastics reign supreme in the seminaries. By a lucky acquaintance, I stayed in the home of a provincial councilor in Novgorod and acquired a smattering of French and German and was able to use the books in his home. What a difference . . . what possibilities.[33]

Finally, the ecclesiastical education in these schools, containing very little which might tie students to Russian traditions and a Russian environment, did produce "rootless" seminarians with an outlook similar to that of young rootless nobles. Perhaps this fact helps to account for the very large number of priests' sons who joined the ranks of the Russian intelligentsia in the nineteenth century.

If we look beyond Platon's educational enthusiasms and convictions to his views on Orthodoxy and the church, there once again becomes apparent the degree to which he was representative of his times. He described the church as "an assembly of men who believe in Jesus Christ . . . and live according to His law," a definition little distinguishing Orthodoxy from any other Christian church or even from a freemasons' lodge.[34] Appropriately enough, Platon is usually mentioned (if at all) in the histories of Russia as the supporter of N. I. Novikov, the leading publicist and Russian freemason of the eighteenth century. Catherine had ordered him to investigate Novikov's reading and religious views, and Platon found in Novikov a model to be imitated by any Christian.[35]

Even this brief sketch of Platon's outlook, intellectual preoccupations, and contributions to the education of several generations of students makes clear that leading churchmen breathed much the same air as that making up the secular cultural and intellectual atmosphere of Catherine's reign. In fact, the problem was not the isolation of educated churchmen from the mainstream of Russia's westernization. Rather, as a consequence of the almost wholly western education which the clergy received, and in light of the ideals it inspired in the church's leading representatives, there was a real danger that the church might become simply a western institution or (in view of the state's use of the seminaries for its own benefit) an instrument of secularization. Certainly for Platon the standard for measuring the progress of the Russian clergy was a western one.

Our clergy are regarded by foreigners as nearly ignorant, for we can speak neither French nor German. But we maintain our honor by replying that we can speak and copy Latin. If we study Latin as we do Greek, then we lose our last honor, for we will not be able to speak or write any language.[36]

When one reflects on the fact that a leading hierarch of the Russian Orthodox church in the eighteenth century could defend the use of Latin in the Orthodox schools on the grounds that Latin erudition and traditions gave the Russian clergy its only distinctions, set it apart from the rest of society, and raised its prestige among the people, then the actual extent to which the church and its schools had become enmeshed in Russia's westernization becomes apparent. Fr. Florovsky quite aptly concludes his survey of the church in the eighteenth century by noting that "Russian theology . . . all of this 'school' theology, in the strict sense was rootless. It fell and grew in foreign soil. . . . A super-structure was erected in the desert . . . and in place of roots came stilts. Theology on stilts: such is the legacy of the eighteenth century."[37]

No one was more acutely conscious than Metropolitan Filaret (Drozdov) of the character of Russian Orthodox education and the dangers as well as the opportunities its western orientation held for the church. Filaret's influence on the Russian church, which began during the reign of Alexander I and increased during the next two reigns, is far too extensive and diverse even to be summarized here. But for the purposes of this essay it is sufficient to examine briefly his background and those of his views on Orthodox education elaborated in the years immediately following Napoleon's defeat in Russia. By doing so, further evidence can be adduced to show that Orthodox education did not retreat behind the walls of isolation. In fact, Filaret's efforts to achieve an awakening of Orthodoxy in the schools contributed to the growth of theological and philosophical knowledge among gentry intellectuals in the 1820s and 1830s. Moreover, during the first years of the nineteenth century, all controversy about these schools centered on the best way to reform them so as to strengthen, not weaken, the western education they provided.

Filaret, the son of a village priest in Kolomna, attended the Trinity Seminary from 1800 to 1803, and after graduating at the top of his class, stayed at the seminary to teach Greek, Hebrew, rhetoric, and poetics. Anxious not to lose a student of his caliber to a secular career, Platon urged Filaret to take monastic vows and, after much delay, he consented to do so in 1808. Filaret seems to have shared some of Platon's distaste for the corrupting influence of society. "The first lesson of *living in society* is learning to become more or less a chameleon," he confided in a letter to his father.[38] But he did not agree with Platon that one should choose a monastic life in which the "sole object is learning." Indeed, he had a rather low estimate of the learning he received under Platon's direction at Trinity Seminary, and he rather uncharitably dismissed his alma mater by remarking that "the entire wisdom [of the seminary] consisted of poems for the eighteenth of November"—Platon's name day.[39] Toward the end· of 1808, Filaret went to St. Petersburg to become a teacher at the invitation of a newly

formed commission charged with reorganizing, improving, and central-
izing the ecclesiastical schools. Here he encountered the diverse and
often contradictory programs advanced by westernizing churchmen, the
imperial reformer M. M. Speranskii, and foreign advisers. These programs provide the necessary background for understanding Filaret's
later work and in themselves reveal how characteristic of the times were
their proponents.

The first elaborate proposal for reforming the church schools during
Alexander I's reign came in 1805 from Evgenii (Bolkhovitinov, 1767-
1837, later metropolitan of Kiev). His suggestions were not far-reach-
ing, but they do shed light on the state of mind of some educated
bishops at the turn of the century. Evgenii's chief complaint about the
church schools echoes the lament of Radishchev's seminarian quoted
earlier. He objected to the sway of Latin which he thought impeded the
creative growth of a western-style education. Since the existing curriculum was "not a scientific program, but only a course in Latin literature," he urged not only a break with Latin, which was being rejected
"in all the best European schools," but also the further development
of instruction by relying on the most up-to-date western books in
Russian translation.[40] Thus, for Evgenii only western ideas constituted
an important and worthy program suited to an educated Orthodox
clergy. Although his specific ideas on reform did not become widely
influential, his proposal for an "academic conference" proved lasting.
Evgenii's idea was to form within each academy a "special society of
learned men" similar to the Society of Friends of Learning or the
Society of History and Russian Antiquities founded in 1804 at Moscow
University. Such an "academic conference" was in keeping with the
pursuits of a western-oriented and erudite bishop like Evgenii.[41]

Evgenii's voice soon became lost in the growing wave of French
influence and example during the years between Tilsit and Napoleon's
invasion of Russia in 1812. Alexander's most able assistant, M.M.
Speranskii, formed the commission which invited Filaret and other
talented teachers to St. Petersburg, and by means of this commission
Speranskii proceeded to overhaul the entire ecclesiastical school network according to the centralized model provided by Napoleon's earlier
organization of the French universities. By introducing a hierarchy of

schools (academy, seminary, and parish schools) subordinated to the commission and not to the diocesan bishops, he experimented with what Filaret later dubbed "educational republicanism."[42] He also experimented with the curriculum of the St. Petersburg Ecclesiastical Academy (as the Alexander Nevskii Seminary was now renamed) by enlisting the aid of Ignatius Fesler (to be discussed below), a German completely outside the heirarchy and even outside the Orthodox church. If Speranskii succeeded in refurbishing the curriculum in St. Petersburg, then he felt confident the new academy could serve as a template for renovating the remaining schools.

However, Speranskii did not carry through these reforms alone or unopposed. In fact, he left the commission before the final charter or statute governing the new schools had been completed. His departure resulted, at least in part, from criticism arising within the hierarchy. Bishop Feofilakt (Rusanov, 1765-1821) took charge of Speranskii's work, yet despite the fact that Feofilakt introduced a new inner spirit into the commission and the St. Petersburg schools, the French orientation remained paramount. He advocated an education that was French and literary, yet antideist. He sought to make aesthetics and literature the capstone of Orthodox learning. Like Evgenii and Speranskii, Feofilakt saw as the aim of Orthodox education the reproduction of the latest western thought in Russian translation, and symptomatically, he championed a student translation of Jean Pierre Frédéric Ancillon's *Mélanges de littérature et de philosophie* to be published as the "first fruit" of the reorganized schools.[43] Although by 1810 Speranskii no longer directly supervised the ecclesiastical school reform, he nevertheless succeeded in reducing Feofilakt's influence by securing the appointment of Ignatius Fesler, a Berlin freemason and defrocked Trappist monk, as professor of philosophy at the St. Petersburg Ecclesiastical Academy. Charged with replanning the curriculum, Fesler immediately substituted philosophy for aesthetics and literatuve as the true aim of the schools.

Fesler's stay at the academy lasted only a few months, but his presence there reflected the new spirit of mystical Christianity, revived freemasonry, and pietism spreading through Russia. In the eyes of many, the artificial, mechanical, superficial rationalism of the past century only inadequately expressed human experience, or scarcely even began to encompass the entire range of human emotions, possibilities, and intuitions. Reason, if it was to have any meaning at all, had to yield to a more deeply satisfying and richer explanation of life. As Speranskii expressed it in a rebuke to Feofilakt:

The goal of philosophical education in the exact understanding of the [ecclesiastical] academy charter is not to continue a murky system of materialism on which all sensual philosophy is founded, but to refute all these useless errors by reawakening reason and preparing it for Christian philosophy, for that philosophy which is—in the words of St. Paul—"not after the rudiments of this world," but after the foundation of eternal truth which is singular and whose source we will seek in vain in the eyes, minds, hands, and other senses.[44]

As it turned out, Speranskii did not succeed in physically removing Feofilakt from the academy and the commission. That was achieved by others. But Fesler's brief presence undermined the authority of Feofilakt, who did not possess sufficient knowledge to expound Kant; and the students, perceiving his limitations, went to Fesler for answers to their questions. In any event, Fesler's dismissal was soon followed by Feofilakt's appointment as exarch of Georgia.

The merits of the various reforms proposed by Evgenii and Speranskii or Feofilakt and Fesler need not be evaluated here; what is of interest is that their respective proposals testify to the shifting western currents at work in Russia during Alexander's reign. Nothing can so easily demonstrate the close connection between the inner life of these schools and the broader movements in Russia than the next task given to Fesler by Prince A.N. Golitsyn, that of coordinating the work of seventy-three evangelical colonies in South Russia as a part of the "spiritual mobilization" for a "pietist revolution" then, after 1812, preparing to sweep over educated and uneducated alike. In fact, the schools were so susceptible to western influence, that they suffered from constant disequilibrium and were insufficiently capable of dis-criminating between that which was beneficial and that which might prove harmful. It was in this context that Filaret took increasing control of the school reform and attempted to link the schools to the stabilizing force of Orthodox traditions.

In the wake of Fesler's departure and Feofilakt's reassignment in Georgia, Filaret became rector of the St. Petersburg Ecclesiastical Academy (1812) and a member of the reforming commission. By 1814 he had redrafted the statute governing the schools originally drawn up by Speranskii and amended by Feofilakt and Fesler. This time, however, the emperor actually signed the statute into law. Filaret's rise to prominence within the schools and the hierarchy coincided with the last phase of Russia's struggle against Napoleon and was greatly aided by Alexander's pietist "conversion" in 1812 as well as by Filaret's close friendship that year with Prince Golitsyn, Alexander's most trusted friend. To an important degree Filaret was one more in a succession of western-oriented hierarchs who came to occupy influential positions in the church.[45] The sources of his outlook were largely western. At Trinity Seminary, Platon's insistence on a solid Latin scholastic routine had given him a thorough grounding in the classical authors and in such Protestant writers as Buddeus, Bingham, and Quenstedt. Later, after he arrived in St. Petersburg, he read western mystical writers including Jung-Stilling and Eckhartshausen, and he tended to approach the Bible in the Protestant manner.

Despite the western sources of his education, Filaret did not remain a scholastic or become a mystic. Moreover, he argued that Platon's warm piety and sentimentalism — those purified "springs of the heart" — had to be joined with genuine Christian learning "through the investigation of truth" if Orthodoxy and the church schools were to put down healthy, strong roots and recapture Orthodox traditions. The Latin scholastic program, he thought, deprived the schools of any natural vitality and had become an "ostentatious ornament on a house with a rotten foundation which is ready to collapse."[46] Of course, much of what Filaret meant by the "investigation of truth" may be summed up as Protestant Biblical theology pruned of its scholastic exposition and shifted onto the base of modern Biblical scholarship. "The best method of theological study, without doubt, consists of reading the Holy Scriptures and examining their true meaning according the their original presentation [i.e., in their original languages]."[47] Nevertheless, he tried to go beyond the prevailing Protestant and other western influences in the schools by demanding that "the best commentaries of the Holy Fathers" be added to Biblical scholarship and Biblical theology.

It is highly desirable that Russian religious learning, which is now being stimulated and which has borrowed so much that is foreign . . . should now show its face in the true spirit of the Apostolic church.[48]

Thus, Filaret's efforts at redirecting the schools aimed at recovering the "true face of Orthodoxy" and defining the relationship of Orthodoxy to the West. In this regard, he anticipated by a generation the Slavophile efforts to pose the question of Russia's relation to the West in ways which emphasized the need to recover Orthodox roots.

Filaret preferred theology to philosophy, and if Fesler's arrival in St. Petersburg might be taken as a benchmark for the growth of German idealist philosophy in Russia, then Filaret's ascendancy among the school reformers marks the beginnings of a Russian Orthodox theology. Yet, whatever his own preferences and despite his opposition to Fesler, Filaret did not intend to reduce the importance of philosophy in Orthodox education. "I think you know," he wrote to his father, "that I love theology, for I find consolation in it. But I must study cold philosophy to which I did not pay sufficient attention earlier. Now I realize my inadequacies."[49] He placed theology and philosophy at the center of the completed statute on ecclesiastical schools, and as a result the schools quickly began to generate serious theological and philosophical thought. For example, Fedor Golubinskii (1797-1854), who entered the Moscow Ecclesiastical Academy in the year that Filaret's statute took effect, discovered the school to be a center of great intellectual excitement. Golubinskii became the secretary of a "student colloquium" which perhaps served as a prototype for the later "circles" organized by the "Lovers of Wisdom" in the 1820s and by other gentry intellectuals during the "marvelous decade" of the 1830s to study Kant, Schelling, and Jacobi.[50] Thus, the reformed academies began to anticipate the new directions in Russian thought as well as reflect the leading intellectual fashions. Several years before other segments of educated Russian society began to study philosophy or theology, the ecclesiastical schools were already acquiring a philosophical tradition.

Of course, any program for constructing an "Orthodox philosophy" or "Orthodox theology" to contrast with western Christianity and western philosophy often required as its material the arguments, positive or negative, advanced by Protestants and Catholics or secular philosophers. But this was also true of the Slavophiles and only emphasizes the similarity between the intellectual experiences of those attending the ecclesiastical schools and those engaged in thought outside church walls. Finally, it should be added that the later growth of German idealism in Russia owed much to the early interest of seminarians who became professors of philosophy from 1812 onward. A.I. Galich (1783-1848) and Daniil Vellanskii (1774-1847), both seminarians (in Sevsk and Kiev, respectively) preached Schelling at the Pedagogical Institute and St. Petersburg University. M.G. Pavlov (of Voronezh Seminary, 1793-1840) along with I.I. Davydov introduced Schelling at Moscow University and was also the mentor of the "Lovers of Wisdom."

This brief summary and description of the Orthodox schools should make clear that they deserve more credit as agents of Russia's enlightenment than they have received in the past. Certainly they had limitations, poverty being chief among them. Further, the hopes entertained by Filaret and other reformers that these schools might exchange scholastic "memorization" for genuine "understanding" often went unrealized. But when one looks at the services they rendered, not only for raising the clergy's educational horizons, but also for supplying teachers in the state's secondary schools and universities, one sees clearly that they were not so deficient as is often asserted. And when one realizes the close relationship between these schools and the growth of Russian law, medicine, and the learned professions, it becomes obvious that the education they provided was not a narrow "clerical" preparation but general training suitable for more advanced work at the universities in Russia and abroad. Finally, if the church schools registered in their curricula the changing themes of Russian thought during the reigns of Catherine II, Paul, and Alexander I, they must not have existed in isolation from educated Russian society. How long after the death of Alexander I in 1825 these schools continued to play a creative role in Russian society still awaits fuller investigation. But clearly they should not be dismissed on the grounds that Orthodoxy had an inherent distaste for the mind. Evidence to the contrary can easily be found in the lives of Galich, Vellanskii, Pavlov, and N. I. Nadezhdin, among those former seminarians who taught at the universities and became the masters of a galaxy of thinkers from the young gentry that included Herzen, Odoevskii, the Kireevskii brothers, Venevitinov, Stankevich, Belinskii, K. Aksakov, Bakunin, and Katkov. It may be appropriate to repeat for Russian philosophy what Samuel Johnson once said of litera- ture: "Not to name the school or the masters of [illustrious] men . . . is a kind of historical fraud by which honest fame is injuriously diminished."

Although it goes beyond the limits of this chapter, an interesting question is the role of the Russian church schools as a creative force in Russia's cultural maturation. During the formative stages of their reor- ganization under Filaret, the church schools took their first tentative steps toward providing an education capable of advancing not only western thought but Russian thought as well. In doing so they became concerned with the recovery and maintenance of Russian social and cultural consciousness and with the transmission of informed tradition which, as James Bowen observes in the quotation at the beginning of this essay, sustains civilization. If thinkers like Dostoevsky and Vladimir Solov'ev believed that Russia could discover something of universal value within itself only by proceeding from the soil of Orthodoxy, then it is possible to suggest that in the long run the importance of the church schools went beyond the number of teachers, lawyers, or doctors they helped to train. They also sustained Orthodox tradition until it became the basis of greater cultural vitality.

NOTES

1. Pittsburgh, Pennsylvania, 1950.

2. *History of Russian Educational Policy (1701-1917)*, New York, 1964.

3. *Education and the State in Tsarist Russia*, Stanford, California, 1969, 17, 19, 33.

4. "The Jesuit Origins of Petrine Education," in J. G. Garrard, ed., *The Eigh- teenth Century in Russia*, Oxford, 1973, 106-30.

5. Reluctantly, because many Russian hierarchs became alarmed that Catherine's demands would prevent the schools from satisfying the church's needs for educated clergy.

6. M.I. Sukhomlinov, *Istoriia Rossiiskoi Akademii. Sbornik otdeleniia russkago iazyka i slovesnosti*, XIV, 4-5.

7. Hugh Seton-Watson, *The Russian Empire, 1801-1917*, Oxford, 1967, 37.

8. E.M. Prilezhaev, "Dukhovnyia shkoly i seminaristy v istorii russkoi nauki i obrazovaniia," *Khristianskoe Chtenie*, 1879, nos. 7-8, 177.

9. *Biograficheskii slovar' professorov moskovskago universiteta*, Moscow, 1855.

10. E.F. Ziablovskii, *Istoricheskaia povest' ob uchitel'skoi gimnazii i pedagogicheskom institute*, St. Petersburg, 1838, 40-46.

11. Roderick E. McGrew, *Russia and the Cholera, 1823-1832*, Madison, Wisc., 1965, 27.

12. *Idem.*

13. *Pis'ma mitropolita moskovskago Filareta k rodnym ot 1800-go goda do 1866 goda*, Moscow, 1882, 32.

14. *Idem.*

15. Prilezhaev, "Dukhovnyia shkoly," 175.

16. McGrew, *Russia and Cholera*, 35.

17. Bogdanovskii, the son of a priest and a graduate of the Mogilev Seminary, studied at the Imperial Medico-Chirurgical Academy from 1853 to 1858. He was a noted anatomical pathologist specializing in surgical pathology, and wrote such scholarly essays on bone transplant as "Opyty perenosa kostei ot odnogo zhivotnago k drugomu," in *Meditsinskii vestnik*, 1860, 10. The pathologist Rudnev, also a seminary graduate and alumnus of the surgical academy in 1860, worked closely with Bogdanovskii.

18. For Vellanskii and other influential "doctor-writers," see L.F. Zmeev, *Russkie vrachi-pisateli*, St. Petersburg, 1889.

19. See the essay entitled "Vozniknovenie i pervonachal'naia organizatsiia derptskago universiteta v nachale XIX v.," *Zhurnal ministerstva narodnago prosveshcheniia*, 1901, 10, 11, 12; 1902, 1.

20. Prilezhaev, "Dukhovnyia shkoly," 185.

21. Leshkov's *Russkii narod i gosudarstvo*, Moscow, 1858 is still of interest to historians. Other prominent seminarians heard Savigny's lectures or followed the new historical school of jurisprudence. V.P. Znamenskii (d. 1835) had shown great promise in both law and literature (see S.K. Smirnov, "Odin iz pitomtsev Speranskago," *Russkii vestnik*, 1886, 1). S.O. Bogorodskii (1804-57), the son of a deacon and a student at Iaroslavl Seminary and St. Petersburg Ecclesiastical Academy, taught law as a professor at Kiev University after his return from Germany. The Barshev brothers, Sergei (1808-82) and Iakov (b. 1807), also played important roles in Russia's legal development. Sergei composed the first course on Russian criminal law, published as *Obshchiia nachala teorii i zakonodatel'stv o prestupleniiakh i nakazaniiakh* (Moscow, 1841). Iakov became a member of Speranskii's commission to codify the laws and profesor of law at Tsarskoe Selo lycée. One last name, I.D. Beliaev, 1810-73, is worth recalling both because of his service to the codification of laws and the history of Russian legislation. In 1845 he was placed in charge of the Senate archives in order to look for

all decrees and other legal enactments which had not been included in the first collection of the laws of the Russian Empire. Within three years, Beliaev assembled 17,000 statutes from the College of Economy. In 1846 he became a member of the Society of History and Russian Antiquities (three times being elected secretary).

22. Prilezhaev, "Dukhovnyia shkoly," 170.

23. Vol. 80 of the *Sbornik otdeleniia russkago iazyka i slovestnosti*, St. Petersburg, 1905, contains a list of volumes for 1867-1905.

24. Richard Pipes, *Russia Under the Old Regime*, New York, 1974, 243.

25. *Polnoe sobranie sochinenii Platona (Levshina) mitropolita moskovskago*, St. Petersburg, 1913, II, 333. Hereafter cited as *PSSP* with appropriate volume no. and page.

26. *PSSP*, II, 335.

27. *Ibid.*, II, 340.

28. *Ibid.*, I, 217.

29. *Ibid.*, I, 7.

30. Alexander V. Muller, ed. and trans., *The Spiritual Regulation of Peter the Great*, Seattle, 1972, 41.

31. S. K. Smirnov, *Istoriia Troitskoi lavrskoi seminarii*, Moscow, 1867, 463-64.

32. Marc Raeff, *Origins of the Russian Intelligentsia*, New York, 1966, 140-41.

33. A. N. Radishchev, *Puteshestvie iz Peterburga v Moskvu*, Moscow and Leningrad, 1961, 34-35.

34. In his catechetical lectures of 1757-58, Platon adds the following: "What is the church? It is not just any gathering, but an assembly of chosen people called from the unclean world by the voice of God." *PSSP*, I, 876-77.

35. One writer has recently noted that after Platon had examined the books Novikov had published, he "reported that they fall into three categories: the first useful, the second mystical — which he 'did not understand,' the third the works of the French Encyclopedists, which he considered harmful. No doubt some of the mystical works were hard enough to understand, even for most Moscow Rosicrucians, but it is noteworthy that Platon evaluated the other two categories just as the Masons did." Donald W. Treadgold, *The West in Russia and China*, Cambridge, England, 1973, I, 126-27.

36. As quoted in G. Florovsky, *Puti russkago bogosloviia*, Paris, 1937, 113.

37. *Ibid.*, 114.

38. *Pis'ma mitropolita moskovskago Filareta k rodnym ot 1800-go do 1866 goda*, Moscow, 1882, 66.

39. I. Korsunskii, "Lira Filareta mitropolita moskovskago," *Russkii vestnik*, November 1884, 275.

40. K. Poletaev, "K istorii dukhovno-uchebnoi reformy, 1808-1814," *Strannik*, 1889, VIII, 533.

41. *Opis' dokumentov i del, khraniashchikhsia v arkhive sviateishago pravitel'stvuiushchago sinoda: Dela kommissii dukhovnykh uchilishch, 1808-1839 gg.*, St. Petersburg, 1910, 33.

42. Speranskii's proposals are reproduced in *Ibid.*, 1-40.

43. See "Oproverzhenie primechanii na knigu gospodina Ansil'iona pod zaglaviem: 'Esteticheskiia razsuzhdeniia' riazanskago arkhiepiskopa Feofilakta," *Chteniia v imperatorskom obshchestve istorii i drevnostei Rossiiskikh pri moskovskom universitete,* 1877, I, Smes', 186-209.

44. I. Chistovich, *Rukovodiashchie deiateli dukhovnago prosveshcheniia v rossii v pervoi polivine tekushchago stoletiia,* St. Petersburg, 1894, 51-52.

45. For a recent examination of Filaret's life and career until 1825, see Robert L. Nichols, "Metropolitan Filaret of Moscow and the Awakening of Orthodoxy," Ph.D. diss., University of Washington, 1972.

46. *Sochineniia Filareta, mitropolita moskovskago i kolomenskago; Slova i rechi,* Moscow, 1873, I, 167.

47. *Polnoe sobranie zakonov Rossiiskoi imperii, s 1649 goda,* St. Petersburg, 1830, XXXII, 25, 673, 30 August 1814, 927.

48. *Sobranie mnenii i otzyvov Filareta, mitropolita moskovskago i kolomen-skago, po uchebnym i tserkovno-gosudarstvennym voprosam,* St. Petersburg, 1885-88, I, 141.

49. *Pism'a k rodnym,* 116.

50. V.V. Zenkovsky, *A History of Russian Philosophy,* trans. George L. Kline, New York, 1953, I, 300-301.

Revolt from Below:
A Priest's Manifesto
on the Crisis in Russian
Orthodoxy (1858-59)

Gregory L. Freeze

The year 1855 marked the beginning of the Great Reforms, not only in the Russian state and society, but also in the Orthodox church. To many contemporaries, lay and clerical, conservative and liberal, it seemed that the church, like other institutions of imperial Russia, needed radical reform. Its problems were legion, its resources meager, its influence waning. Diocesan administration suffered from venality, malfeasance, and arbitrariness; the seminaries were a shambles, afflicted with poverty and pedagogical disarray; the parish clergy had become a virtual caste, impoverished, isolated, and disparaged. Although "liberal society" (*obshchestvo*) at first took little interest in these problems, some laymen and officials busily began preparing secret proposals for church reform. The conservative religious writer A.N. Murav'ev prepared a secret *zapiska* (note) that candidly described the church's problems, attributed them to the domination of the church by a lay overprocurator, and urged a restoration of synodal authority.[1] An offi-

Note: This article forms part of a broader study ("The Emancipation of the Russian Parish Clergy: The Great Reforms and Counter-Reform in Imperial Russia, 1855-1885"), which has been supported by the International Research and Exchanges Board and the Fulbright Faculty Research Program. The author wishes to express his gratitude to the officers and staffs of Soviet archival institutions, particularly the Central State Historical Archive in Leningrad and the Manuscript Division of Lenin Library in Moscow.

cial in the Ministry of Interior, P.N. Batiushkov, worked out an elaborate project for reorganizing parishes and clerical service, reforming
the seminaries, and disbanding the clergy as a hereditary estate
(*soslovie*).[2] P. A. Valuev, a bureaucrat prolific in the composition of
reform projects, also took up the question of the church and in
1861-62 persuaded Alexander II to create a "special commission"
(*Osoboe prisutstvie*) for directing a transformation of the church and
clergy.[3]

What triggered public interest in church reform, however, was not
secret memoranda but an exposé of church problems entitled *Description of the Rural Clergy* (*Opisanie sel'skogo dukhovenstva*), published
anonymously in Leipzig in 1858 and smuggled into the empire. Written
by an obscure provincial priest, Ioann Stepanovich Belliustin
(1819-90),[4] the book turned the "clerical question" into a major
public issue. It made educated society keenly aware of the problems in
the church, earned the tsar's evident support, and even was alleged to
be the cause of student disorders in the St. Petersburg Ecclesiastical
Academy. The book had the contrary effect upon church conservatives, who were appalied by it and its influence; according to D.I.
Rostislavov, a liberal reformer, "one metropolitan was so thunderstruck
by the book's content that it fell out of his hands."[5] Ten years after
the publication of Belliustin's volume, the newspaper *Nedelia* compared
its sensational effect to that of Alexander Radishchev's *Journey* in the
1790s.[6] That was no exaggeration: Belliustin's book became a *cause
célèbre*, marking a sharp turn on the road towards the ecclesiastical
Great Reforms.

Notwithstanding its importance, the Belliustin "affair" has received
virtually no attention in general histories or even in specialized monographs.[7] The reasons for this neglect are varied: secular historians have
generally ignored the church in imperial Russia, official church historians had little use for the wayward, radical Belliustin,[8] and the priest
himself declined to publish his autobiography "under the existing conditions of the press."[9] All this only reflects a broader problem — the
primitive level of historical research on the church, a field where even
the most elementary data have yet to be assembled and analyzed. As in
the Belliustin case, presumptions remain unverified, important

questions unasked, rich archival materials unused. Was Belliustin a radical seminarian (à la Chernyshevskii) or a conservative clerical frondeur? Were his allies enlightened westerners, Slavophiles, or bureaucrats? How did "l'affaire Belliustin" affect the relationship between church and state? Was Belliustin a mere tool of the government for humbling church hierarchs? Was it government repression that caused church conservatives to publish abroad their own "illegal" book in rebuttal to Belliustin's?[10] Drawing upon previously untapped archival materials, this paper will examine the Belliustin affair in order to illuminate the crisis in the parish clergy, the origins of ecclesiastical liberalism, and the complex politics of church reform under Alexander II.[11]

Belliustin's background does not, at first glance, resemble that of a future radical. Like virtually all Russian priests in the mid-nineteenth century, he was born to the clerical estate, a group almost castelike in its social isolation, cultural separateness, and endogamous hereditary order. He received the customary education of a priest's son, attending first an elementary church school (*dukhovnoe uchilishche*) in Staritsa and then the diocesan seminary in Tver, where he excelled and graduated in the first division of his class (*pervyi razriad*).[12] Like many seminarians, he married a girl from the clerical estate in order to inherit her father's position and obtain an appointment—otherwise difficult in a day of supernumerary candidates.[13] After serving four years in his wife's home village (Vasilino in Tver diocese), in 1843 he secured a better position in the cathedral of a district town, Kaliazin, where he earned a reputation for diligence and dedication.[14] Besides discharging the regular duties of priest,[15] he was appointed catechism instructor for the town, served as the official priest and exhorter at the Kaliazin prison and represented the church at civil courts in cases involving local clergy. In 1852 he became the religious instructor at the government's district school, with a substantial salary from the Ministry of Education. His distinguished service did not go unrecognized by the church, which awarded him various honors in 1849 and 1854 and a bronze cross in 1855.[16] Later his parishioners expressed similar admiration, filing petitions that attested to his extraordinary zeal in matters religious and educational.

Despite this recognition, however, Belliustin nourished deep-rooted grievances against the church and its monastic hierarchy. Perhaps the one most commonly shared with other priests was his dissatisfaction with clerical service itself. He recounts of his first years as a village priest in Vasilino that, like most youths who had spent long years in the seminary, he was unprepared for the crushing routine of the rural priest, who alternately ministered sacraments and ploughed fields. Later he wrote that "rural life, with all its exhausting toil, trifles and troubles, with all its filth, its endless needs, with all its useless and often unsuccessful concerns — such a life could not be pleasant and joyful, and I was in no way prepared for all this and did not know how to go about doing most of these things."[17] He despaired of finding common interests with his fellow clergy, who cared not in the least about "learning and literature, even of a religious sort," and declared that "it was impossible to get close to them without the maximum use of stupefying drink."[18] He tried to run a parish school for the village children, but it failed because the peasants refused not only to give material support but even to release their children from work in the fields.[19] Belliustin did not, however, find refuge in the genteel society of the landed nobility, notoriously supercilious and contemptuous toward the parish priest. Nor did the priest overlook the gentry's maltreatment of serfs: his diary plainly records the outrage he felt after ministering last rites to four peasants dying from their masters' abuse.[20] Although his transfer to Kaliazin in 1843 brought him some of the amenities of life, Belliustin could not remain satisfied in his new position for long. Like many clergy he had to support a large family (twelve), and his income simply did not suffice for his sons' education and his daughters' dowries, especially after the runaway inflation of the 1850s.[21]

Apart from his disgruntlement with service, Belliustin chafed most at career frustrations. Priesthood had become a frozen status, offering little opportunity for upward mobility, however ambitious and talented the priest might be. By the mid-nineteenth century virtually all the priests in central Russia were seminary graduates, and the bishops parceled out the choice appointments — in Moscow, or St. Petersburg, or in a provincial capital — only to those who had attended the ecclesiastical academy (which was roughly the church's equivalent of the university).[22] The precedence given to "learnedness," that is, learning, affected not only the monastic clergy, enabling the "learned monks" (*uchenoe monashestvo*) to gain dominance in the hierarchy,[23] but also the parish clergy, where the best positions were controlled by the bishop and awarded on the basis of formal education rather than service achievements. Belliustin had not attended the academy, even though his seminary class rank—in the *pervyi razriad*—qualified him to matriculate. He himself later attributed this decision to "family and important circumstances"—a plausible explanation, given the acute shortage of positions and the opportunity presented to him in Vasilino.[24] But another source reports that Belliustin *did* intend to enter the St. Petersburg Ecclesiastical Academy and was foiled at the last minute by the Archbishop of Tver, Grigorii (Postnikov), who attended the graduation examination at the seminary and for one unsatisfactory answer gave Belliustin such a low mark that it spoiled his chances for the academy.[25] Whatever the reason, he lacked the credentials for the best positions, and as a priest in the cathedral of a poor district town he seemed to have reached the high mark of his career.

Belliustin, however, still hoped to overcome his deficiency in formal education by demonstrating achievement in scholarship.[26] Despite his extraordinarily heavy responsibilities in Kaliazin, he worked feverishly to prove his "learnedness" with a major piece of original writing. Shortly after his transfer from Kaliazin he began his first book, "Christianity and Science in the Nineteenth Century," primarily a critique of David Friedrich Strauss's well-known *Das Leben Jesu*. He then prepared a second work, "Orthodoxy and Catholicism," which began as a translation of another foreign work but developed into a polemical refutation.[27] At the same time, he worked assiduously to collect old manuscripts and in the early 1850s began publishing his findings in a local serial, *Tverskie gubernskie vedomosti*.

But all his efforts came to naught. The Archbishop of Tver ignored his first manuscript, returning it after a year without comment or approval. Later, apprised of an opening at a church in Moscow, Belliustin submitted his work to Metropolitan Filaret, hoping that the prelate would be sufficiently impressed to pass over his lack of an academy degree and grant him the appointment. Beside himself with joy when Filaret summoned him to Moscow for a personal interview, he was unprepared for the metropolitan's crushing judgment: "I examined both your writings and find that there is nothing here but empty philosophizing—which can be of no use whatsoever. To reconcile the irreconcilable—science and faith—means only to flail the water idly."[28] The encounter was a traumatic experience that Belliustin recounted often with pain and bitterness.[29] The priest's historical work also met with rebuff from the church censorship, which in the early 1850s was even more repressive than that of the government.[30] When Belliustin submitted a brochure-length manuscript (". . . And Two Sketches from the Lives of Tver Hierarchs"), a seemingly harmless work that praised two past hierarchs lavishly, the censor—a monk—complained that it was a vapid panegyric, "written as a rhetorical exercise in the compilation of laudatory words." He also expressed bewilderment over the work's purpose ("For whom and for what is it intended to be published?") and was suspicious of the ellipses—what was the omitted part? he queried. Noting their duty to forbid bad as well as harmful writing, the censorship committee refused permission to publish the work and so informed Belluistin's diocesan superiors.[31] Local authorities, too, looked askance at his publishing efforts. The priest wrote one acquaintance that "the consistory does not cease persecuting me in the most cruel way for publishing articles, even anonymous ones, and it would be the end of me if I were to sign my name."[32]

The result of Belliustin's career frustration was an intense antagonism toward the church elite—the "learned clergy" who dominated the church and held its authority. That meant above all the monastic clergy, from whose ranks were selected the bishops, rectors, and censors—all largely on the basis of formal academic records. Belliustin felt a profound aversion for monks and in a diary entry of 1849 gave full vent to his feelings: "O monks, an evil greater than any other, Pharisees and hypocrites: *quousque tandem abutere* with your rights? *Quousque tandem* will you trample law and justice? You promote and award distinctions to those who have the means to feed you, like oxen; you reward those who can pay; you persecute and destroy the poor. . . . *Quousque tandem?*"[33] He claimed that shortly after Filaret rejected his work, a monk published a similar essay in a church periodical; "What does that mean?" he asked bitterly.[34] He sardonically itemized

the "canons" of conduct for "learned" monks: (1) a diocese or monastery is an estate, from which one can take all that is good and valuable;
(2) everything is permissible for monks, but if any should do something
really horrendous—for example, strangle or stab his mistress—then
keep everything as secret as possible and use all your powers to defend
him before the courts; (3) spare no money in order to rise from archimandrite to bishop, and then to membership in the Synod."[35] Yet,
claimed Belliustin, the bishops showed no mercy for the parish clergy,
meting out brutal punishment and leaving the priest defenseless before
the venal officials of the diocesan administration. Later he would single
out Archbishop Grigorii as typical of such bad bishops: "Oh, God alone
knows how many priests, honest and worthy, perished under the rule of
Grigorii—and for no reason at all."[36] Belliustin's hatred for Grigorii
knew no bounds; the priest gleefully repeated rumors that the prelate
was a homosexual who preyed upon young boys in the seminary.[37]

But learned monks were not the only object of Belliustin's enmity—
his resentment toward "learned priests" with academy degrees ran
almost as deep. He complained sarcastically that "the academy, which
probably possesses some mysterious secret for making all its students
into geniuses and consequently deserving of all favors, confers the right
to a position in the capitals—not service, however irreproachable,
honest, and useful it might be." Belliustin was not offering abstract
reflections; he had his own career in mind, complaining bitterly that "I
cannot obtain [a position in the capitals]—I   am not a *magistr* or
kandidat [degrees conferred at the academies]." All his service counted
for nothing: "Even if one finished the seminary as the best student and
did not enter the academy for family and extremely important reasons,
even if one served more than sixteen years irreproachably (and not only
irreproachably but with a certain distinction—two years ago I received
an award for my labors, which have been quite demanding)—all that
means nothing."[38]

The priest, perhaps as compensation, tried to expose the "learned
clergy"—especially monks—as being actually indifferent or hostile to
learning. In 1853 he maliciously wrote to an acquaintance about an
incident that had occurred in Kashin at Korobanov Monastery, which
had recently been bequeathed a large trunk. "The monks joyfully set

about opening the locked, sealed trunk," wrote Belliustin, "hoping to find in it something especially valuable (in their judgment)." When they found only old manuscripts and documents—the value of which they could not appreciate—they were ready to burn the trunk, papers and all, and were dissuaded from doing so only by a warning that the authorities would assume that real valuables had been found and pilfered.[39] Nor were the obscurantists who governed the diocese favorably disposed toward, indeed they actively discouraged, the attempts of parish priests like Belliustin to engage in scholarly activity. "From my experience," he wrote, "I have learned what it means to belong to a *soslovie* where love for scholarship is considered the greatest of crimes, deserving every punishment and penalty."[40] A few years later, in an unpublished portion of the manuscript for his *Opisanie sel'skogo dukhovenstva*, he argued that parish priests had failed to participate actively in the development of church culture and thought because of the "academy" clergy: "Those who became monks, as a result of their 'Academic sagacity,' view with the greatest indignation the attempts of any nonacademy priest to take up serious work and to publish his writings, and with the most merciless cruelty they revile the published work and its author."[41]

As Belliustin's career in the church stalled, he turned his attention increasingly to the secular world, to the conservative segment closest to the church. By far his most important contact was Mikhail Petrovich Pogodin, historian, publicist, and the editor of the *Moskvitianin*. In August 1852 Belliustin wrote Pogodin that "one of my strongest desires is to read your journal," but unfortunately, he lamented, the cost of subscription lay beyond the means of a poor provincial priest. He therefore offered to send articles to Pogodin in exchange for the journal, adding one stipulation: "I respectfully propose one condition, a trifle in substance, but extraordinarily important to me: that is, that my own name not be placed under my articles and that no one—particularly my (church) authorities—know about my writings."[42] Pogodin agreed, and thus began a correspondence that would last nearly twenty years. Significantly, in these early prereform years Belliustin wrote like a conservative Slavophile, castigating the "Europeanism" of the enemy camp and lauding Pogodin's journal as the main bulwark of national culture. The

priest complained that "the Russian spirit" was lacking in other journals, invoked God's wrath on "Kraevskii & Co. [for] corrupting many
souls," and "praised God that Russia still has [in Pogodin] a man of
knowledge and learning, devoted with his whole heart to the fatherland."[43] The two also shared a keen interest in antiquities and old Russian manuscripts; Pogodin, an avid collector and unabashed speculator,
used Belliustin as a provincial agent to ferret out and procure valuable
documents and books. Belliustin, who published many small pieces of
local history, collected old documents from monasteries and churches
for himself as well; he sent Pogodin copies and on occasion even some
originals for the latter's vast collection.[44]

Before 1855 most of Belliustin's writing fell within the fairly safe
area of history, his articles and documents appearing not only in Pogodin's journal but also in *Moskovskie vedomosti*.[45] Although most of
this work was innocuous enough, some of it fully justified the priest's
demand for anonymity. He sometimes gave to his historical work a
curious twist, emphasizing documents that revealed past abuses by the
hierarchy or resistance by the parish clergy.[46] Much more dangerous
was his interest in "moving tables," the experiments in "spiritual mag-
netism" that were quite fashionable in the 1850s (even in court circles)
and claimed to provide direct communication with the deceased.[47]
Belliustin wrote excitedly of his personal experiences, assured the skep-
tical Pogodin that the "magnetic tables" were no hoax, and even submitted an article on the subject. He added an urgent reminder, however,
to protect his anonymity: "Nowadays they do not burn people at the
stake for such activities, it is true; but for us (clergy) to this very day
there exist moral stake-burnings, more terrifying and murderous than
the real ones."[48]

The year 1855 marked the dawn of a new era: Nicholas's death, the
debacle of the Crimean War, and the evident bankruptcy of the old
order generated hopes for reform not only among liberal "society"
but also in such erstwhile conservative nationalists as Pogodin and
Belliustin. Pogodin, like many of his contemporaries, interpreted
Russia's defeat in the Crimean War as evidence of the old regime's failure, and even before Nicholas's death he submitted letters to the
emperor that were sharply critical of the old order and emphasized the

urgent need for change.[49] Belliustin too was caught up in the new atmosphere of reform. He published very little on the serf question, perhaps because of censorship or lack of special expertise, but his private correspondence reflected deep concern and interest. He expressed alarm at the upsurge of peasant discontent ("There is terrible excitement among the peasants here, and one [rumor] is worse than the next"),[50] but he was no ally of the *krepostniki* (defenders of serfdom) or even the "enlightened" bureaucrats seeking reform. The priest was especially critical of reform drafted in the comfortable chambers of a Petersburg chancellery, partly because it boded ill for peasant interests and partly because the ingenious blueprints for reform were not grounded in reality and practice.[51] Belliustin gave more attention to a closely related issue, the need for public education, which seemed especially urgent as the nation edged toward emancipation. Drawing upon his teaching experience in Kaliazin, he tried to explain "why our district schools develop so poorly," and published a number of important articles in the journal of the Ministry of Education (*Zhurnal Ministerstva narodnogo prosveshcheniia*).[52] His work on education, together with his research on old manuscripts, significantly broadened his range of contacts in high society. By the late 1850s his correspondents included a glittering array of notables—Slavophiles such as Iu. S. Samarin and V. A. Cherkasskii, the archaeographer N. V. Kalachov, and government officials such as S. N. Urusov and I. D. Delianov.[53]

But his chief contact remained Pogodin, and their mutual interests gradually came to focus on reform in the Orthodox church. Pogodin, who had once inspected a seminary for the overprocurator in the 1840s had a better idea than most laymen about the condition of the church and its staggering problems.[54] His interest deepened after his meeting with Belliustin to prepare a work "describing the life of clergy in district towns and villages." The priest agreed, vowing to heed Pogodin's imperative—"write only the truth," without hyperbole and rhetoric. Their common conviction was the urgency of fundamental reform. "You are right, a thousand times right," wrote Belliustin. "It is necessary to reform the clergy radically so that it corresponds to the purpose for which it was created."[55] Belliustin consulted many other priests for ideas and information and finally, nearly two years later

(April 1857), completed the main text. A supplement followed in December of the same year.[56]

Belliustin's untitled *zapiska* was a comprehensive analysis of the church and its problems and raised questions about virtually every facet of clerical life and service.[57] It was structured essentially as a chronological account of a "typical" priest's life, from schooling to daily service in the parish, beginning with a lengthy critique of church schools and seminaries and offering a graphic description of the problems in administration, faculty, curriculum, and student life. Belliustin stressed that the seminary utterly failed to prepare youths morally for clerical service, for most students were obliged to rent rooms from the lower townspeople and soon acquired the worst vices—even cases of syphilis were not unknown among the seminarians. He fulminated against the venality of school administrators, who in some cases punished or even failed students whose fathers refused to give the customary bribe, and also criticized the poor instruction provided by church schools, arguing that pupils learned precious little because of incompetent teachers and outmoded pedagogy. The curriculum too was partly to blame; especially after the "Protasov reforms" of 1839, it burdened the seminarians with so many extraneous matters (such as modern technology in agriculture) that they were unable to master any of the basic subjects, including those really essential for the priesthood. Belliustin also voiced a complaint long current when he attacked the domination of Latin, "a dead language, which will be as useful in real life as Sanskrit." He complained that "a youth exhausts his talents for six whole years on a language that he will forget in the first two years of his priesthood, for in all his life he will never encounter a single letter of this language." Belliustin proposed to simplify the curriculum and retain but one of Protasov's innovations—the study of medicine, which in his opinion could provide vital assistance to rural parishioners.

The *zapiska's* picture of priestly service was no less bleak and depressing. The entry into service was itself riddled with injustice, merit and ability counting for little; the parish clergy formed a rigid order, where priests' positions were commonly sold, inherited, or given as dowry—a system that produced *mariages de convenance*, marital conflict, and bitter feuds between disgruntled in-laws. Like most church reformers, Belliustin proposed the prohibition of selling or inheriting clerical positions and that candidates for the priesthood be allowed to marry women from any social estate. Once a priest obtained a position, wrote Belliustin, he faced a life of penury, hardship, and perpetual humiliation. The village priest could partially support himself by farming the land (thirty-three dessiatines) belonging to the parish chruch; but he derived most of his income from the gratuities that parishioners gave for communion, marriage, burials, and various other religious rites. Since these were supposedly voluntary and could be reduced or withheld at will, the priest was left almost totally dependent upon the parishioners. From them he had to solicit larger gratuities and request free labor (*pomoch'*) at harvest time. Belliustin pointedly noted that the priest could find neither refuge no fellowship in gentry society; although the nobles no longer flogged the village priest (as they had been wont to do in times past), they treated him with contempt or at best condescension.

Nor could the priest take refuge in the church and ecclesiastical society. At his own church he had to contend with the sacristans (*prichetniki*), who performed menial tasks and served as readers during liturgies and rites. As students who had been expelled from the church schools or seminaries for "obtuseness" or bad conduct, they were permanently consigned to their low rank of sacristan and remained a blight on the church, notorious for their general misconduct, drunkenness, and insubordination before the priest. Like other reformers, Belliustin urged that this hereditary group be excluded from the clergy and replaced by temporary, hired laymen. The *zapiska* was no less critical of diocesan authorities. Largely because the government allotted only niggardly budgets for ecclesiastical administration, the church suffered from rampant extortion and corruption—the "gifts" and "incidental fees" (*aktsidentsii*) that greased the wheels of administration and justice. Belliustin complained bitterly that the impoverished clergy were constantly obliged to dole out bribes to diocesan officials, clerks, and district superintendents (*blagochinnye*). He held the bishops themselves accountable for failing to protect the subordinate clergy and asserted that some bishops even participated in the abuse. To enable the parish clergy to defend themselves, Belliustin proposed a reform that would become popular in the 1860s: replace the superintendents (appointed by the bishop) with elected priestly elders or *popovskie starosty*, an office that had expired in the eighteenth century and left the parish clergy defenseless before the church bureaucracy.

To the main text Belliustin attached appendixes on several other important problems. One essay on the schism or Old Belief denied that the church was making headway against the schismatics, despite the reassuring—but false—statistics in the bishops' annual *otchety* (reports). In a second article he emphasized that the parish clergy in the towns were just as impoverished as their brethren in village churches. In the past, the government had given aid exclusively to the rural clergy, and most laymen still instinctively connected the "clerical question" with the village priest (*sel'skii sviashchennik*), unaware that the clergy in small provincial towns were equally destitute. In another essay Belliustin offered his solution to the economic problems of the clergy, one that virtually all priests would favor in the early 1860s—a regular government salary. Although the government rejected the idea on fiscal grounds and critics warned that it would transform the parish clergy into one more branch of the hated bureaucracy, Belliustin and his fellow priests argued that only this reform could sunder the bonds of economic dependence upon the parish, enable the priest to attend fully to his pastoral duties, and make the clergy into a respectable profession that would attract outsiders. The *zapiska* ends with an appeal to the emperor to intervene personally and launch the long overdue reform.

Most of Belliustin's specific observations and proposals were scarcely radical—they would be echoed again and again by secret reform commissions, official reports, and articles in the church journals of the 1860s. His critique of church schools, for example, foreshadowed the complaints of the first seminary commission of 1860: concern about the curriculum, moral development of pupils, economic support, and competence of faculty remained matters of central importance as the commission sought to rebuild the church's educational system.[58] In fact, Belliustin's analysis of schools earned praise from some prelates; Innokentii, for example, eagerly inquired about the book and later declared that "the most zealous defenders of the present [seminary] find little that is exaggerated" in the volume.[59] His description of the clerical order and the travails of priestly service within a few years became commonplace in church documents and the press. Complaints about the hereditary order, the low juridical status, and poverty became the main focus of the special commission that Alexander created in 1862; when it collected cahiers from diocesan committees, bishops, and parish clergy in 1863, the documents followed lines already delineated in Belliustin's *zapiska* five years earlier.[60] The problems of diocesan administration also attracted widespread attention; by the mid-1860s the authorities contemplated reform in the church's judicial system, censorship, and local administration, including the "democratic" election of district superintendents by local clergy.[61] All this is not to say that it was Belliustin's book that shaped the coming reforms; rather, it summed up the undercurrent of clerical opinion on the eve of the Great Reforms, expressing common aspirations, common grievances, common interests.

Pogodin was immensely pleased with the *zapiska*. He kept a firm editorial hand on Belliustin, occasionally questioning the veracity of an anecdote or rumor, and he deleted some of the numerous examples taken from Tver diocese in an attempt to conceal Belliustin's identity.[62] Pogodin also struck out some substantive sections—Belliustin's attribution of the Orthodox schism to the monastic clergy, a rhetorical passage comparing bishops to landed aristocrats, and a proposal to equate church awards with those of the civil bureaucracy.[63] Pogodin then had the manuscript copied, adding still another anonymous *zapiska* to the countless number already in circulation. One copy reached the overprocurator. A. P. Tolstoi, and the tsar's confessor, Archpriest V. B. Bazhanov.[64] Pogodin also showed the *zapiska* to ecclesiastical acquaintances, who affirmed its verisimilitude and added corroborative testimony from their own personal experiences.[65]

Even as the *zapiska* first began to circulate, Pogodin took an audacious step. In the summer of 1857 he met a former pupil, N. I. Trubetskoi, who badgered him for permission to publish the work abroad through his foreign contacts. Although Pogodin later claimed that he offered the *zapiska* spontaneously, his diary reveals a prolonged inner struggle before he finally relented and gave a copy to Trubetskoi.[66] He was, most likely, convinced of the futility of yet another *zapiska*, sharing Belliustin's belief that the unpublished work would be read sympathetically "at the top" but then dispatched to the archive with no effect whastsoever.[67] With the die cast, Pogodin suddenly implored Belliustin to submit immediately the final parts, causing the surprised author to inquire about the urgency.[68] Trubetskoi took the finished sections abroad and, early in 1858, the *zapiska* appeared as a small, thin volume in a serial printed in Leipzig (*Russkii zagranichnyi sbornik*), bearing the title *Opisanie sel'skogo dukhovenstva*, with no indication of authorship.

When Pogodin finally apprised Belliustin in the fall of 1857 of what he had done, the priest was petrified with fear. "There is now such chaos in my head," he wrote, "that I cannot put two ideas together sensibly." He categorically opposed publication, "under any circumstances, in any form, if I have any rights whatsoever over my work," and reproached Pogodin for never having even hinted of such a possibility. When Pogodin replied that he should bear the risk for "the general good," the priest bitterly spurned these homilies and reminded Pogodin that he wrote the *zapiska* partly "to improve what is bad" but also "to help improve my situation, [my children's] upbringing, my family's conditions." He added that "if you had only hinted to me that this is how it might end, I swear to the living God that I would have burned the work and not a single soul would have known about it."[69] Belliustin's terror was revealing, an expression of the profound dread that lower clergy had come to feel toward their bishops during Nicholas's reign, especially in Tver diocese where Archbishop Grigorii had earned a particular reputation for arousing fear in the parish clergy.[70] Belliustin's immediate response reflected his trepidation, which was to be overcome only by the emancipation in the reform epoch.

He had good cause for his near hysteria. However valid the book's description, it was offensive in style if not content; as Belliustin himself observed, "This was originally a private work [not intended for publication], and I did not deem it necessary to indulge in sly circumlocutions."[71] His untempered candor was most evident in the treatment of monastic clergy and church hierarchs, acerbic comments that were hardly softened by disclaimers that the author does not "despise" the monastic clergy.[72] Belliustin not only questioned their canonical right to govern the church, but also used abundant hyperbole to condemn the monks' oppression of the parish clergy, as in his assertion that "the relationship between priests and hierarchs is like that between Negroes and plantation owners [in America]."[73] Even more dangerous for Belliustin was the volume's foreign publication. As he learned later, "my guilt, in their words, does not consist in writing the book but in [permitting] all Europe to know what goes on here."[74] Not only did the work embarrass the church before western eyes (and, even without Belliustin, the hierarchs had long been defensive), it also provided ammunition for the diligent Catholic propagandists who had already alarmed government and church officials by their activities in the former Uniat areas of the western provinces.[75] Worse still, Belliustin's book was even prefaced by an epigraph from the works-of a Russian Jesuit, I. G. Gagarin, and a later issue of *Russkii zagranichnyi sbornik* advertised Gargarin's book *On the Reconciliation of the Russian and Catholic Churches.*[76] The Catholic connection, if known,[77] would have been fatal and it may have incited Belliustin's furious rebuke against Pogodin: "[My] composition is now in the hands of those who tirelessly seek all opportunities to ridicule that which we revere in the depths of our soul! . . . New food for malice and slander!"[78]

Belliustin's book caused an immediate sensation in St. Petersburg. Though rare and expensive, the illegal volume quickly circulated in the upper layers of government, church, and society. A. V. Nikitenko, that punctilious *rapporteur* of intellectual affairs, recorded the book's appearance on 16 July 1858 and after reading it concluded that "the condition of our clergy presents a horrifying picture!" He added that the book had reportedly been presented to Metropolitan Grigorii (Belliustin's former nemesis in Tver) and church authorities, who "are furious and have a called it a libel."[79] A few months later the church authorities blamed the *Opisanie* for the disorders at the St. Petersburg Ecclesiastical Academy, where students protested against a hated inspector, urged that none of their number become monks, and attempted to establish ties with students in the Kiev academy. Metropolitan Isidor wrote Metropolitan Filaret that "it is worth noting that [the students] were familiar with the book published abroad about the rural clergy, which gave rise to insistent demands that cannot be satisfied with the resources now at our disposal."[80] When Belliustin learned of these events a few months later, he was elated and wrote to Pogodin that the events at the St. Petersburg Academy only prove the truth of his book: "How is it that you did not write me a word about the [students'] movement in the St. Petersburg Academy surrounding my manuscript? After all, they simply rebelled against those emissaries from the darkness of Hell! And naturally so. Those who have never experienced all this cannot believe the manuscript, but the backs and sides [of these seminarians] provide powerful pieces of evidence."[81]

Predictably, the Synod launched an investigation and soon began to close in on the unsuspecting priest, who no doubt had received assurances from Pogodin that his identity was privy to no one. The first hint of trouble came in October 1858, when a stranger unexpectedly approached the priest during a visit to Tver. The man, who identified himself as Michel de Proudenkoff from "l'Académie de Rome," professed an interest in touring the local area with Belliustin. When the suspicious priest spurned his his requests, Proudenkoff declared: "In vain you affect such modesty, pretending to be someone who knows and understands nothing; after all, we know who writes what and for a long time we've known about you."[82] Frantic, Belliustin suspected a provocation, and wrote Pogodin with certainty that Proudenkoff "wears not a government uniform, but the blackest of cassocks [that of a monk]," and was probably an agent dispatched by Metropolitan Grigorii.[83]

The Synod finally took formal action against Belliustin. In a letter to Pogodin, the shaken priest described how he was summoned to appear on 14 January 1859 before the local archimandrite and answer the following questions:

1. Under what motivation, for what purpose, and when did you write the composition entitled *Opisanie sel'skogo dukhovenstva*, which was then published abroad?
2. Under what motivation, for what purpose, when, and to whom did you transmit your work for publication abroad?
3. At the present time do you regard the information in your composition as just, inoffensive, and harmless?

At the interrogation Belliustin was reminded that "for confession to the crime the punishment will be mitigated, but [otherwise] the laws will be applied in all their severity." Incredulous that the Synod could have conclusive proof of his authorship, the priest denied complicity or culpability by seizing on the technicality that he wrote a manuscript *zapiska*, not a book entitled *Opisanie sel'skogo dukhovenstva*: "I not only did not write but also have not even read a work bearing the title *Opisanie sel'skogo dukhovenstva*; having never seen [this book], I do not even know whether such a book exists anywhere, in Russia or abroad." If the charges are pressed, he wrote Pogodin, "try to see to it that I can defend myself before the courts of the civil government [not those of the church]."[84]

The denouement of the affair was indeed sensational. The Synod decided to impose an extraordinarily harsh punishment: life exile to "Solovki" (Solovetskii monastery), in the barren reaches of the far north.[85] It evidently intended to handle the case administratively, without further inquiry or formal review. Belliustin later wrote with bitter sarcasm that "the *Most Holy* Synod ordered that I be exiled permanently to Solovki—without a trial, without any refutation of my testimony."[86] At that point he was saved by the emperor, who intervened personally to quash the Synod's decision. As early as 10 January 1859 a friend in Petersburg, Kalachov, informed Belliustin of the latest rumor in high society: "There are some good people who have taken your side, including (so it is said) the Imperial family, which has read your work and found in it much that is true and completely new to them."[87] Two months later Belliustin wrote his son Nikolai in Moscow that he had been rescued at the last moment by the tsar himself, who "saved me from the revenge of the monks."[88] Curiously, the church archives show no trace of the affair; a search through the Synod, overprocurator, and censorship files disclosed no hint of Belliustin's interrogation, reports from censors or bishops, the Synod's resolution, or the tsar's intervention. Once the tsar forbade punishment, the Synod or Overprocurator Tolstoi evidently destroyed whatever file had been assembled.[89]

Apparently safe for the moment, Belliustin sought a new appointment with redoubled zeal. Promotion had long been his ambition, and even as he first began to write the *zapiska* in 1855, he hoped to use Pogodin's influence to obtain a better position, preferably in Moscow, but at least in Tver. Nothing came of these efforts, however.[90] Now the priest had still more compelling reasons than financial gain to seek a transfer; the tsar had rescued him on this occasion, but he remained under church jurisdiction and vulnerable to retribution at a later date. Only a clerical position outside the regular jurisdiction of the Synod and bishop – for example, a court or military chaplaincy – could guarantee security. Belliustin had reason to hope for such an appointment, for he now enjoyed considerable sympathy in high society and received large sums of money from Pogodin, Urusov, and others.[91] Grand Duchess Elena Pavlovna – well known for her role in the emancipation of the serfs – took an interest in Belliustin's case, and the priest implored Pogodin for support. "In her hands," he wrote, "is the power [to have me appointed] without the Synod and give me a corner in her Oranienbaum – and for one of her wealth what a trivial loss to give me some kind of salary and an apartment!"[92] Simultaneously, Belliustin sought a military chaplaincy from the tsar's confessor, Bazhanov, who agreed to give the priest a position in the regiments of the grenadier corps.[93] Belliustin, though anxious "to flee anywhere from the diocesan jurisdiction," nonetheless insisted upon an appointment with an income sufficient to support his large family.[94]

All these efforts failed. Despite a personal interview and evident interest in his case, Elena Pavlovna did not offer him a position; according to Belliustin, she was dissuaded by calumnious gossip.[95] Nor did he obtain a military chaplaincy. That paid too little (only two hundred rubles per annum compared to his present income of nearly four hundred rubles) and, worse still, there were no prospects of moving up later to a more lucrative post in the Guards regiments.[96] Nevertheless he agreed to accept the position if the bishop of Tver would transfer his post and property in Kaliazin to a future son-in-law – a curious demand for one so critical of the clergy's hereditary order. The bishop rejected this request, however, and the whole arrangement collapsed.[97] When Prince Odoevskii tried to find Belliustin a place in the Naval Ministry, Grand Duke Konstantin Nikolaevich rebuffed the attempt: "I hasten to inform you that, to my great regret, I can do nothing for the priest

Belliustin, whom, moreover, I do not know at all."[98] Another acquaintance sought to place Belliustin at the Smolnyi Institute, but
failed because of opposition from local church authortities.[99]

As Belliustin unsuccessfully contrived to find a lucrative and secure
position, church conservatives attempted to rebut his damaging indict-
ment by publishing a small brochure under the title *Mysli svetskogo
cheloveka o knige "Opisanie sel'skogo dukhovenstva"* ("A Layman's
Thoughts about the Book 'Description of the Rural Clergy'"). Approved by the St. Petersburg Committee of Ecclesiastical Censorship
and first published as an article in *Dukhovnaia beseda* (a Petersburg
journal founded by Metropolitan Grigorii), the pamphlet assailed
Belliustin's *Opisanie* for aiding Catholic propagandists, who, it alleged
(wrongly), had already translated it into French and German. Further,
it claimed, the book had wrought even greater harm inside Russia,
where it enjoyed wide circulation and popularity. The pamphlet did not
offer a substantive refutation of Belliustin's book, but merely quoted
the more rhetorical outbursts to demonstrate its "one-sidedness," som-
berly concluding that "this harmful and irresponsible book, gradually
penetrating into all strata of society, high and low, is causing tragic
results everywhere."[100]

The author of the pamphlet was A. N. Murav'ev, the conservative
who earlier had himself urged reform in the church. In contrast to
Belliustin, however, he blamed the church's problems not on the
monastic hierarchy but on the lay overprocurator, who exercised real
authority over the church and especially in the days of Protasov had
caused it considerable harm.[101] Early in 1859 Murav'ev had written
Filaret that a rejoinder to *Opisanie* was urgently needed and later it was
rumored that Filaret had even helped to edit the pamphlet.[102]
Subsequently, in a private letter to Pogodin justifying the pamphlet,
Murav'ev rebuked the historian for his role in the affair and warned that
Catholic propagandists would mercilessly exploit *Opisanie*. He
staunchly defended the hierarchs against charges made in it and reiter-
ated the argument of his own reform *zapiska*—that the church's
problems were due to its control by the government, not to the bishops
malfeasance.[103]

Murav'ev's challenge did not go unanswered. Belliustin, reluctant to enter the debate under his own name, pleaded with Pogodin to publish a reply and hold "public opinion" on his side.[104] Even before receiving that request, Pogodin had already published "An Explanation" in a Moscow journal. After castigating the pamphleteer for hypocrisy, he gave a brief account of the preparation of the *Opisanie* and his own role in the affair. Stressing his precautions to ensure the book's veracity, Pogodin claimed that his editing had consisted of nothing more than striking out passages that might betray the author's identity, leaving accountability for the text in the hands of the anonymous author; but he assumed full responsibility for the main offense—the publication of the *zapiska* abroad.[105] A further rejoinder to the pamphlet appeared in June, when the radical intellecutal N. Dobroliubov published a sharply critical review of *Mysli svetskogo cheloveka* and implicitly defended Belliustin. Though denying that he had read or even seen the illegal *Opisanie*, Dobroliubov—a priest's son himself—rebuked the pamphlet for its crude invective and argued that church reform was indeed urgently needed. The censors permitted Dobroliubov's article to appear, and many other journals prepared to join in the controversy.[106]

Just as the nation appeared on the verge of a full-scale debate over the church, the censorship intervened to choke off further discussion. As in the case of serfdom, the authorities feared that debate had gone too far, threatening to unleash passions and aspirations that would only complicate the tidy process of reform from above. In March 1859 the church censors rejected a manuscript called "The Voice of a Seminarian from the Provinces" because it contained "in places comments too caustic for an ecclesiastical student."[107] Another article ("On the Polemics about the Book 'Description of the Rural Clergy'"), which had already been authorized by the government censors for the journal *Illiustratsiia*, was interdicted by church censors in July.[108] The following month the same censors banned another critique of *Mysli svetskogo cheloveka* that was to appear in *Otechestvennye zapiski*.[109] But the turning point came in July 1859, when the tsar—concerned about the public debate on a number of delicate issues—ordered state and church censors to eliminate all further debate on church questions.[110]

That ban, however, had no effect upon a new foreign publication, *Russkoe dukhovenstvo*, a collection of articles published in Berlin. Its seven articles sharply criticized the infamous *Opisanie*, but only in very general terms. The anonymous editor (Nikolai Elagin) set the book's tone in his preface, which reproved Pogodin for his "ignominious role" in the affair and even hinted that the government was permitting the "harmful book" to circulate freely inside Russia. One long article, apparently written by a priest, conceded some truth to Belliustin's account, but argued that *Opisanie* presented only the negative side. Another article upbraided society for insufficient deference toward the clergy and attributed many of the latter's failings to the laity's niggardly support. Two articles defended the monastic clergy: one, a prolix essay, vindicated monasticism; the other justified the right of "learned monks" to dominate positions of authority over the white clergy. The rest of the volume consisted of a reprint of the Murav'ev pamphlet and an essay on the "historical service" that the clergy had rendered to Russia.[111]

Why was the book published abroad? Although it was widely rumored that church conservatives had been so obliged in order to escape censorship pressure from a government contemplating reform, this seems improbable. It was the church authorities themselves who had demanded an end to the public debate, and church censorship committees held the forefront in prohibiting the publication of "unseemly" and "harmful" articles. More to the point was the motive of the volume's editor, Elagin: foreign publication, he believed, would arouse much greater interest in the book. In a letter to Metropolitan Filaret in December 1858, Elagin argued that Alexander Herzen's immense popularity and influence were due "not only to his originality" but also to the illegality of his publications, which have become a kind of "forbidden fruit" for educated society.[112] Early in 1859 Elagin decided to publish a volume directed against Herzen and another work directed "against the book published in Leipzig about our rural clergy, in which the episcopal rank is ridiculed and our clergy's educational and moral upbringing are condemned."[113] Most important, Elagin's book, even if published abroad without prior approval by the censorship, was hardly "illegal." He himself wrote to Overprocurator Tolstoi in September 1859 to explain its purpose, at the same time sending complimentary copies for Tolstoi and several bishops.[114] The government censors approved the book for public sale and circulation, and forwarded the case to the St. Petersburg Committee of Ecclesiastical Censorship for review. The censor, Archimandrite Sergei, reported that "this book, containing polemical ideas of good inclination, can be permitted for the public."[115]

Because *Russkoe dukhovenstvo* was a "legal" book, Dobroliubov was able to review the volume and thus circumvent the censorship ban on essays concerning the "clerical question." He rejected the book's criticism of *Opisanie* for publicly exposing the church's problems; on the contrary, declared the radical journalist, only an open discussion can clear the path for effective reform. Such publicity was particularly needed for the church, which rarely forms the subject of articles in secular journals—a transparent allusion to the axe of censorship. Dobroliubov also pointedly noted the different statuses of *Opisanie* and *Russkoe dukhovenstvo*: "The volume of refutation (*Russkoe dukhovenstvo*) was sold in Russia immediately after its appearance abroad, and no one demands that it be prohibited; it is recognized as well-intentioned and harmless. But *Opisanie sel'skogo dukhovenstva*, even now, when we have heard so much about it from various repudiations, is still not permitted for sale and is read clandestinely, as contraband."[116]

The sharp conservative attacks notwithstanding, Belliustin's hopes for radical reform burned white-hot in the fall of 1859. Excitedly he spread a report from "one of the members of the Synod" that the tsar himself supported fundamental reform in the church: "From the very top [the Tsar] the following proposal was submitted in His [Majesty's] own handwriting: 'Consider: (1) Is it not useful to convert monasteries into hospitals and monks into feldshers and doctors? (2) Is it not useful to remove the white clergy from the influence of the black monastic clergy? (3) Is it not useful to make the sacristans [*prichetniki*] into hired laymen? (4) Present a report on the progress made in improving the condition of the rural clergy.'" Confident that he and Pogodin would have a leading role in the coming reforms, Belliustin wrote that "you will have to demand materials from me and I must again take up the interrupted work." The priest warned that reform must be removed from the hands of the Synod: "Now one must communicate to the very top [the Tsar] this idea: 'These questions must not be decided by the

Synod, which definitely thinks and acts contrary to the ideas of the Tsar and defends the authority of the monks. Rather, as in the present question, experts from all corners of Russia should be chosen."[117] And as late as January 1869 he reported rumors of "a hope that V.B. Bazhanov soon will become the metropolitan for the entire white clergy."[118]

In these months Belliustin stood at the very pinnacle of his influence and power. He transmitted to the empress an article on "schools for girls," a subject of considerable interest to her and one in which Belliustin had earned some recognition.[119] To the emperor he submitted an article on the plight of widowed clergy, which he had originally intended as part of his *zapiska* but completed only after the manuscript had been taken abroad.[120] The question of widowed priests and deacons and their right to voluntary defrocking had since become a lively issue: the Synod in 1859 proposed to remove the harsh disabilities imposed on clergy who voluntarily defrocked themselves; the penalties (periods of long exclusion from any form of government service) had been established arbitrarily during Nicholas's reign and made it exceptionally difficult for clergy to quit the clerical estate, even when they had no desire to remain or actually had compelling reasons to leave.[121] The barrier was especially harmful to widowed clergy: the clerical family was an economic unit and without a wife to manage the household and perform other functions, priests and deacons soon fell into difficult straits. Unlike laymen, they could neither remarry nor retain alien women in their house, and the right to voluntary defrocking had long served as the natural solution to their dilemma. Belliustin estimated that forty percent of the clergy were young widowers and urged the removal of artificial barriers to their exodus. At the same time that he was nurturing his ties with the court, he continued to seek a safe appointment, pressing his negotiations with Bazhanov and keeping alive his hopes elsewhere.[122]

Within a few months, in early 1860, Belliustin suddenly fell precipitately from favor at court. The ostensible reason, according to his own account, was a sudden withdrawal of support by Bazhanov, who had read two of the priest's articles and pronounced them "heretical."[123] Belliustin does not identify the articles, but they were most likely unpublished *zapiski* presenting his extremely liberal views on the schismatics and popular religious belief.[124] But the priest claimed that the true cause of his sudden disfavor was calumny, enemy rumors of his alleged "drunkenness" and accusations of other irregularities—all of which he vehemently denied, citing his service record, the reports of the local district superintendent, and parish petitions.[125] This may indeed have played a certain role, but Belliustin did not grasp the essential reason—Alexander's ambivalence toward the question of church reform. The tsar's only sure commitment—it would recur repeatedly in the 1860's—was to rejuvenate and strengthen the Orthodox clergy in the western provinces. It was a baldly political concern, a desire to build a strong religious bulwark against political and national disaffection in the turbulent region. Beyond that narrow perimeter, however, Alexander's interest quickly waned, especially when confronted with ecclesiastical opposition. Swept away by the euphoria of reform expectations in 1859, Belliustin failed to perceive his imperial patron's narrow designs or the effect of his own increasingly radical proposals upon the cautious emperor.[126]

Evidence of official distrust was soon forthcoming. Belliustin's mail began to vanish: in April 1860 he complained that part of Pogodin's last letter was missing, and in July he reported that nine letters had recently failed to reach him.[127] With bitter irony he wrote in the following month that "such is progress in our country: previously two or three letters disappeared and they were satisfied with that, but now the whole correspondence vanishes."[128] Simultaneously, his last hopes for an appointment to a crown chapel faded, as well-placed figures interceded against him.[129] He also heard ominous threats from the local bishop, who declared: "I know him [Belliustin]: a harmful person, of whom we should long ago have rid ourselves; it is necessary to change the local superindendent [*blagochinnyi*], who still supports him with attestations [of good conduct and service]."[130] In despair, Belliustin even contemplated defrocking himself in order "to tear myself away from this fatal environment which is called the clerical rank (and all my thoughts are now aimed at that)."[131] He tried actively to become a teacher in the Ministry of Education but there too met with disappointment: he was offered a religious instructorship in Arkhangel province,

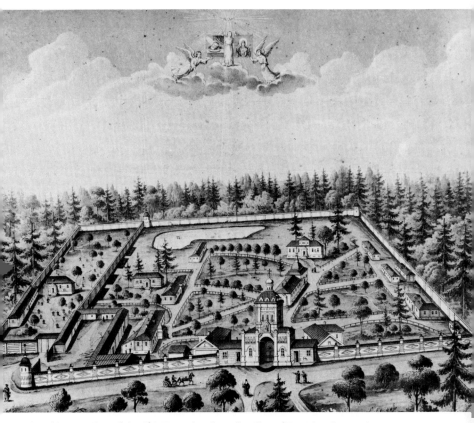

Figure 1. View of the *Skit* Honoring the Beheading of St. John the Baptist at Optina Monastery. The Eastern Orthodox *skit* organizes a strict and solitary monastic life. Church services are not performed daily as in regular monastic routine, but only on Saturdays, Sundays, and some feast days. The monks spend the greater part of their time in solitary contemplation of God, in prayer, and reading spiritual literature. The *skit* is intended to convey an impression of a wilderness apart from the world. Fasting is observed throughout the year, except when the church specifically does not require it. As frequently as possible, each monk confesses to an "elder" (*starets*) and seeks his spiritual guidance. St. John the Baptist *skit*, built in 1821, was the most famous hermitage in Russia and housed the renowned Optina "elders."

Figure 2. Interior of Bethany Monastery Founded by Metropolitan Platon (Levshin) of Moscow. A. P. Stanley, nineteenth-century British historian of the Eastern church, described Bethany as a "gay Italian-like retreat," which corresponded to Platon's monastic ideal.

Figure 3. The Holy Synodal Typography on Nikol'skoe Street in St. Petersburg at the End of the 1840s. From a lithograph with tone by P. Benoist (1813-after 1870).

Figure 4. Gethsemane *Skit*
Near the Holy Trinity-St.
Sergius Monastery. Founded
by Metropolitan Filaret
(Drozdov) following his exile
from the Synod by
Overprocurator Protasov in
1842. In contrast to Bethany
(Fig. 2), Stanley characterized
Gethsemane, which
commemorates the beginning
of Christ's suffering and his
arrest, as an "austere revival
of a mediaeval hermitage."

Figure 5. Interior of Gethsemane *Skit.* View of the individual cells.
Metropolitan Filaret is in the foreground.

Figure 6. Archbishop Feofan (Prokopovich) of Pskov. From a painting by G. A. Afonas'ev. Photograph courtesy of Professor James Cracraft.)

Figure 7. Metropolitan Filaret (Drozdov) of Moscow. Filaret's austere and stern monastic temperament won him many critics. The historian S. M. Solov'ev declared that he had a "hot head and a cold heart." Alarmed at the facile optimism of contemporaries, Filaret confessed, "I fear that earthly joy which thinks it has nothing to fear." (Photograph courtesy of Professor Edward Kasinec.)

Figure 8. Two Generations of Professors and Rectors of Moscow Ecclesiastical Academy. *Above left,* Professor A. V. Gorskii, 1812-75. His paternal love for students won him the sobriquet "papasha." A devoted scholar, his monumental inventory and description of the manuscripts of the Moscow Synodal (Patriarchal) Library required eighteen years and remained unfinished when he became academy rector in 1864. *Above right,* Archbishop Filaret (Gumilevskii) of Chernigov, 1805-66. Called "Gumilevskii" (from *humilis*) since his seminary days in Tambov because of his "humility," Filaret, like his close friend Gorskii, earned a reputation for scholarship. He founded the journal *Writings of the Holy Fathers* with the aim of reviving Russia's Eastern Patristic tradition. The drawings of Gorskii and Filaret were made by D. I. Katal'skii during lectures. *Center,* Fedor A. Golubinskii, 1797-1854. His lectures, or "inspired improvizations," combining eighteenth-century rationalism and pietism with Kant and Jacobi, "shaped the souls" of his audience. *Below left,* Professor Igor V. Amfiteatrov, 1815-88, an outstanding lecturer at the Moscow Ecclesiastical Academy whose brilliant synthesis of European writers left the students "enraptured or even outright worshipful." *Below right,* Professor Sergei K. Smirnov, 1818-99, also on the editorial board of the journal *Writings of the Holy Fathers,* is best remembered for his several histories of Russian ecclesiastical academies. (Photograph reproduced with permission of The New York Public Library.)

Professor A. V. Gorskii

Archbishop Filaret (Gumilevskii)

Fedor A. Golubinskii

Professor Igor V. Amfiteatrov

Professor Sergei K. Smirnov

Figure 9. A Parish Priest in Modern Times. Taken during Nevin O. Winter's visit to the Ukraine during the Russian Revolution.

Figure 10. Khar'kov Pilgrims on a Journey to Kiev's Famous Monastery of the Caves, 1917.

Figure 11. Members of the National Council (*Sobor*) of the Russian Orthodox Church in 1917-18. *Center,* Tikhon, the Metropolitan of Moscow, elected President of the Council and later chosen Patriarch of all Russia. *At his right,* the Metropolitan of Novgorod; *at his left,* the Metropolitan of Khar'kov. *From left to right:* the Archbishops of Kherson, Mogilev, Grodno, and the Metropolitans of Iaroslavl, the Caucasus, Vladimir, and the Archbishop of Tver. *Upper row, from left to right:* the Archbishops of Viatka and Kolomna and the Bishops of Chernigov, Kaluga, Olonets, Kamchatka, Smolensk, and Nikol'sk. *To the left of the Metropolitan of Novgorod,* two Vice-Presidents of the Council, Fr. Lubimov and Professor Prince Evgenii Trubetskoi.

Figure 12. Easter Celebration on St. Nicholas Day in Red Square, May 1918. The new Bolshevik government had purposely declared the holiday a work day, but Moscow's parishes assembled in the square singing Easter hymns.

Figure 13. His Holiness Tikhon, Patriarch of Moscow and All Russia. Before the Revolution, Tikhon had served as Bishop of North America from 1898 to 1907. (Photograph courtesy of Professor Edward Kasinec.)

Figure 14. Professor Nikolai N. Glubokovskii. Known as Russia's "miniature Tillemont" because of his detailed studies of the Church Fathers and his fidelity to sources, Glubokovskii, 1863-1937, earned a wide reputation in Russia, Europe, and America. He was a professor at the St. Petersburg Ecclesiastical Academy. (Photograph reproduced with permission of The New York Public Library.)

but had to decline the post as too distant and poorly remunerated.[132]

By 1861 the Kaliazin priest was clearly in official disfavor. Whereas in the past he had consistently received awards for meritorious service, such honors now ceased; in one case the archbishop even struck Belliustin's name from a list of parish teachers nominated for awards.[133] In 1861 the position of archpriest became vacant in his cathedral and, as senior priest, Belliustin was the natural successor. The parishioners supported his candidacy, filing a petition with the bishop that lauded him as a model priest and indefatigable schoolteacher.[134] Nevertheless, the bishop deferred a final decision, agreeing only to appoint Belliustin as "temporary executor of the position of archpriest." Belliustin accepted this provisional assignment, but resigned angrily in 1864, when the bishop refused to make it official and permanent.[135] In the same year, the tsar himself secretly had Belliustin banned from St. Petersburg, instructing the archbishop not to give him the needed travel permit.[136] The Kaliazin priest, no longer entertaining illusions of a lucrative, influential appointment in St. Petersburg, moved steadily leftward in his general politics. By the mid-1860s he ranked as a prominent clerical publicist, a lacerating critic of the government as well as the church.

The Belliustin affair was an important watershed, a sharp dividing line between the Nikolaevan epoch and the new era of ecclesiastical Great Reforms. It played a central role in fashioning a reform concensus in society, government, and church; the passion of the book, the drama of the affair, the ensuing debate—all served to make the clerical question into a major public issue. The book itself also exerted direct influence on the coming reforms: its criticisms and solutions appeared repeatedly and widely in the 1860s. And, as one of its principal achievements, it aroused the emperor's interest and nudged him in the direction of reform. Although that interest proved rather narrow and essentially political, the emperor's role in the Belliustin affair led many to expect a fundamental transformation in the church.

These expectations wrought extraordinary strains in church-state relations. They redoubled the hierarchs' distrust of the government, evoking fears of uncanonical reforms and further violations of church privilege. Revealingly, church conservatives alleged that Belliustin was a "tool" of the government, which, they claimed, allowed his book to

circulate freely while secretly supporting the obscure priest from Kaliazin. That allegation only aggravated the dissatisfaction with the church
of state officials, who for reasons of economy and convenience wanted
a reformed church that could deal effectively—without coercive police
support—with such problems as religious disaffection. Resistance to reform by leading bishops further deepened the government's impatience,
and the recalcitrance of the hierarchy finally impelled the minister of
interior, P.A. Valuev, to argue that the hierarchs themselves were in
need of reform. He suggested that they be included in the State Council
to help draw them into the "modern world."

Finally, Belliustin's revolt from below heralded a whole new era of
politics within the church. With its clear statement of the white clergy's
interests and grievances against their monastic superiors, his book sharp-
ened a long-standing antagonism and exposed it to public view. In 1861
the minister of interior warned the emperor that the conflict between
white and black clergy had reached dangerous levels and that it had
even inspired radical, "socialist" strivings among the parish clergy.[137]
That report was an exaggeration, but it did attest to the new boldness
and assertiveness of parish clergy and to the breakdown of prereform
discipline and submissiveness. Belliustin had vividly demonstrated that
a parish priest could defy church authority with impunity; within a few
years parish clergy everywhere began to cut the bonds of diocesan control and publish widely in secular and church journals, thus coming to
represent a new force in church and society. The focus of all this
activism was a whole new movement, "clerical liberalism." Though
lacking a firm organizational base, it sought to confer new rights and
freedoms on the clergy—a greater role in church governance, a higher
status in society, a secure and respectable income, new forms of expression and action. For "progressive" priests clerical liberalism's
program was crucial to both church and clergy; it would generate a new
professionalism in the priesthood and defend the special interests of the
clerical class. But such a program clashed sharply with the privileges and
prerogatives of the traditional powers; not only bishops, but also
bureaucrats and parishioners, found cause to oppose it. Thus marked by
consensus and conflict, reform and reaction, this new epoch of church

politics finally came to an explosive climax in the turbulent years of 1905 and 1917.

NOTES

1. A copy of the Murav'ev *zapiska*, hitherto unidentified, is preserved in the "secret section" of the synodal archive in Tsentral'nyi gosudarstvennyi istorich-eskii arkhiv SSSR, fond 796 (Kantseliariia Synoda), opis' 205, delo 603, listy 1-12; hereafter TsGIA and, where appropriate, the customary form of Soviet archival notation: f. (fond), op. (opis'), g. (god), otd. (otdelenie), st. (stol), k. (karton), razd. (razdel), d. (delo), ch. (chast'), l., ll. (list, listy), and ob. (oborot). For a later memorandum by Murav'ev, see "Zapiska A.N. Murav'eva o sostoianii pravoslavnoi tserkvi v Rossii," *Russkii arkhiv*, 1883, kn. II, 175-203.

2. A copy of Batiushkov's most important memorandum is to be found in Rukopisnyi otdel, Gosudarstvennaia biblioteka im. V.I. Lenina, f. 316 (Metropolitan Filaret), op. 1, k. 65, d. 22, ll. 1-23; hereafter cited GBL.

3. See the author's "P.A. Valuev and the Politics of Church Reform (1861-1862)," forthcoming in *Slavonic and East European Review.*

4. Belliustin's legal name was Beliustin, which he used in official documents and some correspondence; in most correspondence and all published writings, however, he preferred the spelling Belliustin.

5. [D.I. Rostislavov], *O chernom i belom pravoslavnom dukhovenstve*, 2 vols., Leipzig, 1866, I, 22.

6. "Vnutrennee obozrenie o noveishikh reformakh dukhovenstva," *Nedelia*, 1868, no. 29, 898.

7. For typical treatment in the more specialized literature, see Igor Smolitsch, *Geschichte der russischen Kirche, 1700-1917*, I, Leiden, 1964, 425-26; A.A. Papkov, *Tserkovno-obshchestvennye voprosy v epokhu Tsaria-osvoboditelia, 1855-1870 gg.*, St. Petersburg, 1902, 30-32. The fullest discussion is to be found in N. Barsukov's monumental biography of Pogodin, but its aim is mainly that of revealing Pogodin's role (N. Barsukov, *Zhizn' i trudy M. P. Pogodina*, 22 vols. St. Petersburg, 1888-1910, esp. XII, 244-52, XV, 115-30.

8. See, for instance, the assessment in *Pravoslavnaia bogoslovskaia entisklopediia*, 12 vols., St. Petersburg, 1900-1911.

9. Belliustin letter of 1887, quoted in S.A. Vengerov, *Kritiko-biograficheskii slovar' russkikh pisatelei i uchenykh*, VI, St. Petersburg, 1904, 430-31.

10. See Jean Gagarin, *The Russian Clergy*, London, 1872, 24-25.

11. The single most important set of materials in the Pogodin archive (GBL, f. 231), which contains numerous Belliustin letters and manuscripts. Besides scattered letters in other archival collections, there are four volumes from Belliustin to his son Nikolai (formerly in Rukopisnyi otdel, Biblioteka Akademii nauk, f. 411/1926 (hereafter BAN), now in the archive of Leningradskoe otdelenie Instituta istorii, f. 115, dd. 1217-20). Other important materials are in the archives of the Synod, overprocurator, and ecclesiastical censorship in TsGIA

(fondy 796, 797, and 807). Belliustin's personal archive is in Gosudarstvennyi arkhiv Kaliningradskoi oblasti (hereafter GAKO), f. 103, to which the author obtained access only after this article was completed; some pertinent materials from f. 103 are summarized and quoted in P.N. Agafonov, "Sviashchennik-publitsist: I.S. Belliustin (K voprosu o liberal'nom dvizhenii v russkoi tserkvi v XIX v.)," Diplomnaia rabota, Moscow State University, 1971.

12. Belliustin's father, Stefan Ioannovich, became a priest in 1820 at a parish in Staritsa, later moved to Tver, and finally settled at a tiny cathedral in Bezhetsk, where he was still serving as late as 1863 (see the 1863 cahier from his church in TsGIA, f. 804 [Osoboe prisutstvie po delam pravoslavnogo dukhovenstva], op. 1, razd. III, d. 404, ll. 1-2). Although such standard references as *Russkii biograficheskii slovar'* state that Belliustin was born and educated in Novgorod diocese, he was in fact from Tver (see the report by I.I. Zav'ialov in *Zhurnal 112-ogo zasedaniia Tverskoi uchenoi arkhivnoi komissii*, Tver, 1912, 12).

13. Reports from 1849 graphically demonstrate that the number of seminary graduates in Tver, as in most other dioceses, far exceeded diocesan needs; the Synod finally established a special committee to consider the problem (TsGIA, f. 797, op. 19, I otd., 2 st., d. 42644 and f. 796, op. 445, d. 345).

14. From Belliustin's service record, summarized by Archbishop Savva in an 1879 file in TsGIA, f. 796, op. 160, g. 1879, d. 831, l. 14 ob.

15. For Belliustin's sermons from the 1840s, see *Zhurnal 112-ogo zasedaniia*, 61-109.

16. *Ibid.*, 12; TsGIA, f. 796, op. 160, g. 1879, d. 831, l. 14 ob.

17. Agafonov, 19, citing GAKO, f. 103, op. 1, d. 1291, l. 149.

18. Agafonov, 20, citing GAKO, f. 103, op. 1, d. 1307, l. 6.

19. Agafonov, 21.

20. See the quotations from Belliustin's diary in GAKO that are printed in M.B., "Dnevnik popa Beliustina," *Proletarskaia pravda*, 16 July 1935, 4.

21. Belliustin to Pogodin, 26 November 1855 and 25 September 1855 (GBL, f. 231/II, k. 3, d. 49/4, ll. 2, 4).

22. For profiles on archpriests, see the 1861 service listings of consistory members, *blagochinnye* and archpriests in TsGIA, f. 796, op. 143, g. 1862, d. 2570, ch. 1-2.

23. See Smolitsch, *Geschichte*, 392-98 and *idem, Russisches Mönchtum: Entstehung, Entwicklung und Wesen, 988-1917*, Würzburg, 1953, 427, 451.

24. Belliustin to Pogodin, 26 November 1855 (GBL, f. 231/II, k. 3, d. 49/4, l. 1 ob.).

25. *Zhurnal 112-ogo zasedaniia*, 16.

26. Belliustin to Pogodin, 25 February 1854 (GBL, f. 231/II, k. 3, d. 49/3, l. 1).

27. Agafonov, 24-28, citing GAKO, f. 103, op. 1, d. 1291, l. 150; a somewhat different version, based on materials provided by Belliustin's son, is given in Barsukov, XII, 245-47.

28. Agafonov, 31-32; Belliustin to Pogodin, 25 February 1854 (GBL, f. 231/II, k. 3, d. 49/3, ll. 1-1 ob.).

29. See Belliustin to Pogodin, 25 February 1854, 25 September 1855, 26 October 1856 and 26 May 1861 (GBL, f. 231/II, k. 3, d. 49/3, l. 1-1 ob.; d. 49/4, l. 4; d. 49/5, l. 6; d. 51/2, l. 1 ob.).

30. See A. Kotovich, *Dukhovnaia tsenzura v Rossii (1799-1855 gg.)*, St. Petersburg, 1909.

31. TsGIA, f. 807, op. 2, g. 1852, d. 1184, ll. 88-88 ob., 89.

32. Belliustin to Pogodin, 11 September 1857 (GBL, f. 231/II, k. 3, d. 49/6, ll. 11-11 ob.).

33. Agafonov, 81, quoting GAKO, f. 103, op. 1, d. 1291, l. 108.

34. Belliustin to Pogodin, 25 February 1854 (GBL, f. 231/II. k. 3, d. 49/3, l. 2).

35. Agafonov, 81-82, quoting GAKO, f. 103, op. 1, d. 1291, ll. 108-9.

36. From an unpublished section of the manuscript for *Opisanie* (GBL, f. 231/III, k. 1, d. 66, ll. 2 ob.-3).

37. Belliustin to Pogodin, 6 January 1859 (GBL, f. 231/II, k. 3, d. 50/2, l. 2).

38. Belliustin to Pogodin, 26 November 1855 (*ibid.,* d. 49/4, l. 1 ob.).

39. Belliustin to Pogodin, 8 April 1853 (*ibid.,* d. 49/2, l. 3 ob.).

40. Belliustin to Pogodin, 4 December 1854 (*ibid.,* d. 49/3, l. 7 ob.).

41. GBL, f. 231/III, k. 1, d. 66, l. 42 ob.

42. Belliustin to Pogodin, 15 August 1852 (GBL, f. 231/II, k. 3. d. 49/1, ll. 1-1 ob.).

43. Belliustin to Pogodin, 25 November 1853 and 1 May 1856 (*ibid.,* d. 49/2, l. 7; d. 49/5, l. 3 ob.).

44. Belliustin to Pogodin, 21 March 1855 (*ibid.,* d. 49/4, ll. 7-8). Eventually Belliustin presented a large number of documents to the Archaeographic Commission, and these are now preserved in the Leningrad Section of the Institute of History (*Letopis' zaniatii Arkheograficheskoi komissii za 1918 g.*, vyp. 31 [Petrograd, 1923], 9; *Putevoditel' po arkhivu Leningradskogo otdeleniia Instituta istorii*, Leningrad, 1958, 369).

45. Belliustin to Pogodin, 8 April 1853 (GBL, f. 231/II, k. 3, d. 49/2, ll. 3).

46. Belliustin to Pogodin, 5 February 1853 (*ibid.,* ll. 1-1 ob.).

47. On the widespread fascination with spiritualism in the 1850s, see V.P. Meshcherskii, *Moi vospominaniia*, 3 vols., St. Petersburg, 1895-98, I, 63-64, and A.F. Tiutcheva, *Pri dvore dvukh imperatorov*, 2 vols., Moscow, 1928-29, I, 122-23, 125, 135-36 and II, 147-49, 173-77, 179, 186. For a general account of this movement, see A. Serafimov, "Spiritizm i spiritualizm," *Dukhovnyi vestnik*, 1865, no. 11, 207-29.

48. Belliustin to Pogodin, 29 November 1853 (GBL, f. 231/II, k. 3, d. 49/2, l. 9); his manuscript article is also in Pogodin's archive (GBL, f. 231/III, k. 1, d. 60, ll. 1-2).

49. Barsukov, XIII, 157-63.

50. Belliustin to Pogodin, 18 January 1858 (GBL, f. 231/II, k. 3, d. 50/1, l. 3); he expressed similar fears to Pogodin in a letter of 20 March 1858 (d. 50/1, l. 7).

51. "It is a miracle the way things are done in Russia: they make a fuss over improving the conditions of peasants but do not wish to ask them about any-

thing! 'Commissions, committees' — all that is marvelous; 'opinions, deliberations' (in journals) — all that is marvelous. But are not journal opinions and all the rest just words, words, words? And can it not happen, as it often does, that theoretical reflections which seem constructed in the best fashion prove unworkable the very first time they are applied in practice?'' (Belliustin to Pogodin, 20 March 1858 [*ibid.*, d. 50/1, l. 7 ob.]). See the similar opinion in his *Opisanie sel'skogo dukhovenstva* (Leipzig, 1858), 51-52.

52. Belliustin to Pogodin, 26 October 1856 (GBL, f. 231/II, k. 3, d. 49/5, l. 7 ob.); for a discussion of Belliustin's work on the educational question and a list of his articles, see *Arkhiv K. D. Ushinskogo*, I, Moscow, 1959, 85ff.

53. Belliustin to E. A. Cherkasskaia, 1 August 1860 (GBL, f. 327/II [Cherkasskaia], k. 5, d. 31, l. 4 ob.); Belliustin to I. P. Kornilov, 15 June 1860 (Rukopisnyi otdel, Gosudarstvennaia publichnaia biblioteka im. M. E. Saltykova-Shchedrina [hereafter GPB], f. 377 [I. P. Kornilov], d. 474, l. 1).

54. M. P. Pogodin. "Ob''iasnenie," *Russkii vestnik*, XXI (1859), sovremennaia letopis', 45-46.

55. Belliustin to Pogodin, 25 September 1855 (GBL, f. 231/II, k. 3, d. 49/4, l. 3).

56. Belliustin to Pogodin, 2 April 1857 and 26 December 1857 (*ibid.*, d. 49/6, ll. 5, 13 ob.).

57. Only part of the original *zapiska* has survived (GBL, f. 231/III, k. 1, d. 66), and quotations here are taken from the published *Opisanie*.

58. See the materials of the seminary reform committee in TsGIA, f. 796, op. 141, g. 1860, d. 367, ll. 1-593.

59. *Pis'ma Innokentiia, Mitropolita Moskovskogo i Kolomenskogo*, 2 vols., St. Petersburg, 1897-98, II, 151, 163-64, 168, 199-200.

60. The bishops' and diocesan committees' reports are in TsGIA, f. 804, op. 1, razd. I; the cahiers from parish clergy are in razd. III.

61. On the election of *blagochinnye*, see the reports for 1866-71 in TsGIA, f. 797, op. 36, IV otd., d. 151, ll. 1-114.

62. On the deletion of examples from Tver, see GBL, f. 231/III, k. 1, d. 66, ll. 2, 2 ob., 6 ob.-7, 9 ob., 10-11; for an instance where Pogodin questioned Belliustin's report of a metropolitan's suspicious relations with a monastery, see Belliustin to Pogodin, 22 May 1857 (GBL, f. 231/II, k. 3, d. 49/6, l. ob.).

63. GBL, f. 231/III, k. 1, d. 66, ll. 7 ob.-8, 14, 15 ob.-18.

64. Barsukov, XV, 125-26.

65. Pogodin. "Ob''iasnenie," 47-48.

66. See the entries in Pogodin's diary for 9 and 12 June 1857 and 6 August 1857 (GBL, f. 231/I, k. 35, d. 1, ll. 47 ob., 49).

67. Barsukov, XV, 125-26.

68. Belliustin to Pogodin, 15 July 1857 (*ibid.*, d. 49/6, l. 9).

69. Belliustin to Pogodin, 22 February 1858 (*ibid.*, d. 50/1, ll. 5-5 ob.).

70. For Belliustin's statement on the legacy of Grigorii's rule by terror, see GBL, f. 231/III, k. 1, d. 66, l. 5; on Grigorii's reputation from his tenure in Riazan diocese, see N. F. Dubrovskii, *Materialy dlia istorii pravoslavnoi tserkvi v*

tsarstvovanie Imp. Nikolaia I, kn. 1-2 (*Sbornik Imperatorskogo russkogo isto-richeskogo obshchestva*, CXIII, St. Petersburg, 1902, 70-71).

71. Belliustin to P.I. Mel'nikov-Pecherskii, 1859 (GPB, f. 37 [A.I. Artem'ev], d. 703, ll. 2-2 ob.).

72. *Opisanie sel'skogo dukhovenstva*, 162-66.

73. *Ibid.*, 112.

74. Belliustin to Pogodin, 26 May 1859 (GBL, f. 231/II, k. 3, d. 50/2, ll. 19-19 ob.).

75. For evidence of the government's mounting concern about religious problems in the western provinces, see the report of the Governor-General of Kiev and ensuing discussions in TsGIA, f. 796, op. 137, g. 1856, d. 230 and f. 797, op. 26, III otd., 1 st., d. 28.

76. *Opisanie*, p. ii (quotation from J. Gagarin's *De l'enseignement de la théologie dans l'église russe*, Paris, 1856, 59); for the advertisement of Gagarin's ecumenical volume (*O primirenii russkoi tserkvi s rimskoiu*), see *Russkii zagranichnyi sbornik*, vyp. 6.

77. The political status of *Russkii zagranichnyi sbornik* remains an enigma. In an introduction to its first issue the editors criticized the publications in England (Herzen's) and France as falling in two opposite extremes, neither telling the whole truth; the editors promised to "defend truth and the fatherland."

78. Belliustin to Pogodin, 8 July 1858 (GBL, f. 231/II, k. 3, d. 50/1, l. 13).

79. A.V. Nikitenko, *Dnevnik*, 3 vols., Moscow, 1955-56, II, 31.

80. Isidor to Filaret, 25 December 1858 (TsGIA, f. 832 [Filaret], op. 1, d. 15, ll. 121 ob.-122); see also Nikitenko, *Dnevnik*, II, 38.

81. Belliustin to Pogodin, 6 January 1859 (GBL, f. 231/II, k. 3, d. 50/2, l. 2).

82. Belliustin to Pogodin, 9 October 1858 (*ibid.*, d. 50/1, ll. 18-18 ob.).

83. Belliustin to Pogodin, 24 October 1858 (*ibid.*, l. 20).

84. Belliustin to Pogodin, 14 January 1859 (d. 50/2, ll. 3-3 ob.).

85. Belliustin to Pogodin, 27 January 1859 (*ibid.*, l. 7 ob.).

86. Belliustin to Mel'nikov-Pecherskii, n.d. (GBL, f. 37, d. 703, l. 2 ob.); see also "Tekushchaia khronika i osobye proizshestviia: Dnevnik. V.F. Odoevskogo, 1858-59 gg.," *Literaturnoe nasledstvo*, XXII-XXIV, Moscow, 1935, 94.

87. N.V. Kalachov to Belliustin, 10 January 1859 (GAKO, f. 103, op. 1, d. 1333, ll. 3 ob.-4, as cited in Agafonov, 92).

88. Belliustin to N.I. Belliustin, 7 March 1859 (BAN, f. 411/1926, vol. 1, unpaginated letter no. 10).

89. To no avail the author carefully searched the inventory of the Synod and overprocurator (including the "secret sections" of each); nor was evidence of the case found in the original protocols and registers, bound in volumes separately from individual archival *dela*, even including the most likely place – the separate volumes of "secret resolutions" (*Kniga dlia zapisyvaniia protokolov na sekretnoi ekspeditsii II-ogo otdeleniia Sinodal'noi kantseliarii*) in TsGIA, f. 796, op. 449, *dela* 166-70 (for the years 1857-60). Nor did the case appear in the archives of the government censorship committee on foreign books (*Komitet tsenzury innostrannoi*, TsGIA, f. 779) or the Petersburg Committee for Ecclesiastical Censorship

(TsGIA, f. 807). That no file survived was also evident in 1879, when the Synod considered defrocking Belliustin for another publicistic venture and ordered that a comprehensive record of his tainted past be compiled; no mention at all is made of the *Opisanie* (TsGIA, f. 796, op. 160, g. 1879, d. 831, ll. 15-17, 112-63). This silence contrasts markedly with the subsequent case of Rostislavov's illegal volumes on the clergy and church schools, from which materials abound—in the archives of the Synod (TsGIA, f. 796, op. 147, g. 1866, d. 1599), overprocurator (TsGIA, f. 797, op. 36, I otd., 1 st., d. 289), Committee on Foreign Censorship (TsGIA, f. 779, op. 1, g. 1867, d. 33), and Petersburg Committee on Ecclesiastical Censorship (TsGIA, f. 807, op. 2, g. 1866, d. 1445, ll. 43-44 ob.).

90. Belliustin to Pogodin, 26 November 1855, 7 April 1858, 1 December 1858 (GBL, f. 231/II, k. 3, d. 49/2, l. 2; d. 50/1, ll. 9, 21-21 ob.).

91. In 1860 Belliustin reported having received 250 rubles from "K.T.," an unspecified amount from Urusov, 300 rubles from the "Society for Aid to Needy Writers" (through P.V. Annenkov), and 300 rubles from Pogodin (Belliustin to Pogodin, 8 January 1860, 2 April 1860, 22 December 1859 [*ibid.*, d. 51/1, ll. 1 ob., 10 ob.; d. 50/2, ll. 29-30] ; Belliustin to Cherkasskaia, 2 August 1860 [GBL, f. 327/II, k. 5, d. 31, l. 4 ob.]).

92. Belliustin to Pogodin, 6 January 1859 (GBL, f. 231/II, k. 3, d. 50/2, l. 1 ob.).

93. Belliustin to V.B. Bazhanov, n. d. (copy in Belliustin to Pogodin, 27 January 1859 [GBL, f. 231/II, k. 3, d. 50/2, ll. 7 ob.-8]).

94. *Ibid.*; Belliustin to N.I. Belliustin, 7 March 1859 (BAN, f. 411/1926, vol. 1, unpaginated letter no. 10.).

95. Belliustin to Pogodin, 8 July 1861 (GBL, f. 231/II, k. 3, d. 51/2, l. 2 ob.).

96. In 1859 Belliustin wrote Pogodin that he received 250 rubles from his clerical position and 143 rubles for teaching in the Kaliazin school (Belliustin to Pogodin, 26 May 1859 [*ibid.*, d. 50/2, ll. 19 ob.-20]). On the failure to secure a suitable position from Bazhanov, see Belliustin to Pogodin, 10 August 1859 (*ibid.*, l. 23).

97. Belliustin to Pogodin, 10 August 1859 (*ibid.*, l. 23).

98. Grand Duke Konstantin Nikolaevich to Prince V.F. Odoevskii, 2 July 1859 (GBL, f. 11/1 [Apraksiny], k. 68, d. 10, l. 2); this letter, a copy, was intercepted and transmitted "in complete confidentiality for the personal knowledge of Count Aleksandr Petrovich [Tolstoi] ," overprocurator of the Synod.

99. K.D. Ushinskii to Belliustin, 2 September 1859 (*Arkhiv Ushinskogo*, I, 59-61).

100. *Mysli svetskogo cheloveka o knige "Opisanie sel'skogo dukhovenstva",* St. Petersburg, 1859, 4.

101. A.N. Murav'ev to Pogodin, 5 June 1859 (TsGIA, f. 796, op. 205, d. 603, ll. 1-15; f. 832, op. 1, d. 83, ll. 132-45 ob.); on Filaret's role, see the report in Odoevskii's diary entry of 18 March 1859 ("Tekushchaia khronika," 94).

102. Barsukov, XV, 127-28.

103. Murav'ev to Pogodin, 5 June 1859 (TsGIA, f. 796, op. 205, d. 603, ll. 1-15).

104. Belliustin to Pogodin, 5, 9, 18 and 26 May 1859 (GBL, f. 231/II, k. 3, d. 50/2, ll. 12-13 ob., 14-15, 16-18 ob., 19-20 ob.).

105. Pogodin, "Ob"iasnenie," 43-50.

106. [N.G. Dobroliubov], *"Mysli svetskogo cheloveka o knige 'Opisanie sel'-skogo dukhovenstva':* [Retsenziia]," *Sovremennik,* 1859, LXXV, no. 6, 340-44.

107. TsGIA, f. 807, op. 2, g. 1859, d. 1292, l. 28 and d. 1359, l. 67.

108. *Ibid.,* d. 1306, l. 41 and d. 1359, l. 148.

109. *Ibid.,* d. 1359, l. 165 ob.

110. See the review of censorship conflicts in 1858-59 in a reform memorandum on church censorship by T. Filippov. "O predelakh dukhovnoi tsenzury," in TsGIA, f. 796, op. 87, d. 205, ll. 40 ob.-46.

111. Elagin to Filaret, 29 December 1858 (TsGIA, f. 832, op. l, d. 32, ll. 120-22.

112. Elagin to A.P. Tolstoi, 5 September 1859 (TsGIA, f. 797, op. 29, I otd., 2 st., d. 246, l. 1 ob.).

113. *Ibid.*

114. TsGIA, f. 807, op. 2, d. 1859, d. 1306, ll. 74-75.

115. *Russkoe dukhovenstvo,* Berlin, 1859.

116. N.G. Dobroliubov [A. Krivitskii], "Zagranichnye preniia o polozhenii russkogo dukhovenstva." *Sovremennik,* LXXX (1860), no. 3, 1-18. The Belliustin volume was indeed included on an 1870 circular listing prohibited books (*Alfavitnyi katalog knigam na russkom iazyke, zapreshchennym k obrashcheniiu i perepechataniiu v Rossii,* St. Petersburg, 1870, 12). For a radical critique of *Opisanie* (evidently by a nonclerical student), see the manuscript published in P.G. Ryndziunskii, "O russkoi tserkvi i russkom dukhovenstve," *Literaturnoe nasledstvo,* LXXIII, Moscow, 1963, 197-206.

117. Belliustin to Pogodin, 6 October 1859 (GBL, f. 231/II, k. 3, d. 50/2, ll. 25-26).

118. Belliustin to Pogodin, 8 January 1860 (*ibid.,* d. 51/1 l. 2).

119. Belliustin to Pogodin, 10 February 1859 (*ibid.,* d. 50/2, l. 9 ob.); Belliustin refers to another unidentified *zapiska* for the empress in a letter to Pogodin of 26 May 1859 (*ibid.,* l. 20).

120. A section of the original *zapiska* completed too late for publication in *Opisanie* is identical to an anonymous *zapiska* transmitted by the tsar to the overprocurator in 1860. The original manuscript is in GBL, f. 231/III, k. 1, d. 66, ll. 30-35; copies of the *zapiska* transmitted by the tsar are in the archives of Metropolitan Filaret (TsGIA, f. 832, op. 1, d. 72, ll. 43-47) and the overprocurator (TsGIA, f. 797, op. 29, I otd., 2 st., d. 249, ll. 34-38 ob.).

121. On the problem of widowed clergy see TsGIA, f. 797, op. 29, I otd., 2 st., d. 249.

122. Belliustin to Pogodin, 27 January 1860 (GBL, f. 231/II, k. 3, d. 51/1, l. 3 ob.).

123. Belliustin to Cherkasskaia, 29 March 1860 (GBL, f. 327/II, k. 5, d. 31, ll. 2-3); Belliustin to Pogodin, 8 February 1860 (GBL, f. 231/II, k. 3, d. 51/1, l. 5).

124. In 1857 Belliustin referred to an explosive *zapiska* on the schismatics; see his letters to Pogodin of 8 and 22 May 1857 (GBL, f. 231/II, k. 3, d. 49/6, ll. 1 ob., 7-7 ob.).

125. Belliustin to Pogodin, 28 March 1860 (*ibid.*, d. 51/1, ll. 8 ob.-9 ob.).

126. See, for instance, P.A. Valuev, *Dnevnik 1877-1884 gg.*, Petrograd, 1919, 190-91.

127. Belliustin to Pogodin, 2 April 1860 (GBL, f. 231/II, k. 3, d. 51/1, ll. 10-10 ob.); Belliustin to Cherkasskaia, 1 August 1860 (GBL, f. 327/II, k. 5, d. 31, 1. 4).

128. Belliustin to Kornilov, 10 August 1860 (GPB, f. 377, d. 477, ll. 3-4).

129. Belliustin to Pogodin, 8 July 1860 (GBL, f. 231/II, k. 3, d. 51/2, 1. 2 ob.).

130. Belliustin to Pogodin, 28 March 1860 (*ibid.*, d. 51/1, l. 9).

131. Belliustin to Cherkasskaia, 29 March 1860 (GBL, f. 327/II, k. 5, d. 31, 1. 3).

132. Belliustin to Kornilov, 15 June 1860 (GPB, f. 377, d. 474, l. 1); Belliustin to Cherskasskaia, 1 August 1860 (GBL, f. 327/II, k. 5, d. 31, l. 5).

133. Belliustin to Pogodin, 8 July 1861 (GBL, f. 231/II, k. 3, d. 51/2, ll. 2-2 ob.).

134. A parish petition of 1875 refers to three petitions to the bishop in 1861 on Belliustin's behalf (GBL, f. 344 [Shibanov], k. 445, d. 10, l. 1); two of the petitions, dated 20 and 28 December 1861, are to be found in TsGIA, f. 796, op. 160, g. 1879, d. 831, ll. 23-25 ob.

135. TsGIA, f. 796, op. 160, g. 1879, d. 831, l. 14 ob.; Belliustin to Pogodin, 25 February 1862 (GBL, f. 231/II, k. 3, d. 51/3, ll. 3-3 ob.).

136. TsGIA, f. 797, op. 34, g. 1864, I otd., 1 st., d. 89, ll. 1-6.

137. See the extract from Valuev's report of September 1861 in TsGIA, f. 908, op. 1, d. 112, ll. 40-47 ob.

PART II: CHURCH AND STATE

Church and State
in Imperial Russia

Marc Szeftel

It is sometimes said that from 1721 onward the relationship between
church and state in Russia displayed the characteristics of caesaropapism and of the Protestant system of *summus episcopus*.[1] Both
claims are exaggerated as the Fundamental Laws of the Russian Empire
clearly show. Essentially what is meant is that Peter I's system of
church-state relations derived from two sources. The legal pattern existing in Protestant states constituted one of them. Byzantine tradition as
interpreted by old Muscovy supplied the other. The Petrine reform of
1721 did not destroy this Muscovite version of Byzantine tradition;
Peter merely adjusted it to conform with his ideas and political requirements. Hence, both the Orthodox church and the Russian state strongly
emphasized the religious and mystical qualities of the tsar's power
which continued to resonate strongly in the popular mind, not only
after 1721 but until the Revolution in 1917.

What was the Muscovite legacy? Following Byzantine example,
Muscovites stressed the intimate association between the temporal and
spiritual powers. Church and state worked hand in hand against any
foreign enemy, domestic rebellion, or heretical challenge in order to
protect a world order established by God. Inevitably such an alliance
made the church dependent upon the tsar for protection. Thus, except

during periods of national crisis on the scale of the Time of Troubles, the church in both Muscovy and Byzantium always strongly felt his power.[2] Nevertheless, a religious coloration imparted in Muscovy to every aspect of public life gave unique status to the authority of the church, which so blended with that of the tsar as to create the impression of diarchy. During the imperial coronation, the thrones of the tsar and the patriarch stood side by side in Moscow Cathedral of the Dormition.[3] If the tsar participated in the church's crucial moments, he did so not because he had the right to govern the church but because as an "Orthodox sovereign" he had a duty to protect it. Two factors bolstered this position. First, the tsar's "autocracy" never was legally defined in Muscovy. Second, there was a limit with regard to the Orthodox church beyond which no member, even a tsar, could pass.[4] Above all, whatever influence he exercised over the life of the church, internally the latter remained completely autonomous, ruled by a national synod which elected the patriarch of Moscow.

The image of the tsar provides an additional feature of this Muscovite-Byzantine legacy. He stood as a living symbol of the Christian tsardom entrusted to him by God, receiving his direct and intimate connection with God through the ceremony of anointment.[5]

Peter's reform modified the Muscovite pattern. From 1690, the Russian monarchy did not summon a single national synod. In 1721, the highest administration of the church underwent reform, not by initiative from the church, but as a consequence of state legislation. Thus, *administratively*, the church passed under state control.[6] Moreover, the secularization of Russian public life, accompanied by a clear definition of autocratic absolutism, removed the last restraints on the sovereign's power over all of his subjects, including the church. Yet the religious and mystical qualities of Muscovite church-state relations persisted in several ways. Until January 1905, or perhaps July 1906 (if not longer), they found expression in the popular awe surrounding the tsar's office. Government phraseology also retained this Muscovite tradition, for it was useful both domestically and in foreign affairs (particularly with regard to Russia's "Slav brothers" in the Balkans). But the greatest emphasis on the Muscovite past continued to be supplied by the church, as a means of limiting the idea of a state church and as a bridge between the Muscovite and imperial orders. In this respect, the rite of coronation took on great importance. On the one hand, it conferred sanctity on the new tsar; on the other, it placed him firmly within the context of traditional Orthodox tsardom. One must remember that whatever the political meaning in this ceremonial may have been, the religious element carried much greater weight.[7]

Except during the coronation ceremony, the emperor participated in the Orthodox church not so much as its ruler but as its faithful member; and that relationship was expressed in articles 62 and 63 of the Fundamental Laws which specified the dominant role of the Orthodox church within the Russian Empire and the emperor's obligation to be a member of the church. These two articles (inserted in 1832, but carried over into the 1906 Fundamental Laws) preserved the religious basis found earlier in Muscovite church-state relations. The church could thereby construe its subjection to the state not as subordination to lay authorities but to the divine right monarch (another link with the Muscovite past). It vitally needed such an interpretation during the years after 1721, for it provided the only means for spiritual survival in the new environment. The persistent ambiguity about the legal limits of state authority over the church proved very helpful. The Byzantine pattern was consequently preserved: the empire could not and would not break its ties with the church, while the church would not separate itself from a state personified by the tsar.[8]

Any continuation of Muscovite tradition after 1721 could not mean the uninterrupted assertion of "caesaropapism." Whatever this term signified in western Christianity, it did not apply to the eastern church which had no authority equal to that of the pope, unless it was the ecumenical councils. The last of these, the Second Council of Nicaea, took place in 787. Much the same could be said of the Byzantine emperor's religious authority as well as of the tsar of Muscovy and the later Russian emperor, who could not issue any laws concerning faith or establish any principles of Christian or ethical doctrine. He was, as article 64 of the Fundamental Laws (1906) stated, the "supreme protector and custodian of the dogmas of the established faith and the keeper of the true faith and all good order in the Holy Church." But this was an exclusively conservative function. The use of the word "caesaropapism" regarding the Russian sovereign (as well as the Byzantine basileus) derives from a misunderstanding or, worse, from ignorance.[9] So much for Byzantine-Muscovite antecedents.

Did the reform of 1721 make the Russian emperor the equivalent of the Protestant *summus episcopus*? Again, as in the case of "caesaropapism," such a view can be questioned because an Orthodox monarch's prerogatives were limited within the dogmatical and liturgical framework of the eastern church. The problem of "caesaropapism" is present, but in a Protestant context. The Church of England has recognized the crown as "the only supreme governor of this realm. . . . as well in all spiritual or ecclesiastical things or causes as temporal."[10] But, on the canonical grounds earlier discussed with regard to Byzantine tradition, the Russian emperor could not exercise such power.

Doubts, however, were cast on the Byzantine-Muscovite interpretation by a note to article 64 of the Fundamental Laws: "In this sense the Emperor is called *Head of the Church* in the Act of Succession to the Throne of 5 April 1797." The epithet "Head of the Church" is used, but only as a note in brevier, as an "aside." Paul I's formula, considered in the context of the Act of Succession to the Throne (*Akt o nasledii prestola*), has been specifically related to only one case, that of the throne passing to a female line whose representative might be non-Orthodox. In this case a choice must be made, "for the Russian sovereigns are heads of the Church." Only if Paul's note had been incorporated into the main body of the text would the emperor have been placed *intra ecclesiam* and *supra ecclesiam*, which might have amounted to caesaropapism *modo anglico*. Such, however, was not the codifier's intention.[11]

Russian constitutional lawyers, on the basis of this analysis, generally considered the monarch's prerogative to be limited to the administration of the Orthodox church, excluding the content of faith, that is, dogmas and spirituals rules.[12] W. Gribowski, however, dissented from this interpretation and accepted it as only a partial contradiction of the terms in article 64. According to him, the monarch could not modify dogmas—only an ecumenical council had that power. As for the rules established by a national church, *they* could be cancelled or amended according to the monarch's will.[13] However far the emperor's prerogative may have extended, one cannot find a single reform dealing with the teachings or the liturgy of the church (and not simply its administration) during the entire synodal period. Gribowski's stricture seems to have been immaterial, except regarding canonizations, which can scarcely be considered administrative acts.

Although Orthodox doctrine made it impossible for the Russian monarch to follow the Protestant pattern of *summus episcopus*, the reform of 1721 incorporated other essential Protestant features. Both "canonical territorialism" and the collegial principle, inspired by the Protestant states (British, German, and Swedish), were bases of the Petrine reform. Bureaucratization of the church constituted still another.[14] The Protestant model was followed as far as canonically feasible. An extreme limit was reached with the oath for the Holy Synod members that was included in the 1720 *Ecclesiastical Regulation*: "I confess under oath that the highest [*krainii*] judge of this Spiritual Collegium will be the All-Russian monarch himself, Our All-graceful Sovereign." The formula "highest judge" parallels that of "highest earthly ruler" applied to the King of Sweden by the Swedish Lutheran Church.[15] Synodal members resented these words, but their obedience was enforced and the oath remained in effect until 23 February 1901, when Nicholas II abolished it as antiquated—at the Synod's request.[16]

Article 64 of the 1906 Fundamental Laws (the former article 43) states that "in the administration of the Church, the Autocratic Power acts through the Most Holy Governing Synod, established by this Power." Although in the strictest sense *upravlenie* meant "administration," one must bear in mind that when this rule was formulated in 1721 and again in 1832 when it became a part of the Fundamental Laws, that is, under absolute monarchy, there was no clear distinction between the monarch's legislative, administrative, or judicial authority. It would thus be more accurate to interpret *upravlenie* in this article as "government," at least before the constitutional reform of 1906. Consequently, article 64 meant that since the establishment of the Synod in 1721, the government of the Russian church belonged to the imperial power, and there was no independent ecclesiastical organ with rights to govern the church beyond those conferred upon it by the emperor. All laws on ecclesiastical matters were expressions of the emperor's authority, sometimes drafted by the Synod, yet at others prepared by a special non-synodal committee for submission to the emperor by the overprocurator—not necessarily after the Synod had studied them. Legislation drew its force solely from imperial confirmation, and not from the authority of the Synod.[17] The overprocurator imparted a strong secular quality to this legislation.

The same was true for the exercise of judicial power by the Synod. The judicial reform of 1864 had no effect on the church, despite efforts by liberal clergymen led by Archbishop Makarii (Bulgakov), the famous church historian. A proposed alteration in the church's legal status was rejected on canonical grounds by almost all bishops. Reform made no headway until 1917.[18]

Within this legal framework which completely restricted the Synod's independence, the life tenure of its four most important members theoretically provided a certain freedom of opinion. Those four (out of twelve members) were the metropolitans of St. Petersburg, Moscow, and Kiev, and the exarch of Georgia. In practice, however, even these members ex officio had to be summoned for each session of the Synod by the overprocurator, which usually meant that this lay official decided which hierarchs would attend. Thus, in 1842 Overprocurator Protasov simply stopped summoning the metropolitans Filaret (Drozdov) of Moscow and Filaret (Amfiteatrov) of Kiev, and this continued until 1855. Even the tenure of the St. Petersburg metropolitan, the presiding hierarch, was not immune to manipulation. For example, in 1915, to suit Rasputin's preference, Metropolitan Vladimir of Petrograd was simply transferred to the lesser metropolitan see of Kiev and replaced by Pitirim, the former exarch of Georgia. The Synod's approval was never asked.[19]

The overprocurator greatly restricted the Synod's freedom of action, gradually concentrating the emperor's authority in his own hands. From 1817, he was the Synod's only spokesman before the emperor, with the exclusive right of report (*vsepodanneishii doklad*). At that point, too, the imperial commands began to be transmitted to the Synod exclusively through the overprocurator, for the presiding metro-

politan lost his contact with the tsar. After 1835, the overprocurator
began reporting on the administration of the church in the Committee
of Ministers and in the State Council, which for all practical purposes
gave him the status of a cabinet minister. The next year, Overprocurator Protasov became the exclusive leader of the entire ecclesiastical
administration by concentrating in a special chancery all the Synod
business. That included relations with public authorities, and all
bishops and clergy, as well as secretaries of diocesan consistories, had
to submit matters directly to the overprocurator.[20] Moreover, from
Protasov's day onward, the overprocurator could, if he disagreed with
them, modify or even set aside the decisions of plenary meetings
of the Synod. According to the testimony of Archbishop Antonii
Khrapovitskii (a Synod member), the proceedings in such cases were
simply destroyed and new decisions were taken.[21] Under these circumstances it is not surprising that constitutional lawyers referred to the
overprocurator as the actual head of the church, while the Synod was
an ecclesiastical collegium with a consultative vote. It was even suggested that article 65 be expanded by adding the words "through the
overprocurator of the . . . Synod, to be appointed by it (i.e., the Autocratic power)."[22]

The dividing line of the 1906 constitutional reform has been crossed
several times in the foregoing analysis, for in practice the legal condition of the church was not much changed after that year. On several
occasions the government stated in the Duma that no change of any
sort had occurred. (Cf. Stolypin's statement on 12 May 1909 and especially that of Overprocurator Sabler on 5 and 12 March 1912.) Liberal
constitutional lawyers disputed this claim by insisting that articles 7,
86, and 107 of the Fundamental Laws did create a new legal situation
for the Orthodox church (although articles 63 and 65 did not represent
any modification). In their view, after 23 April 1906 the church con-
formed to the same legislative procedures which governed all other
aspects of Russian life, that is, mandatory consent by the chambers for
any change or repeal of an ecclesiastical law.[23] If the relationship
between church and state had been legally unclear before the October
Manifesto, this and the 1906 constitution merely obscured things fur-

ther, for a contradiction existed between the chapter of the 1906 Fundamental Laws concerning religion and the articles referring to the legislative process generally.

With Overprocurator Luk'ianov (1909-11), the Russian government first attempted to cooperate with the Duma on the issue of the church's legal position. Then, with Overprocurator Sabler, the government tried to circumvent the new legislative procedure, using article 87 of the Fundamental Laws for the bill on ecclesiastical academies which thus remained interim legislation until 1917. But the necessity to ask the Duma for *new* budgetary appropriations did not permit sabotage as a continuing policy, and whatever the Synod's theoretical objections may have been, in practice it complied with the new legislative order. The overprocurator introduced fifty-nine bills of law concerning the church in the Third Duma.[24] Some of them related to purely ecclesiastical matters such as the organization of parish communities (a bill that had been introduced by Luk'ianov but withdrawn by Sabler).

This incongruous, ambiguous, and even dangerous situation for the church reinforced the feeling that the time was ripe to recreate an autonomous religious body such as a national synod to replace the existing Holy Synod in ecclesiastical matters.[25] But article 86 of the Fundamental Laws would not allow a national synod any legislative capacity even in purely ecclesiastical affairs. To create a special ecclesiastical legislative organ independent of the chambers would have required the circumscription of the Duma's legislative monopoly. Only the emperor could take the initiative in constitutional revision, decide for either a return to the pre-1906 arrangements or the recreation of a national synod, and precisely define the extent of imperial prerogative.[26] Nicholas II did not take that initiative.

The Synod tried to ignore the Duma, but the latter controlled all *new* appropriations. Only one per cent of the Synod's 1906 budget was subject to the Duma's action; the rest was "iron clad." But new needs were arising, while old ones were demanding increased funds. Hence, despite every reluctance, the church administration constantly introduced new bills in the Duma. As these were discussed and voted on, the Duma's control over the synodal budget expanded to include even the consolidated ("iron clad") items, simply because the old and the new

items were financially connected. Still more importantly, appropriations were being conditioned according to Duma desiderata that went
beyond strictly financial considerations into other fields only indirectly
related. Thus, from one budget to the next, from one bill to another,
the Duma's influence on the administration of the church grew inevitably. Legislative inertia in Russia generally and in the church particularly was great, and inertia favored Duma control. But even enemies of
Duma control in the budgetary committee after nine years of prodding
became frustrated by the church administration's legislative impotence
and insisted in 1916 on the Duma's right to interfere. E. Kovalevskii
gave a particularly eloquent speech about the 1916 synodal budget
which describes this impotence:

We started from details, but the *vedomstvo* answered that they are
connected with the system as a whole. Then we raised general problems; the answer was that they transcend the normal secular legislation
concerning the Church. When the Duma narrowed its desires to specific shortcomings of the system, they were declared to be in the
province of the ecclesiastical Synod, the talk about which took another
five years. When it became clear that a national synod is a thing of the
distant future, the Duma began to point out especially scandalous
aspects of the existing relationship between the ecclesiastical and secular regulations, such as the problem of dissolution of marriage for military people (War problems). A special committee was formed to study
the problem, but again without result.[27]

Still, the budgetary pressure produced some results: the methods of
ecclesiastical accountancy improved and the church at least prepared
some important bills.

The Duma gradually became a field of action and a means of pressure for the clergy itself. The reformed State Council had a special
clerical delegation (six members elected by the Synod). Obviously, it
represented only the hierarchy, both monastic and married ("white").
The Duma's electoral law did not provide for an ecclesiastical curia and
the clergymen in the Duma represented mainly the smaller landed
gentry. There were six clerics in the First Duma and thirteen in the
Second (most were antigovernment). After the 3 June 1907 electoral
reform, their number greatly increased. Forty-five clergymen joined the
Third Duma, of whom only four belonged to the opposition; nine were

members of the Octobrist center, while the rest represented various
shades of rightist opinion. On the eve of the elections to the Fourth
Duma, Overprocurator Sabler proposed to Bishop Evlogii (of the
moderate Right) that he organize a clerical party with the aim of using
episcopal influence in the elections to fill the new Duma with progovernment clergymen. Sabler suggested a goal of 100 clergy deputies (out
of 440 Duma members). Evlogii declined the suggestion on the grounds
that political clericalism might only prove harmful to the church.
Nevertheless, pressure was exerted on the clergy from above, and this
contributed to the election of many conservative laymen to the Fourth
Duma. The number of clergymen increased slightly: forty-six members
of the Duma of whom all but four were progovernment.[28] But the over-
whelming majority of those forty-six did not belong to the higher
clergy, and they displayed more independent behavior during the years
when the Progressive Bloc dominated the Duma. Thus in 1916 *all* the
priests in the Duma submitted a petition asking that "the administration of the Russian church be transformed according to the principles
of conciliarism (*sobornost'*), with the state relinquishing its view that
the Orthodox clergy is an instrument of domestic policy." This certainly meant overdue reforms for the Orthodox diocese and parish and
also implied the convocation of a national synod which had been in the
making since 1906 but continuously postponed *sine die*. When examining the Synod's budget, the Duma redoubled the pressure it had steadily exerted since 1912 for a national synod and recommended that it
be convened "as soon as possible." A council of the Russian church assembled in 1917, but by that time the Revolution had overtaken the
imperial government.[29]

Whatever the relative weight of church and state during the imperial
era (and there cannot be any doubt that the state dominated the relationship), the two forces were closely intertwined. The state gave the
Orthodox church complete support in many essential ways. Orthodoxy
was the dominant faith of the empire, enjoying a monopoly on religious proselytism. It exercised censorship over the religious content in
all books. Bishops delegated clergy to attend ex officio the meeting of
zemstva self-government institutions. Governors were required to act as
the church's *brachium seculare* on behalf of Orthodoxy's struggle with

heresies. But most of all, the church enjoyed the state's material support. This became a necessity after ecclesiastical landed property was
secularized in 1764. Deprived of its traditional means of existence and
not having developed any new ones, the church found in state support
the only alternative. An appropriate community organization based on
self-government and self-taxation would have been a possible solution
to this problem, but no such organizational premises existed in eighteenth-century Russia, and the population's reluctance to contribute
voluntarily afforded no encouragement to find other resources. When
the church did not have enough money, Catherine II's government
resorted to land and apportioned some to the clergy. These grants increased in subsequent reigns with salaries being added later. Donations
provided an important additional source of church income. The advent
of representative institutions in 1906, linked with regular and open
budgetary procedures, increased the church's sources or revenue and its
budget grew each year.[30]

The church repaid the state by supporting the tsar and his government. Such fidelity had a very long ancestry, for, as article 4 of the
1906 Fundamental Laws reminds us, it was rooted in the words of St.
Paul's Epistle to the Romans 13:5, and undoubtedly followed the
Byzantine tradition reflected in the ceremonial of the emperor's coronation. But the system established in 1721 added features inspired
neither by Christianity nor by Byzantine custom. They made the
church a part of the Russian political system, a fact made apparent in
the wording of the oath administered by the church to the entire
Orthodox population at the accession of every monarch. It included
the obligation to inform the authorities of anything which might be
"of detriment, harm, or damage to the interests of His Imperial Majesty," and to avert that danger, if possible. Moreover, priests were required to disclose to the police any information regarding plots or
attempts against the emperor or his government, even when that knowledge had been obtained during confession (*na dukhu*). Such a requirement was obviously uncanonical. Diocesan authorities and district
supervisors (*blagochinnye*) were required by law to make certain that
deserters, vagabonds, and men without passports were not sheltered in
the villages under their jurisdiction. The clergy had to proclaim imperial

manifestoes, statutes, and decrees in the churches, and the church had also to use its authority to silence or at least weaken all opposition to the government. Such support for the tsar and his government reached a climax with Overprocurator K.P. Pobedonostsev (1880-1905), who upheld the idea that not only should the moral and religious training of the population be provided by the church, but that this training should serve the political ideology of the Russian state. Pobedonostsev's views prompted the creation in 1884 of a system of parish schools (*tserkov-no-prikhodskie shkoly*) under synodal authority. These were to compete with the politically less reliable network of primary schools under the Ministry of Education (the so-called "*zemstvo* schools"). With considerable help from the treasury, the number of parish schools grew rapidly, but their quality was lower than that of the "ministerial" schools, and they did not attract many pupils. After the constitutional reform of 1906, the new budgetary situation worked to the disadvantage of parish schools and further widened the gulf between the two systems. The Duma did not refuse additional appropriations for the ecclesiastical schools, but it insisted on higher standards while energetically promoting the extension of "ministerial" primary schools. During the farewell reception for the deputies of the Third Duma in the summer of 1912, Nicholas II expressed his great displeasure at the Duma's action. But it could scarcely have been avoided. Pobedonostsev's idea of indoctrinating the population through the parish schools (which would amount to a virtual monopoly over primary education) was not successful.[31]

Beyond budgetary matters, church-state relations remained essentially unchanged by the constitutional reform. It remains to be discovered if possibilities for change actually existed which might have allowed the church greater liberty on the eve of the First World War (or, rather, on the eve of the March Revolution of 1917). To answer this question one must make an effort to discount the importance of Rasputin, who from March 1911 until the very end of the monarchy increasingly bedeviled church-state relations. Or, if not discounting the Rasputin affair, one must at least try to put it in a broader perspective. After all, the episode arose from unique dynastical and historical circumstances hardly to be repeated in the future. Despite all its negative features, the Rasputin scandal might have even rallied the church's defensive reserves and stimulated its desire to achieve independence from the state. At any rate, the post-1906 representative institutions created for the Orthodox church some freedom of action which had not existed previously. Support from public opinion also grew to an extent not possible before. Some observers found hope in these new conditions, and the debates and resolutions in the Duma about a national synod demonstrated that such hope had foundation. Thus, some light at the end of the tunnel could be seen for the Russian church during the last years of the empire.

NOTES

1. A. V. Romanovich-Slavatinskii, *Sistema russkago gosudarstvennago prava,* Kiev, 1886, 173.

2. G. Ostrogorsky, *Histoire de l'état byzantin,* Paris, 1956, 56-57.

3. E. V. Barsov, "Drevnerusskie pamiatniki sviashchennago venchaniia tsarei na tsarstvo," *Chteniia,* 1883, I, 91, 98, 101.

4. I. Smolitsch, *Geschichte der russischen Kirche, 1700-1917,* I, Leiden, 1964, 134-36.

5. Ostrogorsky, *Histoire,* 57.

6. Smolitsch, *Geschichte,* 134, referred to it as *Staatskirchentum.*

7. *Ibid.,* 147-53. See Fundamental Laws, 23 April 1906, chap. 5, art. 57; *Svod zakonov,* I, pt. 1.

8. Smolitsch, *Geschichte,* 159-60.

9. Cf. A. W. Ziegler, "Die byzantinische Religionspolitik und der sogenannte Cäsaropapismus," *Münchener Beiträge zur Slavenkunde: Festgabe fur P. Diels,* Munich, 1953, 81, 97. See also H. Dalton, *Die russische Kirche,* Leipzig, 1892, 20ff.

10. Ronald D. Ware, "Caesaropapism," *Handbook of World History,* ed. Joseph Dunner, New York, 1967, 138.

11. Smolitsch, *Geschichte,* 142-43 and 145-47. See also A. Palme, *Die russische Verfassung,* Berlin, 1910, 136: "The emperor is not *summus episcopus* (he does not belong to the clergy!). Ecclesiastically, the head of the church is the Synod as successor of the patriarch." This statement calls for the remark that neither the partiarch (in Muscovite times) nor the Synod (despite the legal fiction that it was equivalent to the standing national synod) had the canonical power of the national synod, let alone of the ecumenical councils.

12. Cf. A. Gradovskii, *Nachala russkago gosudarstvennago prava,* St. Petersburg, 1883, 151.

13. *Das Staatsrecht des russischen Reiches,* Tübingen, 1912, 50.

14. Cf. in this connection A. V. Kartashev, *Ocherki po istorii russkoi tserkvi,* II, Paris, 1959, 323-30, 345-48.

15. Ware, "Caesaropapism," 138.

16. Kartashev, *Ocherki*, 353, 424-25.

17. M.I. Gorchakov, *Tserkovnoe pravo*, 1909, 206.

18. Smolitsch, *Geschichte*, 174-77.

19. John S. Curtiss, *Church and State in Russia: the Last Years of the Empire, 1900-1917*, New York, 1940, reprinted 1965, 45, 392-93.

20. This bureaucratization of every aspect of the Synod's activity under the overprocurator is symbolized by the three letters *V.P.I.* (*Vedomstvo Pravoslavnago Ispovedaniia*, that is, the Department of Orthodox Confession) which appeared on all its correspondence. On the origin of this term see Smolitsch, *Geschichte*, 199-200.

21. *Otzyvy eparkhial'nykh arkhiereev po voprosu o tserkovnoi reforme*, III, St. Petersburg, 1906, 191. Here one must emphasize that the Synod's decisions had to be unanimous with no dissenting opinions mentioned in the proceedings.

22. B. Nolde, *Ocherki russkago konstitutsionnago prava*, II, *Sovet Ministrov*, St. Petersburg, 1909, 144; Palme, *Die russische Verfassung*, 136-37.

23. Nolde, *Ocherki*, 65, 181-84; N. Lazarevskii, *Russkoe gosudarstvennoe pravo*, St. Petersburg, 1913, 372-74; N. Palienko, *Osnovnye zakony i forma pravleniia v Rossii*, Iaroslavl, 1910, 55, 68-70. Palienko also emphasized the wording of article 10 of the Fundamental Laws which distinguished between the power of administration and that of legislation; only the former belonged to the emperor with regard to the church. Most specialists of ecclesiastical law shared this opinion. Cf. E. Temnikovskii, *Polozhenie Imperatora Vserossiiskago v russkoi pravoslavnoi tserkvi v sviazi s obshchim ucheniem o tserkovnoi vlasti*, Iaroslavl, 1909, 38-40, 70; P. Verkhovskoi, *Uchrezhdenie Dukhovnoi Kollegii i Dukhovnyi Reglament*, I, Rostov-on-Don, 1916, 595. The government's point of view, however, had the support of some scholars. Cf. N. Suvorov, *Uchebnik tserkovnago prava*, Moscow, 1913, 210, and, especially, P. Kazanskii, *Vlast' Vserossiiskago Imperatora*, Odessa, 1913, 162f., 224, 253.

24. See *Obzor deiatel'nosti Gosudarstvennoi Dumy 3-go Sozyva*, St. Petersburg, 1912, I, 171.

25. Lazarevskii, *Russkoe gosudarstvennoe pravo*, 373-74. Out of 442 Duma members, only 382 were Orthodox or Old Believers; there were 25 Roman Catholics, 19 Lutherans, 2 Armeno-Georgians, 2 Jews, and 10 Moslems (*Ezhegodnik gazety 'Rech'' na 1912 god*, 125).

26. See P. Verkhovskoi, *Ocherki po istorii russkoi tserkvi v XVIII i XIX stol.*, I, Warsaw, 1912, 123, 127.

27. Article 249 of the 1841 *Statute on Ecclesiastical Consistories* considered as basic and necessary evidence in adultery cases a testimony under oath of two or even three witnesses to the illegal sexual relationship. Cf. the *Stenograficheskii otchet* of the Fourth Duma, Session 4, II, 2187-95. See also Marc Szeftel, "The Representatives and their Powers in the Russian Legislative Chambers (1906-1917)," *Liber Memorialis Sir Maurice Powicke*, Louvain-Paris, 1965, 235.

28. See Curtiss, *Church and State*, 202-3, 341-42; also Smolitsch, *Geschichte*, 214-16, 324-25.

29. Curtiss, *Church and State*, 289-91; Smolitsch, *Geschichte*, 329-30.

30. Thus it increased from approximately 30 million rubles in 1908 to more than 53 million rubles in 1914! Cf. Curtiss, *Church and State*, 35-38, 128-30 and 346-48. Also Smolitsch, *Geschichte*, 185-91, 356.

31. The one day school census taken on 1 January 1911 produced the following results: "ministerial" schools — 59.6% of all schools, 68% of all pupils; Synod schools — 37.7% of all schools, 29% of all pupils. Cf. Curtiss, *Church and State*, 72-74, 182-83, 349-54.

The Inquisitorial Network
of Peter the Great

Alexander V. Muller

The Russian Orthodox church, in its institutional aspect, was profoundly affected by the accelerated drive toward secularization and
modernization that marked the reforms of Peter the Great. Of Peter's
administrative changes, the most noteworthy was the suspension of the
office of the patriarch of Moscow and its replacement by the Most Holy
Ruling Synod. The suppression of the patriarchate, which had been
established in 1589, was accomplished not by any direct, positive act of
abrogation, but by allowing it to fall into disuse and disappear. The tsar
withheld permission for a council of bishops to convene for the purpose
of electing a successor to Patriarch Adrian after his death in 1700. In
place of the old office, some of whose functions passed temporarily
into the hands of a caretaker, a permanent assembly of churchmen,
together with a later admixture of laymen, was founded in January
1721. Called the Ecclesiastical College, it was similar in organization
to a new array of governmental "colleges" which began functioning
two years earlier as organs of state administration. In February 1721,
at its first session, the Ecclesiastical College was renamed the Most Holy
Ruling Synod. By this designation it continued to be known until after
the fall of the monarchy in 1917, when the patriarchate was restored
(though only briefly, until the present restoration in 1943).

As the most striking transformation effected by Peter the Great's ecclesiastical policy, the creation of the Synod understandably has attracted the most historical attention. However, efforts were also made to expand, tighten, and rationalize control over intermediate and lower levels of church administration. One of these measures was the creation of an inquisitorial network. A number of churchmen were chosen to become "inquisitors," in which capacity they were intended to improve the quality of superintendence over ecclesiastical functioning and thereby promote administrative efficiency. This reform proved to be superficial and shortlived. Nevertheless, viewed in combination with other measures that were more successful and in the broader context of administrative changes taking place within both church and state, it provides an illuminating insight into the intentions, methods, and goals of the Petrine reform movement.

In origin, structure, and function, the office of ecclesiastical inquisitors was closely related to that of the secular fiscals, a staff of state functionaries who, under the supervision of an overfiscal, carried out administrative and judicial surveillance on behalf of the highest bureaucratic organ of state administration, the Ruling Senate. On 5 March 1711, the Senate was directed by a decree from the tsar to select, regardless of his rank, "an intelligent and worthy man" for the post of overfiscal. Among his duties were the unobtrusive supervision of all administrative matters, detection of improper legal judgments, and scrutiny of the collection of revenues. He was empowered to summon before the Senate officials of any rank for malfeasance and there to bring charges against them. To spur his diligence, it was provided that he should receive half the collected fine for any of his reports resulting in a conviction, the other half being credited to the state treasury. Should he fail to obtain a conviction, he was not to be held accountable for the charges he had lodged. In carrying out his duties, the overfiscal was to be assisted by a group of subordinates called provincial fiscals, each supervising an administrative function. They in turn were to preside over the lowest stratum of the organization, the fiscals, who as investigators, had almost as much authority as the overfiscal himself. Except for lacking the capacity to initiate proceedings against justices in courts of highest instance or against members of the general staff, an ordinary fiscal enjoyed the same power and freedom of action as the overfiscal. Those against whom a fiscal brought charges were specifically forbidden to harbor resentment because of the accusation, under penalty of severe punishment and confiscation of all property.[1] The scrutiny of the fiscals percolated through all echelons of the civil bureaucracy, from the level of the central colleges down through the provincial adminstrations and into the cities. Moreover, special units of fiscals were founded for the army and navy. V. O. Kliuchevskii justly describes the fiscals as the Senate's "organ of active control" because they possessed such broad powers of investigation, judicial immunity, and personal inviolability.[2]

The activity of the secular fiscals soon spilled over into areas of ecclesiastical competence. On 2 March 1711, before there were as yet any fiscals, universal obedience to the newly established Senate had been decreed by the tsar. This requirement was explicitly phrased to include, in the first place, members of the clergy. When the fiscals came into being, they were viewed as agents of the Senate, thus, having to be obeyed when, in August 1711, they were granted power to inspect the financial condition of the patriarchal and episcopal administrative agencies in Moscow and the provinces.[3] Prior to this, the church had already been compelled to yield to state judicial control in legal disputes arising between laymen and members of the clergy, and also to relinquish (until the founding of the Synod) economic control over certain of its holdings through the restoration of the state-controlled Central Administration of Monasteries. Now, with the advent of the fiscals, the hierarchy perceived that it was confronted by a state agency with no compunctions about keeping watch over the proceedings of strictly ecclesiastical tribunals and, indeed, even over the conduct of the clergy itself.[4]

Protests arising from the clergy and others concerning the fiscals could not be ignored, particularly about abuses stemming from their immunity from prosecution for false accusation. On 17 March 1714 a decree placed the fiscals under certain restraints, including a statute of limitations on matters covered in their reports. In addition, a fiscal was henceforth liable to incur the same penalty as a convicted defendant if it could be proved that his accusation was made maliciously or selfishly.

Thus the causes for some of the hierarchy's most vehement complaints about the fiscals' function, if not about their very existence, were removed.[5]

Yet it remained awkward to have secular fiscals sit in surveillance of church-related activities, particularly after the formation, announced in the manifesto of 25 January 1721, of a new and unprecedented organ of supreme ecclesiastical administration, the Ecclesiastical College (as mentioned earlier, promptly renamed the Most Holy Ruling Synod). For, even though it was an institution created by the state to carry out its own interests and was formally subject to the tsar as its "final judge," it was nevertheless supposed to give a semblance of control over matters properly lying within the ecclesiastical sphere.[6]

To rectify this incongruity and promote increased efficiency in diocesan or, more properly, eparchial administration, a new impetus was given to local ecclesiastical superintendence by the *Ecclesiastical Regulation*, the same enactment that formulated the rationale and organizational blueprint for the Synod. Under article 8 of matters pertaining to the episcopate, bishops were directed to order that there be appointed in all cities ecclesiastical stewards (*zakashchiki*), or ecclesiastical superintendents (*blagochinnye*), who were to conduct themselves "just as if they were ecclesiastical fiscals." Although the organization and duties of "ecclesiastical fiscals" were not spelled out in the Regulation and had to await further elaboration, the intent of this article in defining their basic function as observers and informers was quite clear. Should they find any deficiencies, they were to report directly to their bishops. It is obvious from this directive that, whatever name they were to go by, the church functionaries called for in article 8 were to occupy a position and carry out responsibilities comparable to those of secular officials within the state administrative organization.[7]

Scarcely half a month after its inaugural meeting, the Most Holy Ruling Synod began implementing the provision in the *Ecclesiastical Regulation* calling for the establishment of "ecclesiastical fiscals." On 1 March 1721 it ordered that there be appointed two protoinquisitors, one for assignment in St. Petersburg and the other in Moscow, each to have as assistants two inquisitors. Moreover, in all eparchies, there was to be appointed one inquisitor for every city of Great Russia.

To obtain qualified personnel for the new posts, the Synod decreed that prominent monks who were skilled in administrative affairs and had shown themselves capable of carrying out the duties of such an office were to have their names inscribed in a register for the Synod's consideration.[8] Two weeks later, on 15 March 1721, after obtaining the desired register, the Synod settled upon its choice of candidates to fill the two protoinquisitorial posts. Appointed to St. Petersburg was the hieromonk Makarii Khvorostinin, whose previous administrative experience included service as chaplain, with the rank of "over-hieromonk," in the navy and as ecclesiastical director on the island of Kotlin, at the eastern end of the Gulf of Finland. Appointed for duty in Moscow was the hierodeacon Pafnutii of the Alexander Nevskii Monastery in St. Petersburg. The remainder of those selected from the register were to be summoned for appointment from the eparchies where they resided, except for six monks already present in Moscow, who were told simply to await the arrival of Pafnutii for their installation and instruction.[9]

This lean inquisitorial apparatus was scarcely adequate for conducting the surveillance of administrative practices at all ecclesiastical levels. Hence, on 19 July 1721 the Synod reshaped the original inquisitorial organization by filling an obvious gap at the intermediate level and augmenting the number of personnel. To assist the protoinquisitor in Moscow, the Synod decreed that three more inquisitors from among the white, or married, clergy be appointed in addition to the two monks already serving in that capacity. One inquisitor from the white clergy was to be assigned to each city and ecclesiastical precinct. Moreover, quite independent of those assigned to eparchies, one monk was to be assigned as inquisitor to each important registered monastery, though the Synod allowed that in the large region formerly under direct patriarchal jurisdiction, such a monk could pursue his inquisitorial functions in neighboring monasteries as well. Finally, the Synod recast the inquisitorial organization to make it correspond more closely to that of the secular fiscals. It provided that inquisitors appointed to eparchies be given a position and rank similar to that of the intermediate category of provincial fiscals, whose counterparts in the ecclesiastical administration thereupon became known as provincial inquisitors.[10]

The foregoing enactment, it may be noted, provided additional assistants only to the protoinquisitor in Moscow. Similar relief was not forthcoming to the protoinquisitor in St. Petersburg, who in other respects too did not fare well at his new post. For in the bleak and as yet undeveloped capital that was supposed to replace old Moscow, the lack of suitable candidates for inquisitorial appointment caused Hieromonk Makarii to ask the Synod's permission to seek them in outlying monasteries. His request was granted, but other seemingly insurmountable difficulties persisted. Makarii informed the Synod that he had no office in which to work, no funds for the rental of living quarters, and no specified number of personnel or means for their support.[11] Finally, on 9 April 1722 the Synod abruptly extricated the hapless Makarii from his predicament by abolishing his post altogether and transferring his jurisdiction to the protoinquisitor in Moscow. As justification it stated that since there was but one overfiscal there ought to be only one protoinquisitor. It further accused the protoinquisitor in St. Petersburg of inefficiency, though it is more likely that the Synod itself, which had strangely neglected repeated appeals from Makarii, was simply unable or unwilling to afford the monetary and other expenditures. needed to maintain such an institution in difficult surroundings.[12]

Although St. Petersburg ceased being a protoinquisitorial center, a new institution was created there for supervising ecclesiastical affairs at the highest level. This was the office of overprocurator. On 11 May 1722, a supreme command from the monarch directed that a worthy military officer, imbued with courage and proficient in administrative affairs, be appointed and given an instruction resembling that of the general procurator. Called upon to act as the monarch's "eye and agent," the general procurator had been appointed in the preceding month, on 22 April 1722, to "sit in the Senate and watch carefully that the Senate fulfills its responsibility." Similarly, the overprocurator in the Synod was empowered to monitor sessions in progress, to make note of the enactments that were passed and keep track of their execution, to offer recommendations for improving the deliberative procedures, and to lodge protests when necessary, thereby halting the proceedings until disputed points could be resolved.[13]

The office of overprocurator was established to supervise the conduct of church administration, yet several characteristics distinguished it from the inquisitorial network with which it shared this charge. For one thing, the duties of the overprocurator, embracing the right of active intervention in cases under consideration and in the deliberative process itself, differed substantially from those of the inquisitors, who possessed no such right. Moreover, direct procuratorial influence was felt only minimally at the lower and broader levels of ecclesiastical superintendence; while for a variety of reasons, not least the overprocurator's dependence on the Synod for his salary, it frequently proved negligible even on matters transacted in the Synod.[14] To be sure, after an initial period of irresolution, confusion, and only partial consolidation, the procuratorship became an important, and occasionally even a preeminent, element in the Synod's functioning. But that was later. During the Petrine period, it was the inquisitorial office that was the more developed.

Contributing to that development was a lengthy instruction issued on 12 December 1722 from the Synod to Protoinquisitor Pafnutii.[15] It attempted to define the duties of inquisitors in terms that had been set forth earlier for secular fiscals in various state decrees and statutes, and to augment them with a description of tasks more relevant to the surveillance of ecclesiastical administration. Besides watching for misconduct by bishops, the inquisitors were given a variety of matters to look out for: that clergymen and monks were duly installed; that the clergy did not carry on illegal trade, engage in misappropriation of resources, or violate the law in their treatment of schismatics by showing them favor or indulgence; and that church authorities did not mistreat peasants under their control, use monetary allowances for purposes other than those intended, or delay the official processing of petitions submitted at any level of ecclesiastical administration. In order that inquisitors might easily acquaint themselves with the order of business at all levels, the church authorities had to give them access to all their records for inspection and scrutiny. The inquisitors could make any extracts they desired so long as they did not impede the normal course of affairs or intrude in matters not concerning them. They were to watch that all clergymen, including bishops, adhered to establishment regulations in every matter, and report on them to higher authorities.

The inquisitors were restricted from going beyond their surveillance function. In only exceptional cases were they to bypass the authorized lines of notification when submitting reports on misconduct. Most emphatically was it forbidden to embarrass the Synod by reporting directly to the Senate, the college chanceries, or other lay officials. They were also prohibited, except when circumstances seemed to warrant suspicion, to inject themselves into civil matters or trespass on the jurisdiction of any other inquisitor. Of greatest importance was the exclusion of inquisitors from all ordinary administrative activity: they were specifically forbidden to issue passports or leaves of absence to anyone; and if in their official capacity they had to summon someone from far away, the necessary paperwork had to be done by the regular church authorities. Once a judicial case was begun on the basis of his report, an inquisitor was not to take any further part in it. The range of inquisitorial operations was clearly and carefully spelled out as being limited to surveillance, notification of higher authorities, and submission of evidence after calling the accused to trial.

From the viewpoint of administrative control, the weakest strand in the network was the provincial inquisitor's high degree of autonomy in the selection process. They could choose anyone at their own discretion for an inquisitorial appointment anywhere within the eparchies under their jurisdiction. That this constituted, at least potentially, a serious flaw in assuring the efficient and incorruptible operation of the inquisitorial network was recognized by the Synod, which on 16 April 1725 issued a special protocol on the matter. The procedural revisions adopted by the Synod showed that it was moving in the direction of including bishops, however tentatively, in the selection process for appointing inquisitors.[16]

The synodal protocol established the requirement that the eligibility of any candidate for an inquisitorial post was to be supported by *written references* obtained from his former place of residence and present monastery, as well as from the place where he received his tonsure into the monastic rank. References pertaining to candidates for the post of inquisitor were to be dispatched to the local bishop;

those for provincial inquisitor, to the Synod. The protocol then went on to provide that candidates for inquisitor were to be taken under advisement by the bishops and provincial inquisitors of their eparchies at the time of their nomination. Confronted with a candidate's name and personal file, a bishop and provincial inquisitor could then presumably render a negative report, which would delay or block the appointment of an individual found to be undesirable or inadequately qualified. In this manner, the episcopate, although indeed granted a certain input in the selection of inquisitors, was designed to operate at a candidate's point of origin rather than his point of reception. The bishop most affected by such an appointment was still given no voice at the last stage of administrative decision. The synodal protocol, therefore, did not introduce anything radically new. While the requirement for verification of personal background did constitute a procedural modification, the basic inquisitorial functions were in no way altered by the protocol or by any other enactment subsequent to the issuance of the instruction of 12 December 1722 to the protoinquisitor.

The inquisitorial network continued to operate along the lines described for almost two years to the day after the death of Peter the Great on 28 January 1725. The Synod then took the first step in dismantling the entire apparatus. The general pretext for this action was to deal with the continued autonomy enjoyed by provincial inquisitors in appointing inquisitors and the abuses to which this practice reportedly led, apparently only partially ameliorated by the synodal protocol of 16 April 1725. The case in point centered on a certain hierodeacon, Aleksandr Tikhonov, who served as provincial inquisitor in the eparchy of Kholmgory. In that capacity, he had appointed a monk by the name of Miron as inquisitor in the important Solovetskii monastery. Miron, however, was suspected by some fellow monks to be a schismatic, an adherent of the Old Belief. Reports of this led to an investigation of Hierodeacon Tikhonov, who, though ill and unable to undergo interrogation at the College of Justice, nevertheless submitted a written deposition in which he admitted his own treasonous guilt in the matter and furthermore proceeded to denounce other provincial inquisitors for reprehensible activities.[17]

The Synod needed no encouragement to seize upon this case as indicating a fundamental fault in the entire inquisitorial network. Accordingly, on 25 January 1727 it issued a resolution giving consideration to provincial inquisitors and inquisitors, and to their "many disorderly acts by which wrongs and antipathies are directed against the clergy and laymen."[18] The resolution took advantage of still another of Peter's ecclesiastical reforms, whose chief features were detailed in a decree of 5 February 1724. The plan envisioned placing an archimandrite in charge of several monasteries, each under the direction of a hegumen. The parochial clergy was to have been divided into "districts" and also made subject to supervision by the archimandrites, who were to compile and forward reports about the clergy to the bishops. This reform was never fully implemented in Peter's reign, and there was not much likelihood for that after his death. Still, the fact that it had been proposed furnished the Synod with an opportunity to say, as indeed it did in its resolution of 25 January 1727, that the inquisitorial office was henceforth unnecessary. Thereupon the Synod resolved that complete informational files be prepared on all provincial inquisitors and inquisitors, including evidence of any wrongdoing, and that those files be forwarded to the Synod for its consideration.

On 15 March 1727, noting that no benefit could be expected from it, the Synod abolished the inquisitorial network. On 7 July, bishops received authority to render judgment in cases involving improper activities by former inquisitors or provincial inquisitors, and subsequent decrees sped the dissolution of the entire institution, sending monks who had served in an inquisitorial capacity back to their monasteries and secular priests back to their previous locations under the jurisdiction of regularly constituted church administrators.[19]

The establishment of the inquisitorial network was thus not a lasting success. The introduction into church administration of the distinctive principle underlying the secular fiscals, which involved organizational detachment from operational administrative agencies and functional restriction to the areas of surveillance and notification, was swept away by the hierarchy without regrets and leaving scarcely a trace after the passage of just six years. If for purposes of ecclesiastical superintendence it proved to be a failure, yet in another and wider sense all of Peter the Great's reforms in the area of ecclesiastical administration made up a considerable achievement in fixing *raison d'état* as the principle of highest public priority. Indicative of this achievement was the continued existence of the Synod and the increasing power imparted to the secular office of overprocurator, the monarch's "eye" in the discharge of synodal affairs. The inquisitorial network, brought into being at secular instigation and having an affinity to organs of state administration, fitted into this overall pattern of development.

NOTES

1. *Polnoe sobranie zakonov Rossiiskoi imperii s 1649 goda*, 1st ser., 46 vols. in 48 and 3 apps., St. Petersburg, 1830-43, IV, no. 2331 (hereafter *PSZ*); *Pis'ma i bumagi Imperatora Petra Velikogo*, 11 vols. in 17, St. Petersburg, Moscow-Leningrad, Moscow, 1887-1964, XI, pt. 1, 125-26, no. 4315; N. A. Voskresenskii, ed., *Zakonodatel'nye akty Petra I*, Moscow-Leningrad, 1945, I, 203-4.

2. V. O. Kliuchevskii, *Sochineniia v vos'mi tomakh*, 8 vols., Moscow, 1956-59, IV, 165; *PSZ*, V, no. 3006; *PSZ*, VI, nos. 3456, 3534.

3. *PSZ*, IV, nos. 2321, 2328, 2414.

4. *PSZ*, IV, nos. 1818, 1829; see also T. Barsov, *Sinodal'nyia uchrezhdeniia prezhniago vremeni*, St. Petersburg, 1897, 199.

5. *PSZ*, V, no. 2786; N.G. Ustrialov, *Istoriia tsarstvovaniia Petra Velikago*, 5 vols., St. Petersburg, 1858-63, V, 31; S.M. Solov'ev. *Istoriia Rossii s drevneishikh vremen*, 29 vols. in 15, Moscow, 1959-66, VIII, 573-74; S.G. Runkevich, *Arkhierei petrovskoi epokhi v ikh perepiskie s Petrom Velikim*, St. Petersburg, 1906, 156.

6. *PSZ*, VI, no. 3734; Alexander V. Muller, ed. and trans., *The Spiritual Regulation of Peter the Great*, Seattle, 1972, 3-4, 6.

7. *Ibid.*, 19-29, 37.

8. V.N. Beneshevich, ed., *Sbornik pamiatnikov po istorii tserkovnago prava, preimushchestvenno Russkoi Tserkvi do epokhi Petra Velikago*, 2 vols., Petrograd, 1914-15, II, 191-92.

9. T. Barsov, "O svietskikh fiskalakh i dukhovnykh inkvizitorakh," *Zhurnal Ministerstva narodnago prosvieshcheniia*, February 1878, 353; *idem, Sinodal'nyia uchrezhdeniia*, 155.

10. *Idem*, "O fiskalakh i inkvizitorakh," 352; *idem, Sinodal'nyia uchrezhdeniia*, 155-56.

11. *Idem*, "O fiskalakh i inkvizitorakh," 354, 361.

12. *Ibid.*, 352, 364; Barsov, *Sinodal'nyia uchrezhdeniia*, 156.

13. *PSZ*, VI, nos. 4001, 4036; F.V. Blagovidov, *Ober-prokurory sviateishago sinoda v XVIII i v pervoi polovinie XIX stolietiia*, 2d ed., Kazan, 1900, 38.

14. Barsov, "O fiskalakh i inkvizitorakh," 384; Blagovidov, *Ober-prokurory*, 74-89.

15. *PSZ*, VI, nos. 3870-4132.
16. Barsov, "O fiskalakh i inkvizitorakh," 357.
17. *Ibid.*, 355, 389.
18. *Ibid.*, 389-90; *PSZ*, VII, no. 4455.
19. Barsov, "O fiskalakh i inkvizitorakh," 390-92.

The System of Nicholas I in Church-State Relations

David W. Edwards

The administrative system of Nicholas I was an extension of his personality, and both were characterized by a strong sense of duty and an obsession with order. He left no area of government untouched in the drive to impose his personal qualities upon his subjects. Nowhere was his desire for duty and order more apparent, or more promptly manifested, than in church-state relations, where it was intensified by his deep devotion to the established Russian Orthodox church. His demands went beyond administrative tidiness to include unanimity in matters of belief. Decisions of the Holy Synod, the governing body of the Russian Orthodox church, were to be "based not on intellect and interpretation, but on the precise meaning of the dogma." It followed, as he told the overprocurator, that in matters of faith "disagreement cannot and should not be [tolerated]."[1] Thus agreement upon religious questions was expected; conformity to Nicholas's administrative organization was essential.

The desire for unity in religious belief and organization is as old as the Russian state itself. This essay does not attempt a full discussion of this current in Russian history but has a more limited objective: to describe the "system" of church-state relations as it evolved during the reign of Nicholas I. Although Nicholas never fully defined the system's form and purpose, it may be argued that both were clearly discernible by 1840. Working through three overprocurators who were increasingly efficient and energetic, the tsar transformed the administration of the church into an organization closely paralleling that of the various state ministries. He and his subordinates worked to create a centralized, bureaucratic, lay-dominated church administration. A further argument, albeit more subjective and tentative, is that during Nicholas's reign the state controlled and directed the church more than at any previous period in the history of Russian church-state relations. Although such a contention demands further investigation, the coincidence of a deeply religious tsar, a powerful overprocurator, and a centralized ecclesiastical administration constitutes strong grounds. This paper focuses upon the gradual concentration of administrative power in the overprocurator and his secular assistants, who not only made concrete Nicholas's conceptions of duty and order, but also attained the highest degree of control yet realized over the Russian church.

In order to put his conceptions of church administration into practice, Nicholas slowly created a staff of loyal and responsive synodal bureaucrats. He transferred the upright, pious, and rather passive Overprocurator P.S. Meshcherskii to the Senate in April 1833 and appointed S.D. Nechaev to replace him. As a well trained and experienced civil administrator, Nechaev knew how to gain influence in his new office.[2] After three years of intense work, he succeeded in changing the spirit of the Holy Synod and increasing the scope of the overprocurator's duties. However, his brief time in office must be seen as a prelude to the powerful rule of Count N.A. Protasov.

Russian churchmen initially hailed Protasov's nomination and flooded his desk with congratulations, for despite Nechaev's liberal use of flattery on synodal members, he had also exercised arbitrary power. Moreover, since Protasov seemed to have had little administrative experience (his civil career began only in 1833), it was hoped that he might not discover the ways to manipulate the complicated ecclesiastical bureaucracy. For his part, Protasov strove to convey an image of piety by establishing a chapel in his home. Metropolitan Serafim

(Glagolevskii) of St. Petersburg recommended Protasov's appointment to Nicholas and described him as a man "well known for his intellect, education, and zeal for the Orthodox church."[3]

Protasov's long term as overprocurator (1836-55) widened the range of state control over the church. As a former military officer, he mirrored Nicholas's ideal of order and duty more perfectly than did either Meshcherskii or Nechaev. His military techniques were reinforced by what some churchmen referred to as his "Roman way." Although he had little sympathy for Roman Catholicism and even worked to destroy the Unia, Protasov's Jesuit education had instilled in him a respect for tradition, the church fathers, and ecclesiastical order. As overprocurator he turned this respect into a program for eliminating theological diversity, suppressing the translation of the Bible into contemporary Russian, and curbing freedom within the church administration.[4] The emperor's search for the ideal overprocurator ended with Protasov, who was by training, intellect, and approach best able to install the Nicholaevan system of church-state relations.

In his efforts to remold the church to suit his administrative conceptions and to deemphasize those points where disagreement might emerge, Nicholas attended to three facets of church organization. First, he methodically examined and supplemented the imperial laws relating to the church. Second, he sought to make the administrative machinery more closely approximate that of the state ministries. Third, he reduced the powers and independence of the hierarchy, virtually transforming it into another wing of the Russian bureaucracy.

A systematic review of laws relating to the church, which formed only one segment of the general codification, brought order to the many legal enactments devised since Peter I's church reform. This orderly arrangement was integrated into the Code of Laws (1833) and remained part of the Fundamental Laws until 1917. Nothing in the code except its organization was new, but the collection reflected a growth in the government's power. All functioning statutes were now contained in fifteen volumes, and the resulting coherence gave strength and solidity to the imperial legal structure. Undertaken at the emperor's order, the codification must be considered the foundation of the Nicholaevan system in religious affairs. The more important laws included the requirement that Orthodoxy be the state religion, that the Synod serve as the agent of the emperor, and that the emperor be a member of the Orthodox church "as a Christian ruler [who] is the supreme protector and preserver of the dogmas of the state faith."[5] Imperial laws touched on every aspect of the church's economic, political, and social life; codification of these laws rationalized state control and strengthened it. Behind the codification stood a paternal solicitude toward the church as a governmental institution; the state undertook to protect the church legally from overt heterodox challenges while guaranteeing material aid to the official religion.[6]

Not only did Nicholas codify and rationalize old laws, he also enacted new legislation which affected the church profoundly. The most important new law was the *Statute on Ecclesiastical Consistories* (*Ustav dukhovnoi konsistorii*) published on 27 March 1841,[7] which expressed Nicholas's antipathy to disagreement or dispute. For example, it emphasized the importance of correctly observing the church's rites and regulations, and measures were designed to prevent the most serious expression of dissent, defection from the faith. Existing religious conflict could be reduced, it was thought, by strictly monitoring the schismatics (*raskolniki*), while diocesan officials could be urged to end these historical squabbles by reconverting dissenters and sectarians.[8] Finally, the statute required that the diocesan consistories make unanimous decisions.

The *Statute on Ecclesiastical Consistories* marked a fundamental shift from the codification of old ecclesiastical regulations to the creation of new laws designed to make the church administration resemble a government ministry. The first step in this direction was taken when the new statute completely overhauled the consistories, increasing the overprocurator's authority and reducing the diocesan bishops' role in the church's management.

The consistories, nominally under episcopal command but actually responsible to the overprocurator, became the administrative and judicial centers of the dioceses, supervising the clergy, church buildings, and the ecclesiastical economy. Consistory reports did not stop with the bishop, but were sent to the Holy Synod. The statute also provided detailed regulations concerning the jurisdiction of diocesan courts, punishments reserved for members of the clergy, and marriage and divorce laws.[9]

Ultimately, the statute's implementation reproduced in the consistories the same pattern of control that allowed the overprocurator to exercise power in the Holy Synod. The consistory secretary became the diocesan counterpart of the overprocurator and was responsible solely to him. His task in the consistory—one in keeping with Nicholas's reign generally—was to achieve unanimous opinions, although when disagreements arose both majority and minority views were recorded. If his own judgment differed from that of the clerics serving in the consistory, the secretary could register his dissenting opinion for the benefit of the overprocurator. The bishop could not veto the consistorial decisions, but he could request the reconsideration of an issue if he believed church law was violated. The bishop was accountable to the Holy Synod; the secretary reported directly to the overprocurator. Nothing escaped notice. In effect, the *Statute on Ecclesiastical Consistories* completely centralized the church's administration.[10]

A significant step in this transformation was making the overprocurator into a de facto minister. In 1827, Nicholas ordered Overprocurator Meshcherskii to report on his area of responsibility at the same time as other ministers.[11] The overprocurator also enjoyed the privilege of direct access to the tsar, without the formality of prior consultation with state secretaries. Nicholas thus regarded Meshcherskii as his independent, personal representative in ecclesiastical matters.[12] Both Meshcherskii and subsequent overprocurators adopted measures to increase their power and prestige and to make their office even more ministerial.[13] The Synod archives were put in order, laws and decrees were systematized, and a history of the Holy Synod and the Moscow Synodal Office was written. In 1835, Nicholas granted the overprocurator de jure equality with the members of the State Council and the Committee of Ministers.[14] Although the overprocurator lacked the several departments and the scores of clerks that formed the normal structure of Russian ministries, Nicholas's favor encouraged the belief that in time the requisite organization would be provided.

Simultaneously, an important additional step was taken in the bureaucratic reorganization of the church. In 1833, Nicholas ordered the creation of a Control Department of Ecclesiastical Affairs,[15] which sought to regularize church government by providing standard employment conditions and uniform accounting practices. A general auditor subordinate to the overprocurator began to check the church accounts, thereby increasing his superior's ability to control its economic life. Within a year, Metropolitan Filaret of Moscow complained about the auditor's close supervision of the Synod, the churches, and the monasteries, which, he argued, discriminated against the Orthodox church, as no other faith in the empire was subject to similar interference.[16] Filaret was, of course, correct, but the price of government subsidies was the careful accounting of these funds. With support came control, and the tsar had established the procedure for overseeing the church's economy.

Nicholas wished to provide a fitting symbol for the Synod's new status and close identification with the other parts of the state machinery. The architect Rossi made plans and estimates for a monumental building to house both the Synod and the Senate. The money for the complex, almost two million rubles, was to come from the capital of the ecclesiastical schools.[17] Nicholas undertook the project, often overseeing the work and even changing some of the plans. The church built in the complex was blessed on 27 May 1835, and a week later the tsar attended the ceremonies opening the new building. In his dedication speech, he referred to the relationship between church and state, or more accurately between the church and Nicholas. Although he had come to the throne unexpectedly and, he maintained, without preparation, the first ten years of his rule had not been without successes. The church must continue to support the state in order to meet the coming challenges. Nicholas also intended to prepare his son and successor, Alexander, for his duties by appointing him to the Holy Synod.[18] Both Nicholas's speech and the appointment of Alexander reflected the emperor's interpretation of church-state relations. Because the state and its ruler needed spiritual aid, the church was duty bound to supply it. To insure that this support was unwavering, the emperor would provide an imperious overprocurator, a magnificent administration building, and even an observant tsarevich. Thus, by 1835 Nicholas's aim of bringing the church into conformity with state institutions had resulted in the creation of a ministerial framework. Only the enclosure and elaboration of that framework remained to be completed.

Following a period of scheming by clerical opponents, Nechaev's tenure as overprocurator ended on 25 June 1836 with his replacement by Count N. A. Protasov.[19] The hierarchs wanted to rid themselves of the overbearing Nechaev but soon found his successor to be no improvement. Upon being appointed overprocurator, Protasov exclaimed to Adjutant General Chicherin: "Congratulate me. I am a minister; I am a bishop; I am a devil knows what." Metropolitan Filaret of Kiev, upon hearing of the incident, remarked that only the last was true.[20] Protasov, however, was more concerned with his imperial master's wishes than the church hierarchy's attitude. His ability to do the emperor's bidding depended in large part upon forging a suitable instrument. This meant the destruction of the collegiate principle, which had characterized the Holy Synod since its founding, and the institution of autocratic rule; Protasov wanted to become "minister of ecclesiastical affairs."[21] Only five weeks after taking office, on 1 August 1836, he presented Nicholas with a wide-ranging report on ecclesiastical administration.[22] In the analysis of his office, he submitted that he lacked the necessary staff and organization to carry out his functions. The tsar received his report favorably and ordered him to begin drafting plans for the needed changes.[23] The overprocurator moved quickly, increasing the size of his staff and creating the Economic Committee in the Holy Synod.[24] Clearly, Protasov was perpetuating, though more systematically, the programs of his predecessors, Nechaev and Meshcherskii.

Early in 1839, Protasov began constructing the capstone to Nicholas's ecclesiastical bureaucracy. In a report to the emperor, he argued that the church government was unable to do its job properly because it was undermanned, irresponsible, and decentralized. The functions of the church administrators had multiplied, but there had not been a corresponding expansion in staff. With the growth of its duties, the Holy Synod increasingly failed to manage its affairs in an orderly fashion. What existed, according to Protasov, was a rambling, inefficient state within a state. To prove his point, the overprocurator referred to the pile of unfinished business at the end of each year and the 50 million rubles for which the Commission on Ecclesiastical

Schools had never accounted.[25] In order for the church to fulfill its great spiritual and educational tasks, it must forsake the collective form of administration and accept the principle of responsible one-man rule. The debates and bickering in the Holy Synod should be replaced by decisive action from the overprocurator.

One week after receiving the report, Nicholas issued ukases fully implementing Protasov's proposals. Under the new administration, increases in staff and financial support were provided to the chancelleries of both the Holy Synod and the overprocurator.[26] Also, the Economic Committee of the Synod became the Economic Department, completely under the overprocurator's control and accountable for all money and property at every level of the church administration.[27] Finally, the emperor decreed the abolition of the Commission of Ecclesiastical Schools and the creation of the Church-School Department,[28] which, like all organs of the church government, was to be firmly under the thumb of the overprocurator. Clerks, as in other ministries, were divided according to their duties, pensions, and uniforms.[29] The office of overprocurator thus came to parallel the Russian ministerships in all fundamental respects. Protasov himself did not hesitate to make the comparison: in a report to the emperor of 16 December 1839, the overprocurator pointed to the reforms' brilliant success and suggested that the department heads of the ecclesiastical administration were entitled to receive the same salaries as their counterparts in the ministries.[30] Protasov's claims were well founded. Building upon the groundwork of Meshcherskii and Nechaev, he had completed the structure of a ministry of ecclesiastical affairs, sitting atop a centralized, bureaucratic lay-dominated church administration.

If the overprocurator was to assume the powers and responsibilities of a minister, it would be necessary to do more than create a legal structure and a larger bureaucracy. Until the upper clergy's independence was reduced both in the diocese and the Synod the emperor and the overprocurator would not fully control the church. Nicholas and his lay appointees chipped away at traditional episcopal privileges, transferring some to secular bodies and abolishing others altogether. A first hesitant step had been taken as early as 1826 with an ukase limiting the bishops' traditional right to address the ruler and forbidding "verbose speeches" by clerics in the tsar's presence.[31] In 1842 and 1843, the Synod stated strongly that bishops were not to give speeches during the emperor's travels. The only exceptions were the three metropolitans (St. Petersburg, Kiev, and Moscow) and the Archbishop of Warsaw.[32] The bishops also witnessed steady inroads into their traditional rights of appointing laymen to ecclesiastical positions, granting priests permission to wander through the country collecting alms, and bestowing rewards upon clergy for outstanding service.[33] These restrictions represented further steps toward church centralization. All power flowed from the center; rewards came only from the Synod; and, with but four exceptions, the only opinions that mattered originated with the clerics and officials sitting in the capital.

In their drive to control Russian Orthodox bishops, Nicholas and his overprocurators also used the power to initiate investigations and recommend disciplinary action. If a bishopric was afflicted by chronic disorder or other irregularities, an inquiry would be undertaken; and a bishop judged guilty of misconduct or incompetence would be reprimanded, transferred to a less desirable see, or forced into retirement. The mere threat of reprisals prompted many of the bishops and priests to think twice before questioning the tsar or secular authorities. Even the powerful Filaret of Moscow yielded in the face of government threats. In the autumn of 1830, Nicholas traveled to Moscow for a first-hand inspection of the suffering caused by the cholera epidemic. During this visit, Filaret gave a sermon urging the continuation of prayers for ending the epidemic and said in passing that nations sometimes suffered because of the sins of their rulers. He referred to King David and Israel, but added parenthetically that "although of course all people sin," Nicholas was not the cause of Russia's misfortunes.[34] Filaret's words raised the suspicions of Nicholas, who was all too prepared to see the allusion to himself. He reprimanded Filaret, and the metropolitan corrected the sermon before it was printed and wrote an apology on 6 October 1830.[35] Every bishop faced similar controls, imposed on the hierarchy by the state and supervised by the overprocurator and, ultimately, by the tsar himself.

Under Nechaev, the government became more actively involved in determining a hierarch's specific post. Bishop Amvrosii of Nizhnii

Novgorod had drawn the wrath of the overprocurator — as well as of many churchmen — for his autocratic abuse of power. Nechaev discussed this case with the emperor, and Nicholas wrote on the report: "Transfer. While in Nizhnii [Novgorod], I myself noticed that he does not have a liking for carrying out the will of the authorities; he must be kept under close surveillance." Amvrosii was subsequently transferred to Penza.[36] He may well have deserved this demotion, but according to the regulations governing ecclesiastical administration, it was a question for the Holy Synod, not the emperor, to judge.

Nechaev also resorted to more insidious means to reduce the bishops' effectiveness in resisting central control. According to the synodal clerk Ismailov:

Suddenly from here and there appeared gendarme denunciations of hierarchs and members of the Holy Synod. The denunciations seem for the most part to be lies; the hierarchs and members of the Synod cleared themselves as well as they could. But the Synod was strongly disturbed and suspicious that the overprocurator himself had participated in the denunciations, having made up his mind to humble the ecclesiastical government.[37]

The government designated Metropolitan Filaret of Moscow one of the primary targets in the campaign to reduce episcopal influence. Filaret, the outstanding representative of the hierarchy during Nicholas's reign, protested the unwarranted monitoring of his activities. In turn Nicholas objected to any constraints on his imperial power and continued the attack upon the metropolitan.[38] In the unequal struggle between tsar and metropolitan, Nicholas eventually triumphed, banishing both Metropolitan Filaret of Moscow and his ally, Metropolitan Filaret of Kiev, from the Synod in 1842. With the departure of these two clerics, Overprocurator Protasov ruled over a docile Synod and truly became "a Patriarch in a soldier's uniform."[39]

Just as Nicholas and his overprocurators worked to limit the independence of the individual hierarchs in the bishoprics, so they endeavored to reduce the power of the highest council of the hierarchs, the Holy Synod itself. The leading clerics in Russia felt a diminution of synodal prerogatives because of procedural changes. The overprocurators arbitrarily violated protocol, unilaterally changed the decrees and resolutions of the Synod, and frequently prevented the recording of the Synod members' opinions during meetings.[40] Furthermore, once the synodal bureaucracy was in place, Protasov funnelled all ecclesiastical business through lay appointees. All questions of policy, from both clerics and laymen, passed through these bureaucrats, who decided what the Synod would discuss.[41] Finally, the hierarchs in the Synod in effect lost the privilege to appoint clerics to vacant episcopal sees. Before the advent of Nechaev, the Synod would choose three candidates for a vacancy but indicate its first choice. The overprocurator would then forward this recommendation to the tsar, who would follow the Synod's advice. Under both Nechaev and, in particular, Protasov, the procedure was fundamentally changed; now the overprocurator, not the Synod, recommended the men for vacancies. According to the official survey of the Orthodox church during this period, Nicholas always requested, and usually followed, Protasov's opinion concerning the appointments of bishops and metropolitans.[42] If a member of the Synod objected to these methods, he could be ordered to return to his see inasmuch as he served at the tsar's pleasure. If a clerk protested against the treatment of the ecclesiastical dignitaries, he would simply be dismissed from his post and perhaps lose the rights of his past service.[43] Sometimes addressing the members of the Synod as "batiushka," a title reserved for parish priests, and at other times screaming at the hierarchs, "Protasov took them in hand as though in the military and at once drilled the crowd of archbishops like a squadron."[44]

Only one small trickle of independence remained in the Synod — the white clergy. The head chaplain of the army and navy and the priest of the imperial family, both members of the white clergy, were invariably named to the Synod by the tsar. Since they held their posts independently of the overprocurator, Protasov could not control or dismiss them. He tried unsuccessfully to abolish the head chaplaincy and replace it with an archbishop of the armed forces who would be a member of the black clergy and more under his control.[45] Although this source of potential difficulty was never eliminated, it could not erode the power which Protasov had labored to create; the victory was his. The members of the Synod, no less than the ecclesiastical hierarchy as a whole, had been worked into the Nicholaevan system of church-state relations by the zealous overprocurator. The upper clergy's hopeless condition was expressed by the scholarly Filaret Gumilevskii in a letter to Professor A.V. Gorskii: "You write with sorrow about the silence of our generals, that is, the members of the Synod. Ah, my friend! If you could see the situation of our generals here, you would shed tears over them — such is their situation."[46]

As the government decreased the independence of the bishops, it also issued instructions which would give them more control over the clerics in their dioceses. These were not antithetical movements but rather two steps toward centralization. Nicholas, interested in the orderly administration of his empire and desirous of knowing all about the lives of his subjects, led this drive. In his effort to collect more information on the church at the local level, he used three methods devised by Peter the Great: the *metricheskaia kniga*, or registry of births, deaths, and marriages; reports on the annual visits of bishops throughout their sees; and the disclosure of all "incidents" involving members of the lower clergy and their churches.[47] During Protasov's tenure, the compilation of the *metricheskaia kniga* became standardized. The collection of vital statistics had long been the responsibility of the priests, and after 1838 the bishops were enjoined to supervise this activity.[48] The priest became a civil servant, and the hours he and his bishop spent at this task were time taken away from their spiritual responsibilities.

Another means of increasing control over the Russian church was the bishops' regular reports. The seventeenth point of the *Ecclesiastical Regulation* of Peter the Great provided for yearly, or at least biennial, visits around his see by each bishop. During the early years of Nicholas's reign, the reports on the clerks and priests of the various dioceses were of uneven quality, a situation which the emperor found intolerable. Not until 1847 was a suitable evaluation form devised. Each hierarch was ordered to complete a detailed examination of his see and conclude with an essay on ways in which the bishopric might be improved.[49] The annual reports presented the government with an opportunity to examine all facets of the activities of the bishop and his staff.

As the supreme governor and judge of his people, Nicholas also desired to know of every unusual "incident" in the churches of his empire. Several unfortunate episodes early in his reign convinced him that the bishops must report more fully to the Synod.[50] Basing his order once again on the *Ecclesiastical Regulation*, Nicholas enjoined the bishops to keep close watch over the parish priests and immediately report to the Holy Synod all incidents involving members of the lower clergy.[51] Although general guidelines had been laid down in 1828, the responsibilities of the bishops and priests in keeping order in the churches were made clearer by a circular from the Holy Synod in 1839.[52] This measure, together with the *metrichskaia kniga* and the annual reports of the bishops, helped the central ecclesiastical authorities to know everything of significance occurring on the local level. Although he borrowed these tactics from the reforming tsar, Nicholas infused them with his own penchant for orderliness. In theory, nothing occurred at any level of the religious pyramid without the knowledge of the emperor, the overprocurator, or the Holy Synod. Vladimir, Archbishop of Kazan, realized the significance of these moves and reflected the utter hopelessness of efforts to change the system: "Now it is impossible to keep anything from the Synod; to us, old men, [life] is becoming difficult, and, having no strength, it is necessary to ask for repose."[53] Although Vladimir expressed the opposition of many upper clergy to the burdens of reporting all to the overprocurator, little doubt exists that the efficiency of church administration improved. Bishops became more aware of the poverty of many parishes, the problems of the families of deceased priests, and the inadequacies of the ecclesiastical schools. But the power to deal with these questions rested not with the local bishop, but with the overprocurator.

From 1825 to 1855, Nicholas and his overprocurators tried to make the church more orderly and obedient. Although Protasov, with his military background and mentality, reflected the tsar's purposes better than did either Meshcherskii or Nechaev, each overprocurator contributed to the drive of the government to create a "ministry of ecclesiastical affairs" and thereby control the church completely. By both open and secret means they established secular domination over the Synod and the church as a whole. By an extension of legal powers and the use of espionage they limited the independence of the bishops. Facing the uncertainties of police reports and the humiliation of the consistories' criticism, most bishops decided to fall in line rather than suffer censure, demotion, or exile. At the same time, they monitored more closely the activities within their dioceses; nothing occurred without the knowledge of the center. Finally, through the codification of the laws and the *Statute on Ecclesiastical Consistories*, Nicholas provided the legal framework for his system of church-state relations. The ruler's conceptions of duty and order thus became the guides for the activities of the church hierarchs. His military mind permeated the power structure of the Russian Orthodox church, creating a centralized, bureaucratic, lay-dominated administration.

NOTES

1. N. F. Dubrovin, "Materialy dlia istorii pravoslavnoi tserkvi v tsarstvovanie Imperatora Nikolaia I," *Sbornik imperatorskago russkago istoricheskago obshchestva*, CXIII, St. Petersburg, 1902, 18. Hereafter cited as *SIRIO*. All references are to volume CXIII.

2. *Ibid.*, 154-55.

3. Quoted in *ibid.*, 395.

4. See especially G. Florovsky, *Puti russkago bogosloviia*, Paris, 1937, 204. Also "Litovskii mitropolit Iosif Semashko," *Russkaia starina*, June 1889, 314, in which Protasov is described as a "pupil and servant of the Jesuits."

5. *Svod zakonov rossiiskoi imperii*, I, St. Petersburg, 1832, arts. 42-43. The code describes the emperor as "Head of the Church" in the remarks added to article 42. Hereafter cited as *Svod zakonov*.

6. *Ibid*, XV, arts. 186-99; XIV, art. 107; I, arts. 44-46.

7. *Polnoe sobranie zakonov*, 2d ser., XVI, no. 14,409 (27 March 1841), 221-63. Hereafter cited as *PSZ*. The Holy Synod published an offprint of the statute under its title *Ustav dukhovnoi konsistorii*, St. Petersburg, 1841. See also A.S. Pavlov, *Kurs tserkovnogo prava*, Trinty-St. Sergius Monastery, 1902, 186.

8. *Ustav*, arts. 1-37.

9. *Ibid.*, arts. 158-279.

10. F.A. Ternovskii, "Iz vospominanii sekretariia Sv. Sinoda F.F. Ismailova (1829-1840)," *Strannik*, September 1882, 83.

11. F. V. Blagovidov, *Ober-prokurory sviatieshago sinoda v XVIII i XIX stoletiiakh*, Kazan, 1889, 371-72. These orders by Nicholas appeared on 21 August and 25 November 1827.

12. *Ibid.*, 372-73.

13. *Polnoe sobranie postanovlenii i rasporiazhenii po vedomstvu pravoslavnogo ispovedaniia rossiiskoi imperii: Tsarstvovanie gosudaria Imperatora Nikolaia I*, 6th ser., I, Petrograd, 1915, no. 258, 372-73, no. 435, 615-20. Hereafter cited as *PSP.*

14. *PSZ*, 2d ser., X, no. 8001, 281, no. 8007, 283; *PSP*, nos. 584-85, 835.

15. *PSZ*, 2d ser., VIII, pt. 1, no. 6657.

16. Cited in Blagovidov, *Ober-prokurory*, 386-87.

17. N. P. Grigorovich, "Imperator Nikolai I-i v sviateishem pravitel'stvuiu-shchem sinod," *Russkii arkhiv*, May 1869, 740-42. Note 1 includes a discussion of the cost of the building and its furnishings.

18. *Ibid.*, 748; *PSP*, no. 608, 863-64. Although Alexander continued to include membership in the Synod on his service list until 1853, he did not attend the Synod's meetings. Igor Smolitsch, *Geschichte der russischen Kirche, 1700-1917*, I, Leiden, 1964, 164; Florovsky, *Puti*, 202.

19. On the background of Protasov's assumption of office, see the following: *SIRIO*, 155; I. A. Chistovich, *Rukovodiashchie deiateli dukhovnogo prosve-shcheniia v Rossii*, St. Petersburg, 1894, 315; N.S. Leskov, "Sinodal' nyia persony i period bor'by za preobladnie (1820-1840 gg.)," *Istoricheskii vestnik*, November 1882, 384-94; Blagovidov, *Ober-prokurory*, 397-98; Ternovskii, *Strannik*, 79-81.

20. "Filaret Drozdov, mitropolit moskovskii," *Russkaia starina*, October 1885, 153-54; V.M. Vestokov, "Innokentii, arkhiepiskop khersonskii i tavricheskii: 1800-1857 gg.," *Russkaia starina*, XXIV, 1879, 657, n.

21. See "Filaret Drozdov," *Russkaia starina*, October 1885, 158; *SIRIO*, 157, 212.

22. Blagovidov, *Ober-prokurory*, 401; I. A. Chistovich, *Rukovodiashchie deia-teli dukhovnago prosveshcheniia v Rossii*, St. Petersburg, 1894, 333; T. V. Barsov, *Sviateishii sinod v ego proshlom*, St. Petersburg, 1896, 351-54.

23. Blagovidov, *Ober-prokurory*, 402-3.

24. *SIRIO*, 214-15, 231. The money for their salaries came from the Commission on Ecclesiastical Schools; *PSZ*, 2d ser., X, pt. 2, no. 9705, 192-96; Blagovidov, *Ober-prokurory*, 403-4. *Gosudarstvennyi kontrol'*, *1811-1911*, St. Petersburg, 1911, 85-86.

25. Blagovidov, *Ober-prokurory*, 407-10.

26. *PSZ*, 2d ser., XIV, no. 12,068, pt. 1, 178-79, pt. 2, 85; no. 12,069, pt. 1, 179, pt. 2, 86.

27. *Ibid.*, no. 12,071, pt. 1, 183-86, pt. 2, 88-89.

28. *Ibid.*, no. 12,070, pt. 1, 179-83, pt. 2, 87.

29. T.V. Barsov, *Sinodal'nyia uchrezhdeniia prezhnago vremeni*, St. Petersburg, 1897, 20.

30. Blagovidov, *Ober-prokurory*, 411; Ternovskii, *Strannik*, 81, states that Protasov became a "true minister."

31. *SIRIO*, 417.

32. *Ibid.*, 415-17.

33. *Ibid.*, 418-23; *PSZ*, 2d ser, V, pt. 1, no. 3878, 818, XV, pt. 1, no. 13,515, 359.

34. Filaret Drozdov, *Slova i rechi*, II, Moscow, 1861, 523-28, esp. 526.

35. "Filaret Drozdov," *Russkaia starina*, July 1885, 11-12. The exact words of the sermon as it was spoken are not available.

36. *SIRIO*, pt. 2, 377-79. The quotation is from 378-79.

37. Quoted in Blagovidov, *Ober-prokurory*, 391. See also Leskov, *Istoricheskii vestnik*, 376, and Ternovskii, *Strannik*, 77.

38. On Filaret, see "Filaret Drozdov," *Russkaia starina*, July 1885, 12-14; Blagovidov, *Ober-prokurory*, 391-92; Leskov, *Istoricheskii vestnik*, 377-78; Ternovskii, *Strannik*, 77-78. A. P. Lebedev, *Cherty nravstvennago oblika moskovskago mitropolita Filareta*, Moscow, 1905, 25-26.

39. *Russkaia starina*, December 1885, 498.

40. Leskov, *Istoricheskii vestnik*, 379; Ternovskii, *Strannik*, 78-79; Blagovidov, *Ober-prokurory*, 394. The source for all of these accounts is the synodal clerk Ismailov: *SIRIO*, 234.

41. For sketches of these men, see *SIRIO*, 159-60; 222-30; Ternovskii, *Strannik*, 82-83.

42. *SIRIO*, 157. See also Blagovidov, *Ober-prokurory*, 397; "Filaret Drozdov," *Russkaia starina*, July 1885, 15-16. Ternovskii, *Strannik*, 79.

43. *Ibid.*, 81-83; *SIRIO*, 161.

44. Leskov, *Istoricheskii vestnik*, 398. See also *SIRIO*, 160-61.

45. "Filaret Drozdov," *Russkaia starina*, October 1885, 165-66; "Razskazy iz nedavnei stariny," *Russkii arkhiv*, 1878, no. 12, 517.

46. Quoted in "Filaret Drozdov," *Russkaia starina*, November 1885, 499.

47. The orders of Peter are found in his *Ecclesiastical Regulation, PSZ*, 1st ser., VI, no. 3718, 314-46. For an excellent translation, see Alexander V. Muller, ed. and trans., *The Spiritual Regulation of Peter the Great*, Seattle, 1972.

48. *PSZ*, 2d ser., XIII, no. 10,956, 91-92; M. Krasnozhen, *Kratkie ocherki tserkovnago prava*, Iur'ev (Tartu), 1900, 154-55.

49. *PSP*, no. 167, 233; *SIRIO*, 423, 444-45.

50. See *SIRIO*, 437-38; Filaret Drozdov, *Sobranie mnenii i otzyvov Filareta mitropolita moskovskogo i kolomenskogo, po uchebnym i tserkovno-gosudarstvennym voprosam...*, St. Petersburg, 1885-88, II, 238.

51. *PSP*, no. 176, 238-40.

52. *Ibid.*; *PSZ*, 2d ser., XIV, no. 12,165.

53. *SIRIO*, 450. Shortly thereafter, Vladimir retired.

Russian Bishops and Church Reform in 1905

John Meyendorff

In principle and in law, the reforms of Peter the Great attempted to integrate the religious functions of Russian society with the centralized imperial administration. Thus, Russian Orthodoxy was considered not really as a "church," enjoying a degree of autonomy, but merely as a body of beliefs shared by the emperor's subjects and requiring state-sponsored social and educational services. Its new organizational structure was designated as the Department of Orthodox Confession, (*Vedomstvo pravoslavnogo ispovedoniia*).

Obviously, Peter's system did not adequately express the traditional Orthodox conception of the church. Even the Byzantine medieval pattern, enshrined in the Orthodox canonical collections, presupposed a "symphonic" relationship between the empire and the priesthood, not absorption of the latter by the state.[1] Whatever might be said of the Byzantine pattern's practical application in Muscovite Russia (where the power of the tsar was in fact more arbitrary than that of the Byzantine basileus), this idea of "symphonia" implies a theological distinction between the ultimate functions of church and state: only discrete realities can function "symphonically"; a department is simply a cog in the state machinery.

Many serious historical studies assume that the Russian clergy lived largely in ignorance of the system's inadequacies, and instead, clergymen supposedly enjoyed a privileged position and opposed any reform of the status quo. The superficiality of this stereotyped notion can easily be demonstrated by examining the statements of bishops in a most significant publication, the three volumes of their official *Replies* (*Otzyvy*) to an inquiry addressed to them on 27 July 1905. The Holy Synod had asked the Orthodox hierarchy to describe those features of Russian church life which in its view needed reform or alteration.[2] Despite the brief time allowed for preparing their answers (by December 1905), the bishops replied punctually. Their comments thus represent a spontaneous, sometimes improvised, reaction to a sudden opportunity for free discussion. The overprocurator had expected the bishops to hold conservative views: one does not normally expect from them revolutionary — or even reformist — thought. Nevertheless, with near unanimity the Russian prelates favored reforms and, even more importantly, they achieved a significant theological and ideological consensus about the principles for greater independence which they considered desirable for the church.

This consensus indicates that independent thought — an important condition for spiritual freedom — had remained alive even within the rigid framework constructed for Russian Orthodoxy by Peter and his successors. Moreover, the *Replies* disclose the educational and intellectual background of their authors, their spiritual genealogy in the preceding decades and even centuries, and their remarkable willingness to recognize and grapple with the theological and canonical issues of the day, including the problems of the lower clergy and laity. Nearly unanimously they demanded the convocation of a church council, proposed innovations for both provincial and central church administration, and foresaw for the clergy a greater role in the country's social and political life.

Farsighted and educated churchmen, including lay professors in the ecclesiastical academies, always regarded Peter's reformed church as abnormal and canonically unjustifiable. Many shared the distaste of the Petrine system expressed by the authoritative Metropolitan Filaret

(Drozdov, 1782-1867) of Moscow. The *Replies* show that generally by the beginning of the twentieth century, the Orthodox hierarchy shared the optimistically reformist mood of the intelligentsia. Churchmen widely accepted A.S. Khomiakov's idea of *sobornost'* as the necessary framework for any possible schemes of reform. These attitudes help explain the several formal steps taken toward church reform in 1904-5. Hence the impetus did not result from any spectacular revolutionary upheaval, but rather from a convergence of opinion among bishops, the intelligentsia, and the leading elements of the clergy. Divergent opinions, of course, soon appeared, but the original reform impulse contained the remarkably uniform view of all these groups.[3]

Under pressure from public opinion, particularly from the *zemstvo* congress held in November 1904, the government enacted a decree on religious toleration abolishing many of the restrictions for non-Orthodox religions. The newly permitted toleration of other churches sharply emphasized how severely the state ruled and controlled the "privileged" official religion, and the indignation provoked by this realization led to the publication of three important statements. As it turned out, these statements proved to be the first steps leading to the council of 1917-18. Political obstacles, however, created delay.

Metropolitan Antonii (Vadkovskii) of St. Petersburg produced the first statement in the form of a memorandum (*zapiska*) to the tsar and the Committee of Ministers, requesting "a special conference of representatives of the Church's hierarchy, with the participation of competent persons from the clergy and the laity." No government official was to be included. The conference would devise proposals providing the church with autonomy and the "right of initiative," guarantees of "freedom from any direct State or political mission," and the freedom to administer its "internal affairs." Metropolitan Antonii also favored granting the parish the status of "legal person" with the right to own property, while deeming it appropriate for the clergy to participate in *zemstvo* activities. One or more bishops were to hold seats in the State Council and have direct access to the Committee of Ministers.[4]

The memorandum's moderate tone and demands reflected more than a desire for greater independence; it expressed the hierarchy's dissatisfaction with the overprocurator of the Holy Synod, who controlled all access to the tsar and his government. By its nature, a truly independent church should have the right to speak for itself.

S. Iu. Witte, the chairman of the Committee of Ministers, sponsored a second statement on church reform presented to a special Conference on Ecclesiastical Affairs under the Committee of Ministers. Encouraged by Witte's sympathy, liberal academy professors had drafted a statement which was much more radical than Antonii's note. Labeling the church's dependency "unlawful" (*nezakonyi*) since it kept Orthodoxy "in a state of paralysis," the Witte-sponsored memorandum went on to argue that *sobornost'* required lay participation in an eventual council and even in the election of candidates for the clergy.[5]

Finally, a third document, a liberal manifesto signed by thirty-two priests of the capital and representing the opinion of leading married clergy, demanded the convocation of a council with an unspecified agenda, which, however, could include such items as the election of bishops by their dioceses.[6]

Emboldened by public opinion and led by Metropolitan Antonii, the Holy Synod requested the tsar to authorize a "local," that is, a national council of bishops. According to canons 4 and 5 of the Council of Nicea, it was to be held semi-annually, but in Russia none had met in two hundred years. Acting upon K.P. Pobedonostsev's advice, Nicholas II refused to grant the Synod's request. Meanwhile, the old overprocurator attempted to delay the reform movement by insisting that the bishops be consulted about the issues. He expected no opposition from a presumably docile and reactionary episcopate to any departure from existing practice. Such is the origin of the *Replies*. The responses actually reached St. Petersburg after the momentous revolutionary events of fall 1905, including the dismissal of Pobedonostsev. In January 1906, a preconciliar commission, whose existence implied the restoration of *sobornost'* in the Russian church, began to prepare for a national council. Many of the most influential bishops expected it to meet after Easter 1906.[7]

The bishops' *Replies* included a number of important topics, especially the composition of the future council. Essentially the debate centered on the possible extension of voting rights beyond the bishops to the clergy and laymen. The bishops' ideas reflected the view frequently appearing in the press.[8] They also discussed the merits of decentralized ecclesiastical administration, the reform of central administration and the possible restoration of the patriarchate, and the extent of competence of ecclesiastical courts (particularly in marital affairs). Given the prominence of lower clergy and laymen in discussions about reform, it is perhaps not surprising to see the bishops deliberating the virtues of regular assemblies of clergy and laity and the degree to which the clergy should be encouraged to take a more active part in the life and responsibilities of society. The parish (as the nucleus of the church) and its canonical and legal status also came under the bishops' close scrutiny. Several areas, such as church property (its acquisition and alienation), theological education, and liturgical practice and church discipline, held special interest for the bishops. A large majority voiced dissatisfaction with the inaccessibility of much of the liturgical rites in the mass of the faithful, with a minority suggesting that the texts be translated from Church Slavonic into modern Russian. Nearly every bishop demanded modifications for achieving the congregation's fuller participation in liturgical worship.[9]

The bishops did not deal directly with the problem of church-state relations, but that issue appears clearly in the background, particularly in relation to proposed decentralization, the reform of church courts, and the participation of clergymen in society. Since a full analysis of the *Replies* would require more space than is available here, only a few brief remarks on these three areas can be offered. These, however, may suffice to encourage others to make fuller use of the abundant materials found in the *Replies*.

The creative and canonical discussions of reform naturally focused on institutions. Only three bishops believed that the existing system of church administration should continue unchanged. Apparently their conservative reaction reflected a fear of reform in the midst of revolutionary unrest. Bishop Lavrentii of Tula, one of the three conservatives, declared that "division of the church—as well as that of the state—can in no case be approved, especially in the present moment of trouble."[10]

The rest of the Russian episcopate unanimously favored the establishment of ecclesiastical provinces headed by regional metropolitans and with regional synods of bishops having some autonomy. Undoubtedly the unpopularity of the centralized synodal bureaucracy headed by a lay overprocurator accounts for this remarkable consensus; yet the bishops also wished to restore a system more in conformity with canon law and church tradition. Certainly the historical studies of the early church and its ministries published by the ecclesiastical academies gave the bishops (or the commissions appointed to draft the *Replies*) material which they utilized.[11] The responses generally asserted that ecclesiastical provinces would give the church more independence, while reorganization would allow it to practice regular conciliarity (*sobornost'*), an objective less easily realized on the national level.[12]

Each ecclesiastical province was to have a canonically based synod, empowered to elect bishops and hear complaints against them. Such complaints, if serious enough, could lead to a bishop's deposition. The crucial issue implied in decentralization was the church's dependence on the state: since Peter I, all bishops had been appointed by a decree of the Holy Synod, which was, in fact, an organ of the state. On this point, several bishops quoted Apostolic canon 30,[13] which considers invalid any episcopal appointment "by worldly rulers"; interpreted literally, it would actually mean that *all* the episcopal appointments since Peter were invalid! Few, however, advocated that it be so applied.

Thus, while basing their proposals on ancient canonical tradition, the *Replies* had to avoid unrealistic and artificial attempts at copying the structure of the early church, which existed under different historical conditions. Several influential bishops were aware of this fact and pointed to the twentieth-century requirement of the Russian church: reestablishment of canonical *norms*, not slavish imitation of ancient structures.[14] The old and respected Metropolitan Flavian of Kiev summarized the problems and goals of the projected reform in four points. (1) Dioceses closely tied to the central administration in St. Petersburg are actually isolated from each other and are unable to meet regional pastoral problems. (2) Conciliarity (*sobornost'*) must first be practiced in regions and "neighborhoods," that is, in the ecclesiastical provinces presided over by their metropolitans. (3) The existing centralized bureaucracy has assumed a power which canonically belongs to the bishops of a region meeting in council. (4) Reform would allow the creation of smaller and more numerous dioceses (in each *uezd*), thereby enabling bishops to be effective pastors of their flocks, not inaccessible high administrators.[15] (On this last point Archbishop Antonii of Volyn suggested that "auxiliary" bishops—an institution borrowed recently from western Christianity—be suppressed and more numerous and smaller dioceses be established.[16]

A substantial number of *Replies* suggested that, in addition to the presiding metropolitan and bishops, the provincial councils include clergy and laity although some wished to grant them only a consultative role.[17] Antonii of Volyn protested virulently against any "democratic" participation by clergy and laity in councils, but his remarks are exceptional.[18] Clearly, the pattern of debate about provincial councils conforms precisely to that surrounding the composition of a national council for the entire Russian church—a debate then going on in the theological periodicals.

The *Replies* also include specific plans for the future ecclesiastical provinces, the number of which varies in the proposals from seven to fifteen. Those who favored seven provinces followed obvious geographic, ethnic, and historical divisions.[19] Such provinces were to include the northwest (St. Petersburg), central Russia (Moscow), the South (Kiev), the Caucasus (Tiflis), Belorussia, the East (Kazan) and Siberia. Other bishops recommended further subdivisions of these vast areas.

The plans for ecclesiastical regionalism could not ignore the national diversity of the Russian Empire. In 1905, national awareness had not yet become a critical issue, but it appears in some of the *Replies.* As a Russian nationalist, Stefan of Mogilev mentioned the danger of Georgian separatism as a disadvantage of regionalism (which he otherwise supported) and suggested that the future "metropolitan of the Caucasus," exercising jurisdiction in areas distinct from those of the Catholicos (national patriarch) of Georgia, always be a Russian.[20] The bishops of Belorussia and the Ukraine refer in passing to the need for preserving a unified "Russia." However, an opposite trend also found free expression. The exarch of Georgia openly claimed that traditional autocephaly (i.e., complete independence) should be restored to the

Georgian church. In his view, religious independence would not lead to political separatism.[21]

A further proposal for autonomy came from Tikhon, bishop "of the Aleutian islands and North America" (and future patriarch of Moscow), who suggested that a separate, autonomous (and possibly autocephalous) church in America be created. He argued that the Russian bishop of this diocese finds himself under completely different political conditions, for he is the head of a multinational religious body which includes not only Russian and Carpatho-Russian immigrants, but also Aleuts, Indians, Eskimos, as well as Serbs, Syrians, Greeks, and others.[22] Tikhon's project, which displayed a remarkable perception of the situation, subsequently served as an authoritative pattern for the creation of the American autocephalous church in 1970.

With the exception of only four bishops, the entire Russian episcopate in 1905 demanded restoration of the patriarchate suppressed by Peter the Great. Three of the dissenters apparently feared any substantial reform, including a council, in a revolutionary atmosphere.[23] The fourth, Paisii of Turkestan, belonged to the opposite extreme. He was afraid that a patriarch might be more easily controlled by the state than a collective body, and consequently he defended a collegiate and elective principle for all levels of church administration.[24]

While defending a restored partiarchate, the majority of bishops criticized the "synodal" regime as uncanonical and contradicting the principle of *sobornost'*. A patriarch responsible for a conciliar form of government would assure the church's independence from the centralized state bureaucracy.[25] Beyond these basic arguments, some *Replies* also reasoned that Orthodox tradition requires every national church to be led personally by the bishop of its major city: among the Orthodox churches, only the Russian church since Peter I lacked this personal leadership.

However, the near unanimity in favor of the patriarchate did not extend to the description of the patriarch's role and responsibility. I. Sokolov, a learned historian of the patriarchate of Constantinople whose opinion on the canonical aspect of the projected reforms had been requested by the metropolitan of St. Petersburg, took the view

that a partiarch acted as the head of a council.[26] The vast majority of
the bishops, however, described the patriarch as only the "first among
equals," so that the council of all the bishops would be the supreme
authority, able to pass judgment upon the patriarch himself.[27] No
unanimity emerged either among the bishops or in the church at large
on the issue of the future council's composition. Some favored a purely
episcopal assembly; others insisted that it also include clergy and laity.

Clearly the *Replies* could not address or solve all problems of central
church authority; they merely anticipated later discussions, on the
meaning of *sobornost'* and its possible institutional expressions, which
took place in the preconciliar meetings and in the ecclesiastical journals
between 1905 and 1917. The solution finally accepted at the council of
1917-18 clearly determined that the patriarch was to be responsible to
a council composed of bishops, clergy, and laity. However, the statute
of 1917 also safeguarded the bishops' particular role by giving them a
collective veto power over all the council's decisions. This solution
(which resembles a sort of parliamentary bicameralism) was anticipated
in the *Reply* by Archbishop Sergii of Finland (the future *locum tenens*
and patriarch) when he suggested a procedure for patriarchal elections.
Three candidates for patriarch were to be nominated respectively by
the house of bishops, by the "lower" house of clergy and laity, and by
the tsar. The patriarch would then be designated by lot.[28] It is worth
noting that Patriarch Tikhon's election in October 1917 was accomplished by lot after nominations by the entire council (bishops, clergy,
and laity, but not the tsar!).

Obviously in 1905 no bishops foresaw either the end of the monarchy or the separation of church and state. Most of the *Replies* desired
a benevolent, liberal Russian state in which the restored patriarchate
would play an independent and socially meaningful role. The vast
majority believed St. Petersburg would be the patriarch's normal residence. Only two bishops thought Moscow, the historic see of former
Russian metropolitans and patriarchs, should again become the religious
capital of Russia.[29]

An inevitable consequence of the system which reduced the clergy
to a closed caste (*soslovie*) was that the priest's role in Russian society
became almost exclusively cultic. The formal administrative obligations

to register births and marriages and limited participation in the state educational system could not provide the clergy with a significant social function. Actually, there is some connection between contemporary Soviet legislation restricting the church to "cultic" activities and the requirements of the Petrine system. The pre-Revolutionary Russian clergy's strong sense of being social outcasts certainly influenced, directly or indirectly, some of the demands and suggestions voiced in the *Replies*. Eventually this social question became the central issue and dominated the debates during the council of 1917-18. For this reason, too, most members of the council vigorously defended the recently developed system of parochial schools as a means for integrating church and society more harmoniously, despite the fact that both the Duma and the Provisional Government considered these schools outdated and financially cumbersome. Another aspect of this same phenomenon can be seen in the "renovated" or "living" church of the 1920s, which to a large extent became a movement of "white clergy" and some socially oriented intellectuals against the most ascetic ideals represented by the monastically inclined episcopate. Only Antonii (Khrapovitskii) of Volyn stood athwart this drive for greater social participation. His vituperative *Reply* in 1905 against "progressive," "republican," and "democratic" priests not only reflected his conservative ideology (in which he was not very consistent) but also his personal aristocratic background (quite exceptional among the bishops). He despised the clergy as a caste, but in this he stood very much alone.[30]

On the whole, the bishops in 1905 succeeded in avoiding such extreme positions and expressed only theological and pastoral considerations. A majority demanded that the clergy be given a voice in the political and social life of Russia not as spokesmen for class interests but as witnesses of Christ's message. As citizens, it was thought, members of the clergy should be given the right to participate in elections to the *zemstvo*, the city duma and the State Duma.[31] Election to such assemblies would assure that a responsible and articulate voice of the church was heard.[32] These demands had already been presented in the memorandum of Antonii of St. Petersburg mentioned earlier. He had suggested that the patriarch and some bishops be ex officio members of the State Council.

While generally advocating a greater social role for the clergy, several bishops also warned against the dangers of politics, quoting ancient canons prohibiting the clergy's assumption of direct political power and legal financial responsibilities. If elected to legislative bodies, it was to contribute to debates dealing with church building, education, welfare, and morality. Clergymen were not to participate in politics as such.[33] Interestingly enough, Bishop Evlogii of Kholm, subsequently a prominent and very active member of the State Duma, was among those who gave such warnings. Actually, the bishops were aware of the difficulty of precisely demarcating those "politics" forbidden to the clergy from those "social responsibilities" which are an unavoidable part of the church's function. Clearly, but understandably, they lacked practical experience in such matters.

The content of the *Replies* by the Russian bishops in 1905 can be analyzed and criticized from different angles. From a theological standpoint, for example, the issue of the respective roles of bishops, lower clergy, and laity at a council, as it was discussed in the *Replies*, cannot be truly solved without first establishing basic ecclesiological presuppositions on the nature of local churches (or dioceses), the manner of electing bishops, and the nature of the episcopal ministry. The notion of *sobornost'* is much too vague and insufficient to give an answer to concrete ecclesiological issues — the ecclesiological ideas underlying the *Replies* would thus require a separate study. Similarly, the influence exercised by the prevailing trends in social thought — toward liberal democracy, romantic *narodnichestvo*, and conservatism — need serious analysis. Finally, the purely historical prosopographic importance of the collection of *Replies* is undeniable, inasmuch as all the major personalities of Russian church history in the revolutionary and post-Revolutionary era are among the authors: Tikhon (Bellavin), bishop of the Aleutian islands and North America, who became the first patriarch (1918-25); Sergii (Stragorodskii), archbishop of Finland, the future *locum tenens*, (1926-43) and patriarch (1943-44); Evlogii (Georgievskii), bishop of Kholm, later metropolitan of Western Europe (1922-46) and leader of the influential Russian Orthodox community in Paris; Antonii (Khrapovitskii), archbishop of Volyn, later metropolitan of Kiev, and eventually the head of the "Russian Orthodox church in exile" in Sremski Karlovci, Yugoslavia; and many others. It should be noted that most of the *Replies* reflect the work of commissions established in dioceses, some of which, especially those working in such intellectual centers as St. Petersburg, Moscow, Kiev, and Kazan, where the local bishop could utilize the resources of the theological academies, have produced reports of great scholarly interest. Elsewhere, the work of the commissions reflects the trends among provincial clergy and church leadership.

All these elements contribute to making the collection of *Replies* probably the most representative and comprehensive document on the Russian church's condition in the Old Regime's last years.

NOTES

1. Cf. F. Dvornik, *Early Christian and Byzantine Political Philosophy. Origins and Background*, Dumbarton Oaks Studies, no. 9, Washington, D.C., 1966, I-II; also my article "Justinian, the Empire and the Church," *Dumbarton Oaks Papers,* XXII, 1968, 45-60; also more briefly the author's *Byzantine Theology: Historical Trends and Doctrinal Themes*, New York, 1974, 213-16.

2. *Otzyvy eparkhial'nykh arkhiereev po voprosam o tserkovnoi reforme,* 3 vols., St. Petersburg, 1906, and *Pribavleniia.*

3. For a general review of the events see A. Bogolepov, *Church Reforms in Russia, 1905-1918,* Bridgeport, Conn., 1966 (reprinted from *St. Vladimir's Seminary Quarterly,* 1965); cf. also J.S. Curtiss, *Church and State in Russia: The Last Years of the Empire, 1900-1917,* New York, 1940, reprinted 1965; James Cunningham, "Reform in the Russian Church, 1900-1906: The Struggle for Autonomy and the Restoration of Byzantine Symphonia," Ph.D. diss., University of Minnesota 1973.

4. Metropolitan Antonii's *zapiska* was published in *Slovo*, 28 March 1905, and reprinted in I.V. Preobrazhenskii, ed., *Tserkovnaia reforma: sbornik statei dukhovnoi i svetskoi periodicheskoi pechati po voprosu o reforme*, St. Petersburg, 1905, 133-36.

5. Text in *Slovo*, 28 March 1905.

6. Text in *Tserkovnyi vestnik*, 1905, 11; reproduced in *Tserkovnaia reforma*, 1-6.

7. *Otzyvy eparkhial'nykh arkhiereev*, III, 276. This was the opinion of Sergii (Stragorodskii), archbishop of Finland.

8. Cf. in this volume Paul Valliere's study on "The Idea of a Council in Russian Orthodoxy in 1905."

9. This aspect of the *Replies* will not be discussed here; the liturgical and disciplinary reforms suggested by the bishops are particularly emphasized in the only (and very brief) existing survey of the *Replies* by N. Zernov, "The Reform of the Church and the pre-revolutionary Russian Episcopate," *St. Vladimir's Seminary*

Quarterly, VI, 1962, no. 3, 128-38 (originally published in N. Berdiaev's periodical *Put'*, Paris, 1934).

10. *Otzyvy*, III, 387.

11. The books most frequently quoted are A.P. Lebedev, *Dukhovenstvo drevnei vselenskoi tserkvi*, Moscow, 1905, and P. Gidulianov, *Mitropolity v pervye tri veka khristianstva*, Moscow, 1905, the second study being the much more substantial. The various ecclesiastical periodicals also devoted numerous articles to the issue during the period 1904-17.

12. Cf. Nikanor of Perm, *Otzyvy*, II, 389.

13. For example, Konstantin of Samara, *Ibid.*, I, 431.

14. Cf. the opinion of Professor A. Brilliantov, included in the remarks of St. Petersburg Metropolitan Antonii, *Ibid.*, III, 117; and Sergii of Finland, III, 227.

15. *Ibid.*, II, 103.

16. *Ibid.*, I, 122.

17. Stefan of Mogilev, *Ibid.*, I, 99-100; Simeon of Ekaterinoslav, I, 77; Flavian of Kiev, II, 75.

18. *Ibid.*, I, 112-20.

19. Cf. the *Replies* from Kursk, Perm, Volyn, Grodno, Olonets, Tomsk, Riazan, and America.

20. *Ibid.*, I, 97.

21. *Ibid.*, III, 510. Georgia, a country Christianized in the fourth century, has been led by a "catholicos" since the sixth century. Political annexation by Russia early in the nineteenth century was followed by the suppression of this Georgian national patriarchate and the appointment of a Russian "exarch of Georgia."

22. *Ibid.*, I, 531.

23. Parfenii of Podolsk, *Ibid.*, II, 490; Lavrentii of Tula, III, 381-82; Dimitrii, auxiliary of Podolsk, II, 491.

24. *Ibid.*, I, 50-52.

25. See particularly the *Replies* from Ufa, II, 54-55; Pskov, II, 205-06; Kiev, II, 103; Moscow, III, 253-55; Warsaw, II, 273; Riazan, III, 577; Volyn, III, 186-94; Orenburg, II, 146-47; Kholm, II, 466; and America, I, 530.

26. *Ibid.*, III, 128-29.

27. Cf., for example, the *Replies* from St. Petersburg, III, 86; Moscow, III, 256; Kaluga, I, 29; Viatka, II, 509; Kholm, II, 466; Stavropol, II, 261; Finland, III, 260, 270; Orel, I, 521; Orenburg, II, 148; Irkutsk, II, 227.

28. *Ibid.*, III, 270.

29. *Ibid.*, Tambov, III, 318; Finland, III, 269.

30. *Ibid.*, I, 112-20.

31. *Ibid.*, Chernigov, I, 111.

32. *Ibid.*, Polotsk, I, 137; Khar'kov, I, 20; Kaluga, I, 33; America, I, 545.

33. *Ibid.*, Voronezh, I, 45; Novgorod, II, 20; Kholm, II, 489; Kazan, III, 436.

The Idea of a Council
in Russian Orthodoxy in 1905

Paul R. Valliere

The Russian Orthodox church was one of the most important institutions to feel the impact of the 1905 revolution. Any modification of its ecclesiastical structure and laws would inevitably have profound consequences for every class in imperial Russian society. Therefore, it is not surprising to find a diversity of opinions about church reform, a circumstance easily confirmed by even a cursory glance at the literature of the period. These opinions are not easily summarized, but debate did tend to focus on certain crucial issues, particularly the relationship of the Orthodox church to the imperial government.

If the issue of church and state became the focal point of discussion, then it must be added that bureaucrats, bishops, sectarians, free-thinkers, aesthetes, and other interested parties approached the question in their own ways and according to their own interests. Each group viewed the question through its own special lenses. However, this essay is mainly concerned with the approach taken by the Russian Orthodox majority within the established church, which saw at the heart of the church-state issue the question of a *sobor*, that is, a national council of the Russian Orthodox church. Supporters of a council argued that not only would such an assembly provide an appropriate context for discussing church-state relations, but it would also offer a partial solution to the problem by giving the church an independent, nongovernmental standpoint from which to address the confused and troubled Russia of 1905. By analyzing the "idea" of a council in 1905, therefore, a clue may be found to the mind of the Russian Orthodox majority on one of the leading problems of the period.

The "idea" of a council must be distinguished from its "problem" or "politics," which are, of course, relevant features of church reform during those revolutionary years. Certainly many contemporaries felt that the problems and politics of a council were more urgent than the basic concept. The difficulty was in convincing bureaucrats to allow a council and in getting the tsar to convene one—a complex task, as the checkered career of Russia's conciliar movement after 1905 shows. Conciliar politics, too, were complicated and derived their urgency and intricacy from the conflicts of power and interest among the numerous parties in the imperial state. These obstacles and polemics often occupied center stage.

Yet despite the maneuverings and conflicts which consumed so much energy, it may be suggested that the central issue was not purely or even primarily a political one, but a theological one which had to be fought and settled on the basis of Orthodox tradition. After all, from the political standpoint, the struggle was essentially a matter of distributing power. The long history of synodal administration had left the imperial government with a great deal of power, the church with very little. If the Synod disappeared, who was going to wield authority in the church and how much power would he possess? Interest groups combated each other to answer this question. These practical politics, however, led to a more difficult problem: the church had lost the habit of exercising power and had no suitable organization for utilizing any new power it might acquire. A simple clash of vested interests could raise this question but not provide an adequate solution. The structure of the church, its relation to Russian society, the proper form of authority, and even Orthodox communal identity were at stake. These matters had to be settled on theological and canonical grounds.

How ecclesiastical politics could transform a practical problem into a theological one is illustrated by the events of early 1905. In December 1904 the imperial government proposed granting religious liberty to non-Orthodox groups, thereby awakening many Orthodox hierarchs to the alarming prospect of being the only religious leaders in the empire without freedom of action vis-à-vis the state. Orthodoxy would find itself at a disadvantage with regard to competitors, particularly the schism. Metropolitan Antonii of St. Petersburg spoke before the Committee of Ministers, which was discussing the government's religious politics, and raised a number of basic questions about freedom for the church, its lower clergy, and hierarchy. However, he hesitated to ask for a council or the restoration of the patriarchate.[1] Overprocurator Pobedonostsev's machinations succeeded in transferring the matter from the Committee of Ministers to the Holy Synod, but to his surprise and dismay the synodal bishops urged that a national council of Russian bishops be called to elect a patriarch. Using the pretext of presenting the tsar an icon, the bishops petitioned him for permission. Nicholas II promised to call a council "when a favorable time shall come."[2] Meanwhile, the Synod solicited the opinions of all Russian bishops on reform and organized the preconciliar meetings (*predsobornoe prisutstvie*), held in 1906. At this point a serious question arose among both clergy and laity: to whom does a council belong? To the Synod? To the bishops of the church? To a restored patriarch? For many Orthodox none of these answers appeared satisfactory. They felt that a council should belong to the whole church: wholeness seemed proper for the Orthodox community.[3] Thus, what began as a practical request for a church council resulted in a theological debate about its nature. All practical suggestions for reform can be fully understood only against this theological background.

The social background of the conciliar movement must also be recognized, for a council could serve too as a powerful social symbol. "Social symbol" here means an idea made concrete with the power to shape social action and sustain a mode of community. Historic religious traditions, whatever else they may be, are in this sense repositories of social symbols. A political analysis of church-state relations must recognize the church's wealth of symbols, yet even the most thorough political treatment cannot exhaust the meaning such symbols embody. On one level, religious institutions exist alongside other organizations and possess certain powers, prerogatives, responsibilities, and limits. On another level, religious institutions transcend these ordinary limits and acquire a mystique or higher value.[4] Russian Orthodoxy contained many social symbols, but the idea of "conciliarity" (*sobornost'*) proved to be one of the richest.

The symbolic status of a council was a matter of particular urgency in 1905, for Russia's religious institutions were feeling the full impact of that vast and complex process of social change called modernization. In fact, the question of church and state in 1905 arose as a consequence of the growing secularization of Russia's social and political life and the new toleration of religious pluralism. These trends, which are a normal facet of modernity, qualified the power of religious symbols and institutions by relativizing them or at least restricting their scope. By 1905, the symbolic aspect of a council had particularly felt the force of these changes. The tradition of summoning councils had been broken two centuries earlier by Peter I's first efforts to modernize Russia. Thus, when the question of the council was raised within the context of a much later shock of modernity, the 1905 revolution, it possessed as a symbol no great security or strength. Yet, despite the sea change which modernity was working on Russia's symbols, they were not necessarily on the brink of disappearing or incapable of expressing human needs. One of the striking things about the symbol of a council is that so many Russians expended so much energy and passion on its behalf.

The Russian word for council—*sobor*—has rich connotations and historical associations which render its meaning more complex than that of its English equivalent. In the Creed, *sobornyi* is used to convey the notion of "catholicity" in the Church Universal. *Sobor* also implies a collective, communal form of social organization, and, moreover, it has a specific historical link with the seven ecumenical councils, whose dogmatic and canonical norms a national *sobor* or council could not violate. There is really no other way to define Orthodoxy as a historic tradition. In this sense, *sobornost'* implies assent to Orthodoxy.

These rich connotations and associations invited a diversity of ideas about a national Russian council. By 1905, nearly all religious publicists agreed that there was something uncanonical in the administration of the Russian Orthodox church and that a return to canonicity required a council. Beyond this general agreement, conceptions varied. They may be arranged spectrally from a minimalist through a moderate to a maximalist interpretation of the council. The spectrum corresponds roughly to the shades of emphasis distinguishing a literal-historic from a spiritualizing-ideal mode of interpretation. In institutional terms, opinions can be categorized according to the role assigned the episcopal hierarchy in the council.

A typical and influential minimalist view is provided by V.M. Skvortsov, an important promoter of Russian Orthodox missionary efforts at home and abroad and the editor of *Missionary Survey* (*Missionerskoe obozrenie*).[5] In a review of ecclesiastical politics in early 1905, Skvortsov leaves in no doubt his satisfaction with what he understands to be the Holy Synod's plan "to petition the Tsar for the reestablishment of the Patriarchate for the honor of Russia and for that reason to gather a national council of eparchial bishops in Moscow to choose a Patriarch and discuss in Council the imminent needs of Church life."[6] He begins by explaining that in January 1905 *Missionary Survey* had intended to advocate publicly the restoration of the patriarchate, but that as editor he had agreed with the censors not to do so for fear of "shaking the foundations of the central church authority." The subsequent, unexpected explosion of discussion about church reform made such fears irrelevant. "Two months ago we neither expected nor intended anything of this sort—and not only we poor mortals but even the very people standing in the forefront of the reform."[7] In this changed environment Skvortsov's ideas seemed very limited. He wished only to see the Russian bishops meet in a council to elect a patriarch, and was shocked by the public's earnest questions about the necessity for this leader, who, he felt, could provide firm direction in uncertain times; he argued "that for the raising of Church discipline a strong authority in the person of a Patriarch is necessary."[8] Not only was Skvortsov alarmed by the public attitude toward this question, he also felt dismayed by the debate over the council membership. He regarded participation by the lower clergy and laity with suspicion, for in his view bishops serve as the guardians of Orthodoxy. Thus, convening a council and electing a patriarch promoted the same end: creation of an independent, centralized, authoritarian, and disciplined church.

Skvortsov's ideas can be defended on historical grounds. The pre-eminent position of the patriarchate finds legitimacy in the *status quo ante* of the seventeenth century. Furthermore, his insistence on episco-pal primacy in a council reflects the historically dominant part played by bishops in conciliar Orthodoxy, particularly in the ecumenical coun-cils. However, a less rigorous stance than Skvortsov's idea of a council could be taken without necessarily denying the bishops a leading role. Moderates in the public debate of 1905 offered a different conception of a bishop and an alternative proposal for council membership. For moderates a bishop was not so much the appointed guardian of Ortho-doxy as an organic embodiment of *sobornost'*, the unity and consensus of the Orthodox community. Thus, the moderate party shifted the issue from episcopal authority to episcopal vocation. They wanted to know whether the bond between the Russian bishops and their local communities in fact expressed the organic unity of the whole church.

The "Memorandum of a Group of Thirty-two Priests of the Capital on the Necessity for Changes in Russian Church Governance" gives a good summation of moderate views. As the most widely publicized unofficial statement on church reform in the spring of 1905, the "Memorandum" calls for the convening of a national council for "the great and holy aim of restoring the canonical freedom of the Orthodox Church in Russia."[9] Institutionally, canonical freedom meant the "self-government" (*samoupravlenie*) of the church through conciliar action in the spirit of *sobornost'*. Episcopal authority was not openly challenged but had to be justified as a derivative of Orthodoxy's organic unity that was rooted in the local parishes:

If recreated norms of canonical Church structure are to find a place in the organizing and securing of ecclesiastical self-government for our Orthodox Church, then in the forefront must come the ordering and development of episcopal governance in strict conformity with the spirit of the canons, which establish broad latitude for *sobornost'* in the Church. This *sobornost'* is rooted in the independent, widely developed life of the parishes as the lowest units, the cells, of Church life; and at the top it is crowned by periodic councils of the whole Church, with the archbishop of the capital city acting as chairman. These councils select from their own number a holy or most holy synod under the chairmanship of the same archbishop for the purpose of the regular administration of the Church during the intervals between these councils. Distinguished from the other bishops by this, his [special] honor, the archbishop of the capital, because of this honor—that is, as the chairman and representative of the periodic councils for the whole Church and the governing synod—bears the title of All-Russian Patriarch.[10]

The intention of this statement is clarified by a number of specific institutional proposals designed to attune the hierarchy to *sobornost'*. The "Thirty-two Priests" of St. Petersburg called for institutional recognition of the equality of all bishops, great and small. They criticized the Russian pattern of large dioceses and urged subdivision. In their opinion, the attendant increase in the number of bishops was desirable because smaller episcopal units would better ensure the close identity of the bishop with his flock. They also called for the restoration of periodic councils in the metropolitanates as a guarantee of middle level conciliar practice in the church and as an antidote to the centralization of *sobornost'* in the All-Russian Council. They found the distinguishing mark of a metropolitan to be solely his position as head of these middle level councils and not in any supposed greatness of his eparchy.[11] These proposals and others in the same spirit which came up often in moderate circles in 1905 aimed to instill the habit of *sobornost'* into every member and office of the Orthodox community.

Skvortsov had nothing good to say about the "Memorandum" of the "Thirty-two," but it is revealing that he did not raise canonical objections to their ideas. He criticized the group's conspiratorial style as being unfit for the church, and chided them for exaggerating the evils of the uncanonical Synod, which Skvortsov himself admits is the church's "Achilles heel." Skvortsov feared their actions would harm missionary work, particularly among the schismatics.[12] His opposition to their views was not canonical, for the group did not formally depart from church law. Instead, these priests emphasized the spirit rather than the letter of the canons. Skvortsov saw canon law as a means to impose discipline and ensure central direction; for the "Thirty-two" and other moderates, canonical order safeguarded freedom:

"Stand fast in the freedom that Christ has given you, and do not submit to the yoke of slavery." (Gal. 5:1) This grand call of the apostle sounds not only for individual believers and not only in its outdated meaning of freedom from the yoke of the old law. It sounds eternally and authoritatively for the whole Church as well, demanding among other things the preservation of the independence and freedom of the Church from everything that enslaves and threatens to enslave it to the external yoke of worldly principles and ends. The Church must not submit to the conditions and requirements of social governmental life no matter the height attained by these requirements, for it will always be only a relative height; the Church must act always as a free power of grace, proclaiming the acceptable year of the Lord. . . . The restoration of Church freedom cannot and must not be accomplished otherwise than through restoring the efficacy of the canons that guard this freedom, in all their fullness and purity.[13]

The church is free. This is the good news that the moderates preached: canon is a rule but not a fetter, for the rule is freedom. There is a quality of exaltation here. The freedom of the church is not relative, which is to say granted by the state or by any other configuration of social forces. It is, in the sense of religious transcendence, freedom from "the external yoke of worldly principles and ends." This evangelical freedom is an end in itself. It is the church's "consciousness of her inner integrity, the witness of the Spirit that dwells within her, that in her innermost self she lives only by His eternal truth, that she is free from worldly principles and knows no other influences or commands but the influences of the Holy Spirit and the injunctions of her divine destiny."[14]

The lay theologian N.P. Aksakov spells out some of the implications of the "Memorandum of the Thirty-two" in a sensitive theological commentary entitled "Canon and Freedom."[15] His criticism of the "Thirty-two" is intended to purify, not alter, their position. Thus he objects to any description of the "Memorandum" as the "opinion" of a "group," for these priests were expressing the "ideal" of canonical freedom which has been valid from apostolic times and about which there can be no argument, hence no "opinions."[16] He also objects to the priests' frequent appeals for "changes" (*peremeny*) in Russian church governance rather than speaking consistently of the need for "restoration" (*vostanovlenie*): "One can make changes as many times and in as many directions as one wants, but there can only be one restoration. A change depends on human opinion and in general on human judgment, but the necessity of restoration derives from the very essence of the Church and the tasks imposed upon her by her Divine Founder. If the legal structure is forgotten or broken, it is unconditionally necessary to restore it; this has the significance of a categorical imperative."[17] Clearly Aksakov is arguing that canonical freedom gives the church a religious transcendence enabling it to rise above the social divisions of party, interest, and opinion. Understandably, he goes on to contend that the church not only "secured external freedom for itself" in the canons, but also that it originally "apportioned its entire life according to the principle of internal freedom." Canonical freedom is more than a prerogative of the church; it is its way of life:

In a church faithful to her norms of self-government, her holy canons, there is no place either for the caprice and despotism of individuals, whatever their hierarchical position, or for the despotism of a victorious majority that somehow rallies and establishes itself; there is in her no principle of monarchial power [edinovlastie] nor any kind of oligarchy, for power belongs only to the church herself in her entirety, and the implementation of this power is accomplished only by means of conciliar definitions, with the constant control of lower councils by higher if the decisions of the lower give room for dissatisfaction and do not secure the peace of the church.[18]

Aksakov also contends that politically the church should express its commitment to freedom in a policy of religious freedom. As a community standing beyond ordinary social divisions, it must use in its social and political mission only the means appropriate to its transcendence. For this reason the church ought to limit itself to "spiritual" and "religious-moral influence on individuals," pursuing a pacific and voluntary approach to social action.[19] Aksakov and most other moderates did not approve of magisterial, not to mention outright authoritarian methods in church affairs.

The moderates' emphasis on the organic quality of *sobornost'* discloses its social aspect; but for them the social element in *sobornost'* could not be detached from the historic institutions of Orthodoxy, and through these unique institutions the church expressed its transcendence of history and society. A certain dualism of church and society was accepted as fitting and even inevitable. "Maximalists" among church reformers were inspired by a quite different vision. They wished to abandon the moderates' dualism in favor of interpreting *sobornost'* as a more comprehensive social reality. This radical shift accompanied a pronounced deemphasis on historical Orthodoxy. The early councils of the church were seen as the first fruits of a greater realization of *sobornost'* to be consummated in the life of a whole people—the Russian people in particular. The maximalist idea of a council might be characterized as theological "populism" (*narodnichestvo*).

A radical lay contingent of maximalists, including Merezhkovskii, Rozanov, and Ternavtsev, aired their views in the Religious-Philosophical Assemblies of 1901-3. These laymen banded together to solve what they understood to be the essential religious problems of Russian culture and of modern culture as a whole: the reconciliation of Christ and the world, church and society, God and man. Traditional Christianity, they argued, insists upon dualism. It demands that the church ascetically deny man and the world, thereby leaving both to the forces of godless secularity. To escape from this spiritual schism, it is essential to acquire a new spirituality, one which can generate a cultural synthesis uniting God's justice with the justice of earth and humanity.[20]

All humanity must labor to create this union of divine and worldly justice; however, Merezhkovskii and his associates expected the first steps to be taken in Russia with the reconciliation of the intelligentsia and the Orthodox church. The party of humanity and the party of divinity would become one; a social unity would result. Through the church—the repository of the Russian people's living faith—the intelligentsia would be united with the people. In Ternavtsev's opinion the church was more "popular" (*narodna*) than any other institution in Russian society. "The intelligentsia does not see this, does not understand this," while ascetically minded hierarchs do not take it seriously enough to begin the social mission that the *narodnost'* of the church implies. According to Ternavtsev, this social mission is "diaconic"; that is, the church must find a religious solution to the problem of property.[21] Renewal of the church's social mission will be a step toward a new society for all Russians. Ternavtsev and other lay radicals had no interest in any dimension of the church which was not "popular"; at the very best they were indifferent to the Orthodox hierarchy. Quite unlike moderate reformers who spoke of renewing the church's organic community, maximalists talked of renewing the organic community of Russian society as a whole. In doing so, the historic church would be transcended by its inclusion in an unprecendented religio-cultural synthesis.

In the maximalist idea of a council, *narodnost'* is the central point. The term is prescriptive and moral, not descriptive: it indicates a community with a deep spiritual consensus. *Narodnost'* is *sobornost'* realized in social action. Rozanov typically expressed the social spirit of the maximalist understanding of *sobornost'*.

Russia, i.e., the Orthodox people, is in the religious and ecclesiastical sphere not something vacuous, but rather the "very body of the Church" in the sense of the Eastern patriarchs' well-known letter to the Roman pope in the mid-nineteenth century, composed in response to his invitation to a council contemplated by the latter [the pope] : "We cannot appear with our people; and without our people we are not the Church; and our opinion without their approval is not the opinion of the Church," answered hierarchs of the East. According to Khomiakov as well as the fundamental teaching of the Orthodox dogmas about the "catholic church," i.e., "the peoples' Church" [o "sobornoi tserkvi," t. e. o tserkvi "narodnoi"] , not the clergy of the Church but the whole Orthodox people is the preserver and guardian and even the final judge of the faith.[22]

Rozanov cites the rejection of the Florentine Union by the laity of the Christian East as an example of the "people" exercising their authority in the church, for the hierarchy had shown strong pro-Union sentiments. He then formulates a startling thought: "The people are the Church, *Ecclesia*, i.e., 'popular assembly.' The word, i.e., 'church,' was already in use with Pericles, and, taking this political term of the ancient self-governing commune as their own *name*, the fathers of the ecumenical councils never even thought of the 'church' otherwise than as a popular *mass*, a whole *nation*."[23] Adherents of historical Orthodoxy could only scowl at this clever play on words.

Because maximalists tended to think about *sobornost'* as mass consciousness, they expended little energy on devising the elaborate institutional proposals that typified the moderate party. However, they did advocate a decentralized church. *Sobornost'* would be realized in Spirit-filled local communes, and, following populist precedent, they thought of the communes as commensurate and compatible units, not reckoning with the possibility of differentiation or conflict. The social organizational model provided by the Old Believer communes appealed to the maximalists as exemplifying the identity of *sobornost'* and *narodnost'*. The pre-Petrine Orthodox parish had a similar appeal and its virtues were often noted in the lively debates about parish reform in 1905. In his remarkable "Memorandum on the Contemporary Situation of the Russian Church" of early 1905, the former Finance Minister S. Iu. Witte laid particular stress on the integrity of the old Russian parish which built its own church building, elected and supported its own clergy, financed educational and philanthropical projects and occasionally even functioned as a peasant bank and local court. The "communal principle" (*sobornoe nachalo*) which knit all these activities together and governed the parish Witte saw as "the distinguishing peculiarity of ancient Orthodoxy."[24]

As the major ideas about a council varied substantially, it is worth determining the practical difficulties of transcending these fundamental divisions. One might logically expect to find minimalists and moderates, who shared a commitment to historic Orthodoxy, moving toward a common ground, with the maximalists standing apart. In most periods of Orthodox history the issues separating minimalists and moderates on the one hand from the maximalists on the other would have produced insurmountable obstacles. Yet the discussion of the council being reviewed here could not have taken place in most periods of Orthodox history. The 1905 debates were conditioned by the unprecendented religious situation imposed by modernity. Alien, external forces of modern secularism and pluralism were changing Russia. The growth of such new studies as modern church history and historical theology altered Orthodoxy's traditional view of its own past, and nationalist sentiments among its peoples complicated its present and future. These historical changes had forced Orthodoxy to grapple with its own relativization. In such circumstances, new divisions and developments could arise within tradition itself, opening the way to an unprecedented communication with nontraditional forces.

One conflict illustrates the problem that developed between the minimalist and moderate parties working together in the preconciliar meetings. The members of section 1 sought to determine the composition of the council and the prerogatives of its constituent groups. A majority of the section called for a council of laity, lower clergy, and bishops, with the first two groups exercising only a "consultative vote" (*soveshchaiushchii golos*) while the bishops possessed a "deciding vote" (*reshaiushchii golos*). A significant minority of section 1 opposed this formula and published its dissenting opinion,[25] a pure crystallization of the moderate idea of a council. It admitted that church reform ought to have "a strictly canonical foundation," but this foundation must be understood as a canonical "ideal," as "the spirit of the canonical principles of the ancient universal church," rather than as the letter of the canon law. "The ideal is eternal, the forms are changeable as life is changeable in its constant progression." The historic canons "are not always and everywhere the same, and, moreover, like any other product of history, being suitable for their own time, they may be unsuitable for ours."[26] The source of the ideal is the Holy Spirit, the living reality and creator of *sobornost'*. A council is an occasion for the manifestation of the Spirit, and every council potentially can attain the measure of *sobornost'* manifested in that "authoritative example and model for the later councils," the Apostolic Council of Jerusalem, described in Acts 15. The Apostolic Council made "no distinction . . . between a consultative and a deciding vote," and lay people and presbyters deliberated alongside the apostles themselves.[27] The minority report also emphasized the communal aspect of *sobornost'*, claiming that "the Orthodox Church, calling itself '*sobornyi*,' i.e., founded on a communal, collective principle [*na nachale obshchinnom, khorovom*], by this essentially distinguishes itself from other church communities, for example, the western, founded upon other principles, such as papal, episcopal, presbyterian, et al."[28]

Professor Ilia Berdnikov of the Kazan Ecclesiastical Academy published a personal reply trenchantly criticizing the "Opinion" of the minority.[29] The key faults he found in the report were subjectivism and the danger that through manipulation of the word *sobornost'* modern modes of community might be substituted for Orthodox ones. Subjectivism derived from the minority's willingness to relativize the historic canons of Orthodoxy without providing a satisfactory structual alternative:

As for the "canonical foundation" upon which the drafters of the separate opinion propose to build the reform of Church governance, it is so hazy, so intangible by reason of its indefinability, that it is altogether beyond our comprehension. What is recommended is some sort of unattainable ideal, which has been realized nowhere and cannot be realized, some sort of inner primal foundation of the Church: Solomon himself would not be able to make it out. The one certainty is that for the drafters of the separate opinion it is not the teaching of the Orthodox Church that serves as this foundation, but something completely subjective.[30]

As for *sobornost'*, a word that "is continually buzzing in our ears in the sessions of section 1," Berdnikov quarreled with the minority's view that it is reducible to a "communal" (*obshchinnyi*) principle of church organization:

Identifying the conciliar (*sobornuiu*) Church as one founded on communal principles, the drafters of the separate opinion apparently think of it as having a character distinct from all Western church communes, not excluding the Protestant. But it is difficult to see what other kind of Christian commune is possible. Coming next in line after the Protestant commune would seem to be one of the democratic type. If so, then one must observe that the Orthodox Church by no means calls itself conciliar in this sense.[31]

Berdnikov concluded by reminding the minority that "*sobornyi*" translates the Greek word "*katholikos*" and thus refers to the worldwide identity of Orthodoxy, which is guaranteed by the dogmas and canons approved by the valid councils. Berdnikov goes so far as to suggest that if the Russian church really wants to live up to *sobornost'* it should consult the views and practices of the other Eastern Orthodox churches before resolving questions at the council, beginning with the question of the council's composition and the prerogatives of the groups involved. He seems to have thought, probably with justification, that such consultation would have a conservative influence on the council idea.

Berdnikov's criticisms were neither obscurantist nor reactionary. The minority did open the way to a subjective evaluation of Orthodox canons by historicizing them, and its sketch of a "communal, collective" Orthodoxy does invite comparison with modern democratic ideas of community. Many moderates who felt that a "democratic" Orthodoxy would evoke a sympathetic response from the party of modernity in Russia probably intended this comparison. Berdnikov's critique demonstrates that in some respects the moderates had more in common with the maximalists standing on the fringes of historic Orthodoxy than with the minimalists. On the practical institutional questions of 1905, such as parish structure, central administration, rights of the hierarchy, and the like, the moderate party often more closely identified itself with the maximalists than with the minimalists. Furthermore, Berdnikov was quite justified in suspecting that modern intellectual and social influences were entering Orthodox thought and practice by way of this alliance.

However, Berdnikov failed to see that his own position was not purely traditional or untouched by the dynamics of modern religious life. His appeal to a pure catholicity as the substance of *sobornost'* amounted to considerably more than a traditional confession of faith in historic Orthodoxy. It represented a kind of religious confessionalism that is as much a product of modernity as the idea of *sobornost'* current in modern circles. Berdnikov's idea of catholicity took shape in an environment quite different from that which formed the feeling and structure of traditional catholicity. The traditional idea did not require such a strained and radical defense, for whatever its problems may have been in earlier times, historical relativism was not one of them. Relativism constituted Berdnikov's central problem. Although he presented catholicity as a concrete, structural alternative to the hazy "canonical ideal" of the moderates, his catholicity in practice turns out to be every bit as transcendental and elusive. Which eastern churches, for example, did Berdnikov propose to consult regarding a "catholic" council — the church of Greece, or the Bulgarian church, or even the recently arabized patriarchate of Antioch? All three had to some degree departed from the traditional role of catholicity in the Christian East. And if he did not choose these but others, then it would be clear that

Berdnikov was selecting historical instances to support an ideal rather than basing his ideal on the unambiguous fact of traditional Orthodox catholicity.

Consequently, in the debate over the idea of a council, the issue between Berdnikov and his moderate and maximalist opponents was not traditional versus modern ideas but modern confessionalism versus whatever constituted the ideas common to moderates and minimalists. These ideas might be grouped together as "liberal"; however, it is possible to be more descriptive. Maximalists and minimalists saw a council as the consummation of a decentralized, federal, voluntary, and charismatic church. For them it represented a decentralized structure of religious community because it presupposed local centers as the primary foundation of *sobornost'*. The moral and spiritual consensus shared by local communities would make federalism possible, thereby actualizing the universal, catholic dimension of *sobornost'*. Moreover, a council stood for a voluntary and pacific means of building, sustaining, and defending community, since *sobornost'* was conceived as a purely moral force. Finally, it symbolized a charismatic community, for it was understood to be a happening of grace, not a historical product: a council gained legitimacy by the Spirit's presence within it.

The term "charismatic" is the most comprehensive of all. It describes the force that energizes and holds together a decentralized, federalist and noncoercive church. It also indicates the mystical, trans-historical status of the Church community. Above all, the term is appropriate to a description of the most striking point of contact between the moderates and maximalists — one lying not in the area of party interests or social ideology but in theology itself — the doctrine of the Holy Spirit. The frequent appeal by both moderates and maxima-lists to the Spirit as the giver and guide of the council stands in contrast to the relative unimportance of this theological theme in the minimalist literature.

The meaning of this meeting of theological views must not be senti-mentalized by denying the very different starting points, motives, and even final formulations of the doctrine in moderate and maximalist circles. The more radical maximalists, such as Merezhkovskii, arrived at the emphasis on the Spirit through their own acute sense of histori-cal expectation as well as their appreciation of this doctrine as one of the more open-ended issues in the traditional Christian revelation, hence one to which their own "new revelations" might be made rele-vant. The moderates came to the same emphasis by a more traditional route. In Orthodox theology the councils were always understood as belonging to the "economy of the Holy Spirit," and to the extent that a party chose to stress the conciliar character of the church, a doctrinal emphasis on the Spirit came naturally, even unselfconsciously. This emphasis always carried the added attraction for moderates of giving a very Orthodox, as opposed to western, tone to their theology, the em-phasis on the Spirit being traditionally a distinguishing mark of Orthodox dogmatics and piety. But whatever differences existed between the two appropriations of the doctrine of the Spirit, the fact of a meeting on this ground indicated a spiritual bond uniting moderates and maximalists.

To some extent this was a bond of shared pathos. Given the dynamics of modernization in Russia in 1905, it is difficult to say how the symbol of a Spirit-led council could have affected the development of modern Russian history. For that matter, it is difficult to say if a place exists for charismatic community in the modern world generally. The force of such doubts can be directed against the work of moderates and maximalists alike. This is not to say that the work of the reformers of 1905 had no sequel, for the council of 1917 stemmed directly from it. Still, this council was hardly a fair test of the significance and efficacy of the church reform movement: it took place amid violent revolution and was for that reason rushed and poorly attended in its crucial final sessions. Some good was accomplished with the revival of the patriarchate, which restored the canonical independence of the church of Russia. But this independence became virtually meaningless in the face of Bolshevik persecution of the church and the de facto suppression of the patriarchate after the death of Patriarch Tikhon in 1925; and it remains fundamentally compromised in the patriarchal church that has existed since 1943. The promise bequeathed by the church reform movement still waits to be fulfilled. Perhaps in some

future era of "great reforms," a new generation of Orthodox Christians
will recover and creatively apply the discussions and proposals of 1905.
These continue to embody the deepest and boldest reflections on the
problems of church, state, and society in the Russian Orthodox past.

NOTES

1. "Dokladnaia zapiska v Komitete Ministrov vysokopreosviashchennago
mitropolita Antoniia: Voprosy o zhelatel'nykh preobrazovaniiakh v postanovke
u nas pravoslavnoi tserkvi," in I.V. Preobrazhenskii, ed., *Tserkovnaia reforma:
sbornik statei dukhovnoi i svetskoi periodicheskoi pechati po voprosu o reforme,*
St. Petersburg, 1905, 133-36. Hereafter cited as *Tserkovnaia reforma.*

2. Quoted in John Shelton Curtiss, *Church and State in Russia: The Last Years
of the Empire, 1900-1917,* New York, 1940, reprinted 1965, 214.

3. "The central question troubling the ecclesiastical-social consciousness of
our day is that of calling of an all-Russian local council, of its composition and of
the relative importance of those rights with which clergy and laity may be
admitted to the council alongside the bishops. Since for the last two centuries a
council has not been summoned in our Church and the very tradition of the
councils of earlier times has been forgotten, it is natural with the restoration of
this ecclesiastical institution first of all to clarify the very idea of *sobornost';* all
the more insofar as the Orthodox Church, calling itself *sobornyi,* i.e., founded
on a communal, collective principle, essentially distinguishes itself by this from
other church communities founded upon other principles, for example, the
Western communities: papal, episcopal, presbyterian, et al." "Otdel'noe mnenie
men'shinstva chlenov I-go otdela Vysochaishe uchrezhdennago pri Sviateishem
Sinode Prisutstviia po voprosu o 'sostave sobora,'" *Zhurnaly i protokoly zasedanii
Vysochaishe uchrezhdennago Predsobornago Prisutstviia,* St. Petersburg, 1906, I,
581. Hereafter cited as *Zhurnaly i protokoly.* For a discussion of the "Otdel'noe
mnenie" see above, 195-96. For a bishop's defense of the opinion that a council
belongs to the whole church see Bishop Sergii's speech of 20 March 1905 in the
St. Petersburg Theological Academy, "Svoboda – dlia tserkvi, no ne dlia nas,"
Tserkovnyi vestnik, March 1905; reprinted in *Tserkovnaia reforma,* 32-33.

4. The state, too, can be the bearer of a mystique that transcends its purely
political role, but this is not a matter that can be treated here.

5. V. Skvortsov, "K istorii vozniknoveniia patriarshago voprosa (So skrizhalei
serdtsa)," *Missionerskoe obozrenie,* April 1905; reprinted in *Tserkovnaia reforma,*
316-29.

6. *Ibid.,* 327.

7. *Ibid.,* 317.

8. *Ibid.* Apparently this quotation is taken from the passage excised from the
January 1905 article on church reform.

9. "Zapiska gruppy iz 32-kh stolichnykh sviashchennikov: o neobkhodimosti
peremen v russkom tserkovnom upravlenii," *Tserkovnyi vestnik,* 17 March 1905;
reprinted in *Tserkovnaia reforma,* 1-6.

10. *Ibid.*, 5-6.

11. *Ibid.*, 4-5.

12. *Ibid.*, 321-22.

13. *Ibid.*, 3-4.

14. *Ibid.*, 2.

15. N. Aksakov, "Kanon i svoboda," *Tserkovnyi vestnik*, 28 April and 5 May 1905; reprinted in *Tserkovnaia reforma*, 440-46, 481-84.

16. *Ibid.*, 441-42.

17. *Ibid.*, 443.

18. *Ibid.*, 442.

19. *Ibid.*, 443-44.

20. The most concise statement of the overall problem and vision of the lay radicals in the Religious-Philosophical Assemblies is V. A. Ternavtsev's keynote address to the first meeting, "Russkaia tserkov' pred velikoiu zadachei," *Zapiski religiozno-filosofskikh sobranii v S. Peterburge*, 8-22. The *Zapiski* were published as supplements to the monthly numbers of *Novyi put'* (St. Petersburg) from January 1903 through January 1904. Pagination is consecutive from 1 to 531.

21. "Russkaia tserkov' pred velikoiu zadachei," 11-13.

22. V. Rozanov, "Trevozhnyi 'slukh'," *Novoe vremia*, 20 March 1905, reprinted in *Tserkovnaia reforma*, 15.

23. *Ibid.*, 15-16.

24. "O sovremennom polozhenii pravoslavnoi tserkvi (Zapiska S. Iu. Vitte), "Slovo," 28 March 1905, reprinted in *Tserkovnaia reforma*, 122-26.

25. "Otdel'noe mnenie men'shinstva chlenov I-go otdela Vysochaishe uchrezhdennago pri Sviateishem Sinode Prisutstviia po voprosu o 'sostave sobora'," *Zhurnaly i protokoly*, I, 579-89. The signatories of the "Otdel'noe mnenie" were V. Nesmelov, M. Mashanov, V. Zavitnevich, N. Aksakov, P. Svetlov, and A. Rozhdestvenskii.

26. *Ibid.*, 579.

27. *Ibid.*, 580-82, 588.

28. *Ibid.*, 581.

29. "Osoboe mnenie professora Kazanskoi dukhovnoi akademii Il'i Berdnikova po povodu otdel'nago mneniia men'shinstva chlenov I-go otdela Vysochaishe uchrezhdennago pri Sviateishem Sinode Prisutstviia po voprosu o sostave sobora," *Zhurnaly i protokoly*, I, 115-24.

30. *Ibid.*, 115.

31. *Ibid.*, 124.

SOURCES AND ARCHIVES

A Bibliographical Essay on the Documentation of Russian Orthodoxy during the Imperial Era

Edward Kasinec

One conceivable reason for the paucity of American scholarship on the Russian Orthodox church is a lack of familiarity with this subject's vast published and unpublished materials. This essay, in attempting to provide some guidance toward ameliorating the situation, has two specific goals: first, to determine the bibliographical environment in which some of the sources for the study of modern Russian Orthodoxy were generated; and second, to indicate some of the peculiarities of that environment which in the past have misled researchers about the church. A solid grounding in bibliographical findings decreases the likelihood that scholars will uncritically accept traditionally established bibliographical categories. This essay is not meant to treat the problem exhaustively, but rather it should be understood as an initial plunge into an ocean of sources. Moreover, the items listed in the bibliography are intended to represent various types of reference aids.

The first of the paper's three parts deals with published documentation. The second addresses the problem of access to published materials. A concluding section provides some observations on unpublished sources, archives, and manuscript collections.

1. Printed Sources

Unquestionably the largest and most important group of published sources includes theological works—Biblical exegesis, dogmatic, moral, polemical, and pastoral theology, catechetics, canon law, church archaeology, patristics, church history, and philosophy. Of course, the highly centralized Russian imperial administration also generated considerable administrative and legislative documentation directly affecting the life of the church during the synodal period.[1]

The question of religious publishing in the Russian Empire has never been adequately explored. A cursory look at some basic reference tools indicates that its role was significant and that during the imperial era the publication of religious materials occupied a place second only to that of popular and children's literature. On the eve of the First World War there were forty-four Russian publishing houses largely devoting their efforts to "theology, religion, morals, and church questions." These printing houses were scattered throughout the empire, although the major church-affiliated institutions were the synodal typographies in Moscow and St. Petersburg, the printing houses of the great Trinity-St. Sergius Monastery near Moscow and the ancient Monastery of the Caves in Kiev. Other houses dealing with religious publishing, such as those of I.L. Tuzov and A.S. Suvorin, were privately owned. Also notable were the publishers I. D. Sytin, Svirelyn, and Prostakov. Together these centers supplied the needs of churches, monastic institutions, parish schools, the Bible Society, as well as the St. Petersburg Society for the Spreading of Holy Scripture.[2] Of course, a significant portion of their output also went to satisfy the needs of private individuals. The following statistics supplied by A.A. Bakhtiarov and corroborated in the Soviet period by M. N. Kufaev (1927) give some idea of the proportions of the synodal printing houses' output in 1885:

The Moscow typography printed 238,760 books and brochures of various titles and 3,778,650 copies of single sheets; the St. Petersburg typography printed 1,474,620 books and brochures and 365,040 sheets. The greatest number of books and brochures printed on the orders of the Holy Synod *in the Moscow typography* were a psalter in Slavonic without red coloring, 30,000 copies, a book of hours without coloring in 40,000 copies, an Octoechos without red coloring in 20,000 copies, an abbreviated prayer book in Slavonic in 24,000 copies; [printed] on personal request: an Acathist to Prince Peter and Princess Fevronia, Murom thaumaturgists, in Slavonic in 10,000 copies, an Acathist to the holy princes Fedor, David, and Konstantin, Iaroslavl thaumaturgists, in Slavonic in 9,000 copies. [The greatest number of books printed in] *the St. Petersburg typography* were the New Testament in Russian in 100,000 copies, the Slavonic Gospels in 59,000 copies, in Slavonic and Russian, 30,000 and in Russian, 50,000 copies. The Gospel in Russian was printed in separate fascicles for each Evangelist (25,000) for a total of 100,000. The psalter was printed in Slavonic in 40,000 copies and in 20,000 copies in Russian. A prayer book for the laity in Slavonic in 20,000 copies, a shortened prayer book in civil type in 115,000 copies, and *Sviatye Kirill i Mefodii apostoly slavianskie* in 141,300 copies. The vitae and acts of SS Cyril and Methodius, the enlighteners of the Slavs, in 115,260 copies, short aphorisms from the lives of SS Cyril and Methodius, the enlighteners of the Slavs, in 115,000 copies; [printed] on private request: a short prayer book for Orthodox soldiers in civil type in 145,000 copies and a hymn of praise to the Blessed Virgin Mary Comforter of All Those in Distress, 10,000 copies.[3]

The vast structure and proportions of the literature on modern Orthodoxy create many problems for the bibliographer. The close relationship between religious and secular life in imperial Russia is an obstacle to selecting a manageable and relevant bibliography on specific topics from a subject as broad as modern religious history. For example, the existence of the office of Chief Military Chaplain of the Army and Navy Forces means that an article of interest to a historian of religion may (and probably will) appear in the *Morskoi sbornik* (Navy miscellany). In turn, a historian tracing the religious life of late-nineteenth-century Russia must also have frequent recourse to such belle-lettrists of the period as Leskov, Tolstoy, Rozanov, or Melnikov-Pecherskii. Many articles of interest also appear in secular historical serials. For example, a piece on Metropolitan Filaret (Drozdov) might easily appear in as many as several hundred serials.

The researcher of Orthodoxy will soon discover that his subject has, bibliographically speaking, already been capsulized and is presented to him in some special ways. One might be termed "geographical," that is, displayed according to diocese (eparchy) or an entire region (*krai*), particularly whenever the church served in the institutionally weak role of missionary, as in the southwest (Kiev, Vilnius, Vitebsk) or in the Amur region. A second focus for Orthodox literature is the person of an outstanding hierarch. Of course, the histories of individual dioceses and the biographies of individual hierarchs are important and interesting, but the sheer numbers of such studies constitute an inherent bias which must be recognized. Largely for this reason, recent research on Orthodoxy during the imperial era has been distracted from such phenomena as local and universal canonization, pilgrimages (*palomnichestvo*), thaumaturgy, folly in Christ (*iurodstvo*), the Orthodox sacraments, and the Orthodox social welfare movement. Similarly, phenomena intensively studied for the medieval period are totally neglected for the modern period, though, for example, the belief in saints obviously did not cease in 1721 — at the beginning of the twentieth century, the canonization of Saint Serafim of Sarov drew several hundred thousand people.

At this point an examination of published sources alone will enable us to isolate three important categories of materials. The first encompasses religious-theological serials, the second, various sorts of histories, the third, memoirs, correspondence, and diaries.

A. Religious-Theological Serials

These may be arranged and analyzed according to the following subcategories: (a) the serials of the capitals, Moscow and St. Petersburg, and regional serials such as the diocesan gazettes (*eparkhial'nye vedomosti*); (b) academic periodicals (both in the intellectual nature of their contents and in the sense of being produced by the four theological academies) and edificatory periodicals (*nazidatel'nye*); and (c) official publications (by the Synod or the local bishops) and the independent organs (*vol'nye*), whether of those for lobbyists for social justice, temperance, charity for the poor, or for the white clergy.

Religious-theological serials in the Russian Empire date from the appearance of masonic, mystical, and pietistic writings in the eighteenth and early nineteenth centuries. They included Novikov's *Utrenii svet* (Morning light, St. Petersburg, 1777-80; reproduced in microfilm);

Vechernaia zaria (Twilight glow, 1782); I.G. Kharlamov's *Besedy s bogom* (Conversations with God, 1787-89); Labzin's *Sionskii vestnik* (Messenger of Zion, 1806, 1817-18); Ia. Utkin's bimonthly publication for the Society of Lovers of Christianity entitled *Dukhovnyi god zhizni khristianina* (Spiritual year of a Christian life, 1816-17); and the *Izvestiia o deistviiakh i uspekhakh bibleiskogo obshchestva* (Reports on the Activities and the Accomplishments of the Bible Society, 1824). After the reorganization of the theological academies in 1814, each school published its own journal. The St. Petersburg academy, for example, issued *Khristianskoe chtenie* (Christian reading; reproduced in microform) from 1821 until the eve of the Revolution in 1917. In 1875 an appendix was added under the title of *Tserkovnyi vestnik* (Church messenger). The academy in Kiev began publishing its journal *Voskresnoe chtenie* (Sunday reading) in 1837, while its successor *Trudy* (Proceedings; reproduced in microform) first appeared in 1860. *Pribavleniia k tvoreniiam sviatykh ottsev v russkom perevode* (The supplements to the works of the Holy Fathers in Russian translation; reproduced in microform), an organ of the Moscow Ecclesiastical Academy, commenced publication in 1843, was discontinued, and later revived by Metropolitan Antonii (Khrapovitskii) as *Bogoslovskii vestnik* (Theological messenger, 1892-1918; reproduced in microform). The ecclesiastical academy in Kazan, newly created in 1842, published *Pravoslavnyi sobesednik* (The Orthodox interlocutor, 1855-1917?) which had at its inception the least "catholic" aim of any of the academic journals, namely, a dialogue with the "Old Believers." The program of *The Orthodox Interlocutor* was established by Metropolitan Grigorii (Postnikov, d. 1860) and Archbishop Agafangel (Solov'ev, 1812-76). It was published with an appendix, *Izvestiia po kazanskoi eparkhii* (Reports on the Kazan diocese, 1867-1917?). In addition, the academic periodicals frequently contained appendixes which published the protocols of the academy.

The first of the eparchial gazettes (*vedomosti*) was founded on 11 November 1859 in Kherson diocese by Archbishop Dmitrii (Muretov). Within two years, four others began publication in Iaroslavl and Chernigov (1860) and in Kiev and Tambov (1861). Such serials as *Tserkovnye vedomosti* (Church news, 1888-1917?), *Vestnik voennogo dukhovenstva* (Messenger of military chaplains, 1890-1910), *Narodnoe obrazovanie* (Popular education, 1896-1917?), the organ of the Educational Council of the Holy Synod, and the *Vestnik gruzinskogo ekzarkhata* (Messenger of the Georgian exarchate, 1891-1917?) also belong to the category of "official" publications.

In addition to these intellectual academic journals, several "edificatory" journals also began publication. Among them were *Dushepoleznoe chtenie* (Spiritually useful reading, 1860-1917?), *Strannik* (Pilgrim, 1860-1917?), S. Uvarov's *Voskresnyi den'* (Sunday, 1888-1917?), S.S. Liapidevskii's *Kormchii* (Rudder, 1888-1917?), and the various *Listki* (Leaflets) published by the Trinity, Pochaev, and Kiev monasteries (from 1884 to the Revolution).

The reign of Alexander II saw a flowering of religious journals, as witnessed by *Uchilishche blagochestiia* (School of piety, 1857-60), a publication in Russian and the Baltic languages by the Riga Ecclesiastical Academy; *Dukhovnaia beseda* (Spiritual conversation, 1858-76), supplemented by *Tserkovnaia letopis'* (Church chronicle), founded by Grigorii Postnikov; Askochenskii's notorious *Domashniaia beseda* (Domestic conversation, 1858-77), and *Rukovodstvo dlia sel'skikh pastyrei* (Guide for village pastors, 1860-1917?); A.V. Gumilevskii edited *Dukh khristianina* (Spirit of a Christian, 1862-65), while Makarii (Bulgakov) founded *Dukhovnyi vestnik* (Spiritual Messenger, 1862-67; reproduced in microform). Still others include *Khristianskiia drevnosti i arkheologiia* (Christian antiquities and archaeology, 1862-78); the *Chteniia* (Proceedings, 1863-1917?; reproduced in microform) of the Moscow Society for the Lovers of Religious Enlightenment; *Dukhovnyi dnevnik* (Spiritual diary, 1864-66), published by the Khar'kov Ecclesiastical Seminary; the *Missionerskii protivomusul'manskii sbornik* (Antimoslem missionary journal, irregularly from 1872); A.I. Popovitskii's sensationalist journal *Tserkovno-obshchestvennyi vestnik* (Church-society messenger, 1874-86), renamed *Russkii palomnik* (Russian pilgrim, 1887); *Missioner* (Missionary, 1874-79), a publication of the Orthodox Missionary Society; *Bratskoe slovo* (Fraternal word, 1875-1917?; reproduced in microfilm), published by N.I. Subbotin and the "one faith" (*edinoverets*) Archimandrite Pavel (Prusskii).

Only a few journals were founded under Alexander III or in the early period of Nicholas II's reign: *Pastyrskii sobesednik* (Pastoral interlocutor, 1884-1910); *Dukhovnyi tsvetnik* (Spiritual nursery, 1885-86); *Dushepoleznyi sobesednik* (Spiritually useful interlocutor, 1888-1917); *Tserkovno-prikhodskaia shkola* (Church-parish school, 1887-94/95); P. A. Ignatovich's *Khristianskii put'* (Christian way, 1894); *Drug istiny* (Friend of truth, 1888-91); *Vestnik trezvosti* (Messenger of temperance, 1894); *Prikhodskaia zhizn'* (Parish life, 1898); and *Tserkovnoobshchestvennaia zhizn'* (Church-social life, 1906). Other journals published during this period were *Tserkovnyi golos* (Voice of the Church, 1907); *Drug trezvosti* (Friend of temperance, 1900-1901); *Bozhiia niva* (God's field, 1902); *Nastavlenie i uteshenie sviatoi very khristianskoi* (Moral instructions and comforts of the holy Christian faith, 1887-1917); *Waimuli sonumetoosa* or *Dukhovnyi vestnik* (Spiritual messenger, 1905); *Missionerskii sbornik* (Missionary miscellany, 1891-1917); *Pravoslavnyi blagovestnik* (Orthodox messenger, 1893-1917), published by the Orthodox Missionary Society; *Missionerskoe obozrenie* (Missionary survey, 1896-1917); *Pravoslavnyi putevoditel'* (Orthodox guide, 1903-7); the Slavophile journal *Blagovest'* (Annuciation, 1883-87); *Vera i razum* (Faith and reason, 1894-1916); *Vera i tserkov'* (Faith and church, 1899-1907); *Pravoslavnyi palestinskii sbornik* (Orthodox Palestine miscellany, 1881-1916); *Soobshcheniia* (Announcements [of the Orthodox Palestine Society], 1886-1926); and *Novosti bogoslovskoi literatury* (News of theological literature, 1904; reproduced in microfilm).

B. Historical Writings

The late eighteenth century in Russia witnessed a renewed interest in historical studies. Local religious and secular authors began to produce a vast number of histories of cities, eparchies, monasteries, and cathedrals, which were often published first as articles in both religious and secular journals and then as separate volumes. Usually the local hierarchs encouraged these meticulous studies of individual shrines, churches, and so on, and unquestionably they played a positive role in unearthing and inventorying archival and manuscript materials. An additional impetus to studying local church history came in the middle third of the nineteenth century with the increased emphasis on history in the curriculum of the seminaries and academies. Two decades later, the Holy Synod requested that the local bishops compile comprehensive historical and statistical descriptions of their eparchies and that special committees be formed for that purpose. The various site descriptions as well as historical and statistical overviews of the eparchies form a large bloc of the literature on modern Orthodoxy. There are many problems connected with this type of literature. For example, it would be interesting to ascertain the value for social and economic history of the monastic and parish histories; in most cases these writings contain lists of benefactors along with their social status. A study of the social composition of a bloc of parishes within a city on the basis of the individual histories might prove useful.

C. Memoirs, Correspondence, and Diaries

The final group of materials under the heading of published sources includes memoirs, correspondence (epistolary), and diaries of individuals associated with the church. Much of this type of documentation was written by the great hierarchs of the Orthodox church and reflects their interests and prejudices. Further, the vast majority of these sources were published in the various eparchial gazettes (*eparkhial'nye vedomosti*) or other serial publications with equally limited circulation, and relatively few were reprinted as separates. Fortunately, in the nineteenth century some of the educators in the theological academies, including N. P. Giliarov-Platonov and D. S. Rostislavov have left us their memoirs, thereby giving a therapeutic corrective to the memoirs of the clergy.

Even this cursory survey of published sources will give some idea of what one can expect to find in western and Soviet collections. One of the first steps in surveying western collections of publications pertaining to modern Orthodoxy was taken almost thirty years ago with the filming by the Library of Congress of such European Slavic collection catalogues as those of St. Sergius Orthodox Theological Academy in Paris and Helsinki University Library's Slavic Division. After the war the Library of Congress published a catalogue of its own already substantial Russian-language holdings on Orthodoxy, and Mr. John Dorosh compiled a useful list of the non-Cyrillic (Latin script) holdings.[4] In addition, the Lieb Library in Basle has been described by Simone Blanc, and a photocopy of the Lieb catalogue is held (and updated) by the Bodleian Library in Oxford along with a manuscript catalogue of Bodley's own John Birkbeck collection. Fr. Jan Krajcar S. J. has written a short overview of the important holdings of the Pontifical Oriental Institute,[5] and short notices have also appeared on some of the smaller American fugitive collections in the *Newsletter* of the (now defunct) Slavic Bibliographic and Documentation Center. Bibliographers and librarians in Germany and Austria have provided us with numerous library catalogues of their holdings of Slavica, collections frequently containing many German and Latin language works on modern Orthodoxy.

Notwithstanding the rich holdings in the West, some of the largest concentrations of published modern Orthodox documentation (aside from those in the Lenin and Saltykov-Shchedrin libraries) are located in the libraries of the Moscow and Leningrad Ecclesiastical Academies. The library of the Moscow Ecclesiastical Academy, which is situated within the confines of the Trinity-St. Sergius Monastery at Zagorsk, about forty miles from Moscow, is located on two floors of the pre-Revolutionary academy's separate building. On the first floor are located a preliminary card catalogue, the newspaper reading room, the serial collections, and the reading room for professors and foreign guests. The stacks and staff working areas are on the second floor. The library also possesses the archives of the bibliographer K. N. Popov, and while its collection of pre-Revolutionary serial publications is vast, it probably contains nothing that cannot also be found in the Lenin Library. (The same, however, cannot be said of the books in the Tserkovno-Arkheologicheskii Kabinet organized by the late Archpriest A.D. Ostapov, largely manuscripts relating to the sixteenth and seventeenth centuries.) The library also contains several unpublished indexes to pre-Revolutionary religious-theological serials, specifically to *Pravoslavnyi sobesednik, Khristianskoe chtenie, Trudy Kievskoi dukhovnoi akademii* and *Bogoslovskii vestnik*. These are carbon copies of indexes originally compiled by V. M. Popov in the Leningrad Ecclesiastical Academy. Finally, since the reconstitution of the theological academies in 1945 there have been written a considerable number of dissertations, some of which are of interest to the historian of Russia and Orthodoxy.

Microrepublications and hardcopy facsimile reprints have, of course, resurrected many sources for the historian of modern Orthodoxy. The role of Jordanville's *Tipografiia sviatogo Iova pochaevskogo* has been especially important in this regard, as has that of the YMCA-Les Editeurs réunis in Paris.

A careful reading of one of the most recent guides to reprints and microforms in the Slavic fields shows that approximately a dozen firms have been responsible for making available upwards of thirty religious-theological serials as well as more than a hundred titles dealing with modern Orthodoxy.[6] These monographic reprints and microform republications may be divided into the following categories: (1) republications of religious service books, descriptions of holdings of Old Church Slavonic manuscripts and printed books, as well as general scholarly works by learned monks and religious figures published during the synodal period; (2) republications of important works by and on such modern religious thinkers as Solov'ev, Berdiaev, Bulgakov, Trubetskoi, Tolstoy, Novikov, Gamaleia, Zenkovskii, the authors of the *Vekhi* collection, as well as Varentsov's collection of religious poetry; (3) reprints of the classic church histories by Makarii (Bulgakov), Golubinskii, and Bishop Porfirii (Uspenskii). But by far the largest group of reprints and microrepublications includes the classic secondary studies of nineteenth-century Russian religious historiography. Among these are many writings on the Old Belief and the sectarians, histories of the seminaries and academies (e.g., the outstanding study by Znamenskii on the Kazan academy), studies by Moroshkin and D.A. Tolstoy on the Jesuits in Russia and by Stelletskii on Prince Golitsyn, Pavlov on the secularization of church properties, Verkhovskoi's detailed study of the *Ecclesiastical Regulation*, and several works by T.V. Barsov on the structure of the Holy Synod.

Several firms have made available microform files of Russian serial publications. In addition to some of the major masonic and academic serial publications, these firms have offered a representative selection (sometimes in incomplete files) of sectarian, edificatory, Old Believer, and religious art serials. These titles include *Baptist* (1907-12, 1914);

Bogoslovskii bibliograficheskii listok (Theological bibliographical leaflet, 1906-16); *Tserkov'* (Church, 1908-14); *Dukhovnyi khristianin* (Spiritual Christian, 1905-16); *Chteniia v tserkovno-arkheologicheskom obshchestve* (Proceedings of the church-archaeological society, 1883-1915); *Inorodcheskoe obozrenie* (Foreign survey, 1917); *Istina* (Truth, 1906); *Izvestiia vysochaiishe uchrezhdennogo komiteta popechitel'stva o russkoi ikonopisi* (Reports of the imperially established committee for the overseeing of Russian iconography, 1902-3); *Novia Iudeia* (New Judea, 1908); *Pravoslavnyi blagovestnik* (Orthodox herald, 1893-1917); *Pravoslavnoe obozrenie* (Orthodox survey, 1860-91); *Pskovskaia starina* (Pskov antiquity, 1910); *Staroobriadcheskii pomorskii zhurnal* (Old Believer littoral journal, 1908-9); *Staroobriadtsy* (Old Believers, 1908-9); *Staroobriadcheskii pastyr'* (Old Believer pastor, 1913-14); *Staroobriadcheskaia mysl'* (Old Believer thought, 1910-16); *Svetoch* (Torch, 1910-12); *Svetil'nik* (Lamp, 1913-15); and *Khristianin* (Christian, 1907-16). One could add to this list *Zhurnal Moskovskoi patriarkhii* (Journal of the Moscow patriarchate), published since World War II but frequently dealing with pre-Revolutionary church topics.

2. Reference Works

For ordering and making accessible the wealth of documentation in his area of study, the historian of modern Orthodoxy has at his disposal a rich array of reference tools, both in western languages and Russian and touching not only on modern Orthodoxy but broadly on the social sciences and humanities as well. Works dealing with religious life were registered in general historical bibliographies of the nineteenth century by V.I. Mezhov and the Lambin brothers, a fortunate circumstance since there are relatively few *specifically bibliographical* tools for the student of modern Orthodoxy and two of the major works deal with the Old Belief and Sectarians: these are A. S. Prugavin's *Raskolsektanstvo . . . Vypusk 1: Bibliografiia staroobriadchestva i ego razvetlenii* (Schism and sect, 1: Bibliography of the Old Belief and its branches) (Moscow, 1887), and F. K. Sakharov's *Literatura istorii i oblicheniia russkogo raskola* (Literature on the history and exposure of the Russian schism), in 3 volumes (Tambov, 1887-1900). Other more general aids.

published in Moscow in 1891 under the title *Ukazatel' russkikh knig i broshur* (Index of Russian books and brochures), cover the literature published between 1801 and 1888. The first fascicle compiled by "N.P." deals with church history, the second with "dogmatic, moral and comparative theology and the Old Belief and Sectarians." Like these two works, A.A. Lebedev's *Russkaia bogoslovskaia literatura za 1888-1892* (Russian theological literature for 1888-1892) (Saratov, 1908) is a bibliographical rarity. Paul Svetlov's *Chto chitat' po bogosloviiu?* (What to read in theology?) (Kiev, 1907) has the rather narrow goal of describing apologetical literature in Russian and western languages.

In addition to the many general encyclopedias published before the Revolution, several specialized ones dealt specifically with Orthodox theology. Sadly, the publication of the encyclopedia, edited by A.P. Lopukhin and N. N. Glubokovskii, stopped in 1911 with the letter *K*.[7] Equally useful to the student of modern Orthodoxy are the many published catalogues of archival and manuscript collections, as well as the library catalogues of religious educational institutions (academies and seminaries). There are also many published catalogues of important private collections with substantial holdings of religious materials. The published descriptions and catalogues of the libraries of such prominent laymen as N.P. Smirnov, D.V. Ulianinskii, S.D. Sheremetev, G.V. Yudin, as well as such prominent religieux as the Metropolitan Flavian (Gorodetskii) of Kiev, devote entire sections to the literature of modern Orthodoxy.

Important, too, are the sale catalogues of such religious publishing houses as A.S. Suvorin's *Novoe vremia* (Modern times) in St. Petersburg as well as the firms of Tuzov and Klochkov.

Because of the church's important role in pre-Revolutionary Russian life, the Imperial Historical Society's biographical dictionary contains a wealth of material on all ranks. But like the *Pravoslavnaia bogoslovskaia entsiklopediia* (Orthodox theological encyclopedia) of Lupokhin and Glubokovskii, the *Russian Biographical Dictionary* is unfinished: four letters were never published and three of the published letters are incomplete. Supplementing this major biographical work are various listings (frequently termed *spiski* or *katalogi*) of hierarchs, heads of monastic institutions, bishops of eparchies, and students of the theological seminaries and academies compiled periodically by the Synod under the supervision of Iu.V. Tolstoi and, earlier in the nineteenth century, by the archaeographer Iu. M. Stroev. Among the most useful reference tools for students of modern Orthodoxy are the guides to the monasteries of the empire by L.I. Denisov (published in 1908) and the exhaustive bibliographical guide by M.V. Zverinskii published between 1890 and 1907.

Religious libraries of the synodal period may be divided into the following categories: (1) academic (those of the four academies, eparchial seminaries, and the parish schools); (2) eparchial; (3) religious society libraries; and (4) the collections of the various deaneries (*okruzhnyia* or *blagochynnycheskiia*) and individual churches.

From the latter part of the nineteenth century, bibliographers and librarians began compiling catalogues for the academy collections. The first edition of the Kazan academy catalogue was published in 1874 (with an addendum in 1884), and in 1880, I. Gorizontov catalogued the Kazan seminary collection. Between 1880 and 1892, the librarians Korsunskii, Troitskii, and Kolosov published a catalogue in four volumes and seven parts of the 21,080 items in the collection of the Moscow Ecclesiastical Academy. Beginning in 1881-82, published acquisitions lists began to appear for this collection. The two-volume catalogue of the Kiev Ecclesiastical Academy appeared the following decade (1890-92).

One of the richest mines of information for the student of modern Orthodoxy lies buried in the vast number of religious-theological serials published during the synodal period. The indexes to these publications are the key to unlocking this treasure, and according to a recently published bibliography of indexes to Russian serial publications, their number may well approach one hundred. Unfortunately, like the memoirs, diaries, and correspondence of hierarchs, many of these indexes were not published as separates, but only in the respective journals. By far the largest group are those to the eparchial gazettes and official religious publications. The edificatory journals, however, are poorly covered.

It is unfortunate that reference aids make up a relatively small proportion of the reprinted items dealing with modern Orthodoxy. Most of what has been made available in reprint and microrepublication consists of listings of hierarchs published by the Holy Synod, reports (*otchety*) of the overprocurator of the Holy Synod, bibliographical listings of the texts for religious schools, classic bio-bibliographies compiled by the Archbishop Filaret (Gumilevskii) and the Metropolitan Evgenii (Bolkhovitinov), listings by P. Syrku and P. Liubopytnyi of the papers of Porfirii (Uspenskii).

Several important bibliographical studies of religious publishing houses have also become available in reprints. These include A.V. Gavrilov's *Ocherki istorii S-petersburgskoi sinodal'noi tipografii. Vyp. 1. 1711-1839* (Outlines of the history of the St. Petersburg synodal typography 1. 1711-1839) (St. Petersburg, 1911) and A. N. Solov'ev's *Moskovskii pechatnyi dvor: Istoricheskaia zapiska o moskovskoi sino-dal'noi tipografii* (Moscow printing office: A historical note on the Moscow synodal typography) (Moscow, 1917).

It has been pointed out that published legislation concerning the church was one of the most important sources for the study of Russian religious life during the synodal period. Because much of this legisla-tion was scattered throughout various serial publications such as the eparchial gazettes and central official serials like *Tserkovnye vedomosti* (Church news), the government and private individuals began to collect it into synoptic compendia. These compendia might be divided into four groups: (1) those collecting all imperial legislation dealing with the established church; (2) collections which gathered legislation in force at the time of compilation; (3) compendia dealing with the Old Believers and sectarians; (4) the decrees (*ukazy*) of the Synod alone.

Another group of reference aids that might be mentioned consists of the various calendars and organizational guides published annually by the Holy Synod and the chancery of the Council of Ministers. These guides are invaluable for researchers, because they give an accurate over-view of the more important officeholders within the church and the re-ligious bureaucracy.

The number of statistical compendia dealing with the Orthodox church in the nineteenth century is few. The chief work of this kind was compiled by Preobrazhenskii and is entitled *Otechestvennaia tserkov, po statisticheskim dannym, 1840/1841 po 1890/91* (The Fatherland church according to the statistics, 1840/41 to 1890/91)

(St. Petersburg, 1897). This useful compilation mirrors the growth of many Orthodox religious institutions, including libraries.

3. Unpublished Sources

It is not possible in an essay of this scope to discuss fully the problem of religious archives and manuscript collections in imperial Russia. This would necessitate not only a statement about the great central repositories in the various capitals of the empire — St. Petersburg, Moscow, Kiev — but would also entail a discussion of literally thousands of church, consistory, and monastic collections scattered throughout dozens of dioceses. All three principal cities of the empire had many monastic, parish, and academic institutions, each with considerable archival and manuscript holdings.

During the medieval period, Russian monasteries, like those in the West, were centers for the copying of manuscripts. Furthermore, they were the primary recipients of benefactions in the form of manuscripts and, after the sixteenth century and the beginning of printing in Muscovy, of printed books. However, unlike Western European monasteries which had rich holdings of the works of classical antiquity, the manuscript collections of Russian monasteries contained historical writings, cosmographies, lexicons, patristic writings, liturgical manuscripts, texts of canon law and lives of the saints.

Some of the largest collections in the empire were centered in Moscow. For example, the Synodal (formerly Patriarchal) Library dated from the early medieval period (thirteenth and fourteenth centuries) and, as a result of many patriarchal benefactions in the seventeenth century, gained a considerable reputation throughout Europe for its collections of Greek and Church Slavonic manuscripts. The description of these manuscripts by the priests Gorskii and Nevostruev (published 1862-69) stands as one of the great monuments of pre-Revolutionary archaeography. Another of Moscow's eparchial collections, that of the Trinity-St. Sergius Monastery, contained hundreds of Old Testament texts, patristic and liturgical manuscripts, as well as priceless documents of canon law, church history, and property deeds. The greatest number were from the sixteenth century, with only a small percentage of the monastery holdings dating from the synodal period.

Therefore, only a relatively small proportion of the manuscript holdings of Russian monasteries of the synodal period actually related to events of the eighteenth and nineteenth centuries; for the historian of modern Orthodoxy the most important materials lay in these institutions' *archives*, which contained important documents for the socioeconomic and even political history of Russia. During the synodal period the Solovetskii and Spaso-Evfimiev monasteries served as places of incarceration for political as well as religious nonconformity. On some occasions the great shrines were used as repositories for major documents of state, as during the reign of Alexander I when the documents relating to the imperial succession were deposited in the tabernacle of the Great Moscow Cathedral of the Assumption. In addition to being published in the religious theological journals, documents from religious repositories appeared in such journals as *Russkaia starina* (The Russian past), the *Chteniia* (Proceedings) of the Moscow Society of Russian History and Antiquities, and *Kievskaia starina* (The Kievan past).

For the historian of modern Orthodoxy, the most important central archival institutions were found in St. Petersburg, especially the Archives of the Holy Synod, the Military-Religious Jurisdiction (Vedomstvo) and the collections of the Alexander Nevskii monastery. During the second half of the nineteenth century, the Commission for the Description of the Archives of the Holy Synod made great strides in analyzing, describing, and publishing inventories (*opisi*) of the holdings. Its members included some of Russia's most distinguished church scholars and such prominent archivists as N. I. Grigorovich, K. I. Zdravomyslov, and A.N. L'vov. The commission not only did outstanding work in publishing a series of descriptions for the synodal fonds, entitled *Opisanie dokumentov i del, khraniashchikhsia v arkhive Sv. Sinoda* (Description of documents and items preserved in the archives of the Holy Synod), but also created a system of unpublished internal catalogues arranged chronologically and by twenty-seven subject areas.

With the establishment of a central organization for inventorying and describing the synodal archives an equally serious effort was mounted to deal with those of the consistories. After the creation of the eparchial archival commissions, the 1870s and 1880s witnessed the organization of historical-statistical committees, which did much to preserve, inventory, and publish the riches lying in the eparchial repositories.

Using the Moscow consistory (*dikasteriia*) as an example, the following types of material might be found in a typical archive: (1) protocols of the consistory; (2) books registering those who confessed in the course of a year (*dukhovnye knigi* or *ispovednye rospisi*); (3) censuses of the clergy (*revizskiia skazki*); (4) decrees (*ukazy*) of the Synod; (5) metrica; and (6) statements on church property (*mezhevye knigi*).

During the first decade of the Soviet regime, a good deal of the careful archaeographic work of the nineteenth century was destroyed. A close reading of provincial journals and such important serial publications as *Delo i dni* (Deeds and days) and *Arkhivnoe delo* (Archival affairs) for the late twenties reveals that the archives and manuscript repositories of many religious institutions were vandalized and hopelessly scattered during the violent antireligious campaigns. Of course, some serious scholarly work based on religious manuscripts was carried on during this period, but the work dealt almost exclusively with documents of medieval provenance. For example, the archives of the Paraclete, Gethsemane Hermitage, Kinoveia, Hermogen Hermitage, and the Chernigovskii, Khotkovskii, and Pokrovskii monasteries, all administratively subordinate to the Trinity-St. Sergius Monastery, were destroyed outright. The collections of such Moscow monasteries as the Alekseevskii, Bogoiavlenskii, Vsesviatskii Edinovercheskii, Skorbiashchenskii, Ivanovskii, Nikitskii, Nikol'skii Edinovercheskii, Novodevichi, Rozhdestvenskii, Sretenskii, Strastnoi, Pokrovskii, and Kazanskii remained unaccounted for after the events of the 1920s.

In addition to these archives, several secular, governmental collections contained important materials relating to modern Orthodoxy. For example, the second division of the archives of the Ministry of Justice in Moscow held the papers of the Economic College (1762-87) pertaining to land holdings, as well as important portions of the senate archives from St. Petersburg. Materials on church holdings were also to be found in the archives of the Ministry of Agriculture and State Property. The

Moscow archives of the Ministry of Foreign Affairs contained documents dealing with the foreign relations of the Orthodox church, while the archives of the Ministry of Internal Affairs in St. Petersburg contained documentation on the Old Belief, sectarians, and foreign denominations in Russia. Finally, the State Archives (Gosudarstvennyi Arkhiv) and the archives of the Ministry of Foreign Affairs in St. Petersburg held documents concerning high crimes, the marriages of the imperial family, and the Petrine church reforms.

Those religious archives which remained substantially intact through the 1920s were nationalized in the following decades and found their way into archival and manuscript repositories subordinated to either the Ministry of Culture (including manuscript divisions of libraries and museums and pedagogical institutions) or the Main Archival Administration, better known by its Russian acronym, GUA (Glavnoe Upravlenie Arkhivov). For the most part the archives of eparchial consistories, as well as of theological seminaries and consistories, were incorporated into collections administered by GUA. Although it is broadly correct to state that institutional archives were incorporated into the orbit of GUA while personal fonds (archives) (*lichnye fondy*, i.e., those of local hierarchs, learned clergy, teachers in the seminaries and academies, and pious lay people) generally found their way into the repositories administered by the Ministry of Culture, one must also take care to note that during the period of nationalization, materials were frequently apportioned with no apparent rationale. Again, taking Moscow religious archives as an example, we might note that the Archives of Ancient Acts (TsGADA) received the archives of the Dukhovnyi Sobor of the Trinity-St. Sergius Monastery as well as the following Moscow eparchy monasteries: the Zaikonospasskii, Spasskii, Danilov, Novospasskii, Voznesenskii, Pafnutev-Borovskii, Savva-Storozhevskii, Iur'ev, and the important collections of such historic repositories as the Chudov, Vysokopetrovskii (site of the Moscow Eparchial Library), Zlatoustovskii Nikolai-Ugreshnyi, Iosifo-Volokolamskii and Znamenskii. Nevertheless, the Moscow Regional Archives (TsGAMO) received from the Trinity-St. Sergius Monastery portions of the archives of the Moscow Ecclesiastical Academy, as well as those of the Moscow,

Perevinskaia, and Trinity-St. Sergius seminaries. In addition, the collections of the Conception, St. Nicholas (Greek), Spaso-Andron'evskii, Simonov, Donskoi, Mozhaisk Luzhets monasteries, the Pokrovskii Cathedral, the nine Moscow ecclesiastical administrations, as well as the archives for the Directory of the Christ the Savior Cathedral, are also to be found in the Moscow Regional Archives.

The archaeographic literature dealing with the institutions and personalia of modern Orthodoxy is vast. For example, discussions of the holdings of Russian monasteries appear not only in specialized archaeographic literature but in general site descriptions as well. Very frequently a general history of a monastery or religious shrine also contains a description of its manuscripts. The various specialized pre-Revolutionary guides (*reestry, putevoditeli,* or *obzory*)—sometimes buried in the pages of religious-theological serials—can. be of great value to researchers who have succeeded in the arduous task of tracing the present location of pre-Revolutionary fonds. General archival practice dictates that unprepared fonds are not to be given to researchers; Soviet archival and manuscript repositories generally follow this principle. Therefore, it is especially important for western scholars to be familiar with pre-Revolutionary descriptions of archival repositories. Detailed descriptions (*opisi*) of archival fonds are given to foreign (especially American) scholars only by exception.

Unfortunately, we know all too little about the business forms of the modern Russian religious bureaucracy, and especially, about the modes in which it created, processed, and .stored its papers, two problems that would be encompassed by the modern discipline of records or paper management. Also unstudied are the various types of documents and their relationship to printed texts. For example, was it always obligatory to print decrees (*ukazy*) and rescripts? Where is the best place to search first for the printed text of a synodal circular or the episcopal resolutions (*resoliutsii*) by a local hierarch?

One can see from this brief review of sources that there is a wealth of published and archival material which is relatively unknown as well as unused. It is clear that if we hope to improve our understanding of Russian Orthodoxy during the imperial era, students of this important subject must carefully investigate such sources. By doing so we can expect to attain a greater and more complex appreciation of Russia under the Old Regime. The following selected references should serve as a useful point of departure in this investigation.

SELECTED REFERENCES

Abramtsev, David F., comp. "Bibliography of the Publications of the Moscow Patriarchate," *Edinaia tserkov'*, III, nos. 5-6, May-June 1949, 26-28 [1942-48] ; VI, no. 5, May 1952, 14-16 [1949-51].

Adres-Kalendar': obshchaia rospis' nachal'stvuiushchikh i prochikh dolzhnostnykh lits' po vsem upravleniiam v rossiiskoi imperii na 1913 god. Chast' I. Vlasti i mesta tsentral'nogo upravleniia i vedomstva ikh. St. Petersburg: Senatskaia Tipografiia, 1913, 14-15.

Akademiia Nauk SSSR: Institut Russkoi Literatury (Pushkinskii Dom). *Rukopisnoe nasledie drevnei Rusi: po materialam Pushkinskogo Doma.* Leningrad: Izdatel'stvo Nauka, Leningradskoe Otdelenie, 1972.

Anderson, V.M. *Vol'naia russkaia pechat' v Rossiiskoi Publichnoi Biblioteke.* St. Petersburg, 1920.

Babine, Alexis V. *The Yudin Library: Krasnoiarsk (Eastern Siberia).* Washington, D.C., 1905.

Basanoff, V. "Archives of the Russian Church in Alaska in the Library of Congress," *Pacific Historical Review*, II, no. 1, March 1933, 79-84.

Bakhtiarov, A.A. *Istoriia knigi na Rusi.* St. Petersburg: A. Transhel', 1890.

Bel'chikov, N.F., Begunov, Iu.K., and Rozhdestvenskii, N.P., comps. *Spravochnik-ukazatel' pechatnykh opisanii slaviano-russkikh rukopisei.* Moscow-Leningrad: Izdatel'stvo Akademii Nauk, 1963.

Berkov, P.N. *Russkie knigoliuby: ocherki.* Moscow-Leningrad: Sovetskii pisatel', 1967.

Blanc, Simone. "Note sur la Bibliothèque Lieb de Bâle," *Cahiers du monde russe et soviétique*, VIII, 1967, 637-39.

Burr, Nelson R., with Smith, James Ward and Jamison, A. Leland. *A Critical Bibliography of Religion in America.* Princeton: Princeton University Press, 1961.

Claus, H. *Slavica-Katalog der Landesbibliotek Gotha.* Quellen und Studien zur Geschichte Osteuropas, X. Berlin: Akademie Verlag, 1961.

Dobroklonskii, A.P. *Rukovodstvo po istorii russkoi tserkvi.* 4 vols. Riazan-Moscow, 1889-93.

Dobrovol'skii, L.M. *Zapreshchennaia kniga v Rossii 1825-1904: Arkhivno-bibliograficheskii razyskaniia.* Moscow: Izdatel'stvo Vsesoiuznoi Knizhnoi Palaty, 1962.

Dorosh, John T. *The Eastern Orthodox Churches: A List of References to Publications Printed in the Roman Alphabet with Indication of Location.* Typescript, Library of Congress, Washington, D.C., 1946.

Fedosov, I. A., ed. *Istochnikovedenie istorii SSSR XIX-nachala XX v.* Moscow: Izdatel'stvo Moskovskogo Universiteta, 1970.

Gendrikov, V.V. "Kratkii putevoditel' po fondam lichnogo proiskhozhdeniia rukopisnogo otdela muzeia istorii religii i ateizma," in *Ateizm, religiia, sovremennost'*, 212-23, edited by V. N. Serdakov, *et al.* Leningrad: Izdatel'stvo Nauka, Leningradskoe Otdelenie, 1973.

Gennadii, G. *Spisok knig o russkikh monastyriakh i tserkvakh.* St. Petersburg: Eduard Pratsa, 1854.

Glubokovskii, N.N. *Russkaia bogoslovskaia nauka v eia istoricheskom razvitii i noveishem sostoianii.* Warsaw: Sinodal'naia Tipografiia, 1928, [71]-115.

Grekulov, E.F. *Bibliografiia literatury po issledovaniiu pravoslaviia, staroobriadchestva i sektanstva v Sovetskoi istoricheskoi nauke za 1922-1972 gody.* Moscow, 1974. [not seen]

Guide to Russian Reprints and Microforms. New York: Pilvax Publishing Corporation, 1973.

Ikonnikov, V.S. *Opyt russkoi istoriografii.* 2 vols. in 4 pts. Kiev: Universiteta Sv. Vladimira, 1891-1908.

Ianzhul, I. I., *et. al. Kniga o knigakh: tolkovyi ukazatel' dlia vybora knig po vazhneishim otrasliam znaniia.* Moscow: D. I. Inozemtseva, 1892, chap. 1, 3-14.

Kasinec, E. "New Archival Treasures for the Historian of Russia and America," *Orthodox Church*, IX, no. 7, 1973, 8.

Klassifikatsiia literatury v organakh gosudarstvennoi bibliografii. 5th ed., rev. and supplemented. Moscow: Izdatel'stvo Kniga, 1971, 219-20.

Krajcar, Jan. "The East European Holdings in the Library of the Pontifical Oriental Institute, Rome," *Slavonic and East European Review*, XLVIII, no. 111, April 1970, 265-72.

Letopis' periodicheskikh izdanii SSSR: 1966-1970. 2 pts. Moscow: Izdatel'stvo Kniga, 1972 [overtitle: Vsesoiuznaia knizhnaia palata], chap. 1, 93.

Library of Congress: Reference Division. *Russia: A Check List Preliminary to a Basic Bibliography of Materials in the Russian Language. Part VI: Church and Education in Russia (1944); Part X: Reference Books.* Washington, 1946.

Lisovskii, N.M., comp. *Russkaia periodicheskaia pechat' 1703-1900 gg. (bibliografiia i graficheskiia tablitsy). Otdel 1: Bibliografiia russkoi periodicheskoi pechati. Otdel 2: Graficheskiia tablitsy russkoi periodicheskoi pechati.* Petrograd: Tip. G. A. Sumakhera i B. D. Brukera, 1915, 224-46, 248.

Likhachev, D. S., and Droblenkova, N. F., eds. *Puti izucheniia drevnerusskoi literatury i pis'mennosti.* Leningrad: Nauka, Leningradskoe Otdelenie, 1970 [overtitle: Akademiia Nauk SSSR: Institut Russkoi Literatury (Pushkinskii Dom)].

Malyshev, V.I. *Drevnerusskie rukopisi Pushkinskogo Doma: Obzor fondov.* Edited by Adrianova-Perets. Moscow-Leningrad: Nauka, 1965.

——. "K voprosu ob obsledovanii chastnykh sobranii rukopisei," *Trudy otdela drevnerusskoi literatury* [=*TrODRL*], X, 1954, 449-58.

——. "Moskvichi—sobirateli pis'mennoi i pechatnoi stariny," *TrODRL*, XXI, 1965, 383-89.

————. "Ob uchete i obsledovanii chastnykh sobranii starinnykh rukopisei i knig," *Issledovaniia po otechestvennomu istochnikovedeniiu: sbornikh statei, posviashchennykh 75-letiiu, S.N. Valka.* Moscow-Leningrad, 1965, 409-11.

————. "Zadachi sobraniia drevnerusskikh rukopisei," *TrODRL,* XX, 1964, 303-32.

Masanov, Iu.I., Nikitinia, N.V., and Titova, A.D., comps. *Ukazateli soderzhaniia russkikh zhurnalov i prodolzhaiushchikhsia izdanii 1755-1970 g.* Moscow: Izdatel'stvo "Kniga," 1975.

Mez'er, A.V. *Slovarnyi ukazatel' po knigovedeniiu.* Leningrad: Kolos, 1924, 79-86, 761-63.

Mezhov, V.I., comp. *Trudy tsentral'nogo i gubernskikh statisticheskikh komitetov: Bibliograficheskii ukazatel'. . . .* St. Petersburg: V. Bezobrazov i Komp., 1873 [= Mezhov. *Bibliograficheskie monografii.* Vol. 1, vyp. 1.].

Muzei istorii religii i ateizma, Leningrad. *Ezhegodnik,* 1957-64.

Olishev, V.G., et al., eds. *Sovetskaia bibliografiia: sbornik statei.* Moscow, 1960 [overtitle: Ministerstvo kul'tury RSFSR: Gosudarstvennaia Ordena Lenina Biblioteka SSSR imeni V.I. Lenina.].

Ot religii k ateizmu: Sistematicheskii ukazatel' knizhnoi i zhurnal'noi literatury po voprosam religii i ee kritiki v 1917-1924 gg. No. 1. Moscow: Ateist, 1926.

Periodicheskaia pechat' SSSR 1917-1949: Bibliograficheskii ukazatel': zhurnaly, trudy i biulleteny po obshchestvennopoliticheskim i sotsial'noekonomicheskim voprosam. Moscow: Vsesoiuznaia Palata, 1958.

Piatidesiatiletie vysochaishe utverzhdennoi komissii po razboru i opisaniiu arkhiva sviateishogo sinoda, 1865-1915: istoricheskaia zapiska. Petrograd: Sinodal'naia Tipografiia, 1915, v-vi.

Rogov, A.I. *Svedeniia o nebol'shikh sobraniiakh slaviano-russkikh rukopisei v SSSR.* Moscow: Izdatel'stvo Akademii Nauk SSSR, 1962, [overtitle: Akademiia Nauk SSSR: Otdelenie Istoricheskikh Nauk. Arkheograficheskaia Komissiia, esp. sec. 6, 7.].

Rozanov, N. "Ob arkhivakh Moskovskoi dukhovnoi konsistorii," *Chteniia v moskovskom obshchestve liubitelei dukhovnogo prosveshcheniia,* VI, 1869, 42-60.

Sbornik svedenii o povremennykh izdaniiakh (po 1 noiabria 1870 g.). St. Petersburg: Ministerstvo Vnutrennikh Del, 1870.

Seydoux, M. "Les Périodiques antireligieux en U.R.S.S.: bibliographie et état des collections dans les bibliothèques occidentales," *Cahiers du monde russe et soviétique,* XI, 1970, 124-43.

Shmidt, S.O. "Tserkovnoprikhodskie letopisi kak istochnik po istorii Russkoi derevni," *Ezhegodnik po agrarnoi istorii Vostochnoi Evropy: 1971.* Vilnius, 1974.

Simmons, J.S.G. *Russian Bibliography, Libraries and Archives: A Selected List of Bibliographical References for Students of Russian History, Literature, Political, Social and Philosophical Thought, Theology and Linguistics.* Oxford: [Anthony C. Hall], 1973, [52]-55.

Slavic Bibliographic and Documentation Center. *Newsletter,* Nos. 1-6 (January 1970-April 1972).

Spisok knig tserkovnoi pechati khraniashchikhsia v biblioteke sviateishogo pravi-tel' stvuiushchogo sinoda. St. Petersburg, 1871.

Sorok let sovetskoi gosudarstvennoi bibliografii (1920-1960): Sbornik statei. Moscow: Izdatel'stvo Vsesoiuznoi Knizhnoi Palaty, 1960.

Szeftel, Marc. "Russia (before 1917)," in *Bibliographical Introduction to Legal History and Ethnology,* edited by John Gilissen. Brussels: Institut du sociologie, 1963-73.

Tugov, Iu. M., comp. *Osnovy nauchnogo ateizma: Rekomendatel'nyi ukazatel' literatury,* edited by D. E. Mikhnevich. Moscow, 1959.

Vol'fson, I. V., ed. *Gazetnyi Mir: adresnaia i spravochnaia kniga.* 2d ed. St. Petersburg, 1913, cols. 467-70.

Widener Library, Harvard University: Shelflist. Church history periodicals, classified listing by call number. 26 September 1967.

Widnäs, Maria. "Valamo Klosterbibliotek," *Nordisk tidskrift för bok-och biblioteksväsen,* XXVII, no. 2, 81-96.

Work Projects Administration: Historical Records Survey, New York City. *Inventory of the Church Archives in New York City: Eastern Orthodox Churches and the Armenian Church in America.* New York, 1940.

Zaionchkovskii, P. A. [ed.], *Istoriia dorevoliutsionnoi Rossii v dnevnikakh i vospominaniiakh: annotirovannyi ukazatel' knig i publikatsii v zhurnalakh.* Moscow, 1976.

——. *Spravochniki po istorii dorevoliutsionnoi Rossii.* Moscow: Izdatel'stvo "Kniga," 1971.

Zernova, A. S., and Kameneva, T. N., comps. *Svodnyi katalog russkoi knigi kirillovskoi pechati XVIII veka,* edited by E. I. Katsprzhak. Moscow: Izdatel' stvo "Kniga," 1968.

NOTES

1. In addition to printed works, mention might be made of iconographic and more tangible religious materials preserved in many museums in both the Soviet Union and the West; however, discussion of these goes beyond the scope of this paper.

2. A sizable file of the reports (*otchety*) of the society are held by the Slavonic Division of the New York Public Library.

3. See Bakhtiarov in the selective bibliography at the conclusion of this essay.

4. In order to avoid duplicating titles throughout the text, the items mentioned are cited fully in the selective bibliography.

5. However, the Krajcar list does not indicate the files of Russian pre-Revolutionary periodicals and eparchial gazettes, official religious serials published during the interwar period in various centers of the Russian immigration (Warsaw, Kharbin, Prague, Berlin, Sortavala), or the noteworthy collection of religious serials published in the Soviet Union during the early twenties. I am grateful to Fr. Charles Indekeu, S. J., for permitting me to examine this remarkable collection.

6. See the *Guide to Russian Reprints and Microforms* in my selective bibliography.

7. To this day, the only completed Orthodox encyclopedia in any language is the twelve-volume *Thriskevtiki ke Ithiki Engiklopédia* (Athens, 1962-70). [Editors' note]

Guide to Further Reading
in Western European Languages

Amburger, Eric. *Geschichte des Protestantismus in Russland*. Stuttgart: Evangelisches Verlagswerk, 1961.

Amman, Albert M. *Abriss der ostslawischen Kirchengeschichte*. Vienna: Thomas Morus Presse, 1960.

——. *Kirchenpolitishe Wandlungen im Ostbaltikum bis zum Tode Alexander Newski's*. Rome: Pont. Institutum Orientalium Studiorum, 1936.

——. *Storia de la chiesa russa*. Turin, 1948. Ger. ed., *Ostslawische Kirchengeschichte*. Vienna, 1950.

Andrews, Dean Timothy. *The Eastern Orthodox Church: A bibliography*. New York: Greek Archdiocese of North and South America, 1953.

Arseniev, N. "La direction spirituelle dans l'église russe." *Contacts*, XIX, 1967, 108-29.

——. *Holy Moscow*. London: S.P.C.K., 1940.

——. *Russian Piety*. London: Faith Press, 1964.

Attwater, Donald, comp. *A List of Books in English about the Eastern Churches*. Newport, R.I.: St. Leo Shop, 1960.

Batalden, Stephen K. "Eugenios Voulgaris in Russia 1771-1806: A Chapter in Greco-Slavic Ties of the Eighteenth Century." Ph.D. dissertation, University of Minnesota, 1975.

Beausobre, I. de. *Flame in the Snow*. London, 1945 [on Saint Seraphim of Sarov].

Benz, E. "Die abenländische Sendung der östlich-orthodoxen Kirche." *Akademie der Wissenschaften und der Literatur*, VIII, Mainz, 1950.

Birkbeck, W.J. *Russia and the English Church during the Last 50 Years*. London: Rivington, Percival and Co., 1895.

Bissonette, Georges L. "Pufendorf and the Church Reforms of Peter the Great." Ph.D. dissertation, Columbia University, 1962.

Boerneke, Leroy A. "The Dawn of the Ecumenical Age: Anglican, Old Catholic, and Orthodox Reunion Negotiations of the 1870's." Ph.D. dissertation, University of Minnesota, 1977.

Bogolepov. A.A. "Church Reforms in Russia 1905-1918." A.E. Morrhouse. *St. Vladimir's Seminary Quarterly*, X, nos. 1-2, 1966, 12-66.

Bohachevsky-Chomiak, Martha. *Sergei N. Trubetskoi: An Intellectual among the Intelligentsia in Prerevolutionary Russia.* Belmont, Mass.: Nordland Publishing Company, 1976.

Bolshakoff, S. *The Foreign Missions of the Russian Orthodox Church.* London, 1943.

Bonwetsch, D.N. *Kirchengeschichte Russlands.* Leipzig, 1923.

Bouyer, Louis. *Orthodox Spirituality and Protestant and Anglican Spirituality. History of Christian Spirituality*, III. London: Burns and Oates [c. 1969].

Bulgakov, S. *The Orthodox Church.* New York, 1935.

——. *The Wisdom of God: A Brief Summary of Sophiology.* New York: Paisley Press, 1937.

Byrnes, Robert F. *Pobedonostsev: His Life and Thought.* Bloomington: Indiana University Press, 1968.

Casey, Robert. "Cultural Mission of Russian Orthodoxy." *Harvard Theological Review*, XL, 257-75.

Chrysostomus, Johannes. *Die religiösen Kräfte in der russischen Geschichte.* Munich: Verlag Anton Pustet, 1961.

Cracraft, James. *The Church Reform of Peter the Great.* Stanford: Stanford University Press, 1971.

——. "The Church Reform of Peter the Great, with Special Reference to the *Ecclesiastical Regulation* of 1721." Ph.D. dissertation, Oxford University, 1969.

——. "Feofan Prokopovich." In *The Eighteenth Century in Russia,* edited by J.G. Garrard. Oxford: Oxford University Press, 1973, 75-105.

——. "Feofan Prokopovich: A Bibliography of His Works," *Oxford Slavonic Papers*, N.S., VIII, 1975, 1-36.

Cunningham, James. "Reform in the Russian Church, 1900-1906: The Struggle for Autonomy and the Restoration of Byzantine Symphonia." Ph.D. dissertation, University of Minnesota, 1973.

Curtiss, John Shelton. *Church and State in Russia: The Last Years of the Empire 1900-1917.* New York, 1940, reprinted, New York: Octagon Books, 1965.

——. "The Russian Orthodox Church and the Provisional Government." *American Slavic and East European Review*, VII, 237-50.

Dalton, H. *Die russische Kirche.* Leipzig, 1892.

Debia, James. *An account of the religion, rites, ceremonies, and superstitions of the Moscovites; extracted from several writers of the best character and authority.* London: J. Downing, 1710.

Dindorf, Meinrad, and Kasinec, Edward. "Russian Pre-Revolutionary Religious-Theological Serials in St. Vladimir's Seminary Library." *St. Vladimir's Seminary Quarterly*, XIV, 1970, 100-107.

The Doctrine of the Russian church, being a primer or spelling book, the shorter and longer catechism, and a treatise on the duty of parish priests. London: J. Masters, 1845.

Dorosh, John. *The Eastern Orthodox Church: A Bibliography of Publications Printed in the Roman Alphabet with Indications of Location.* Washington, 1948.

Dunlop, John B. *Staretz Amvrosy: Model for Dostoevsky's Staretz Zossima.* Belmont, Mass.,: Nordland Publishing Company, 1972.

Dyrud, Keith. "The Russian Question in Eastern Europe and in America, 1890 to the First World War." Ph.D. dissertation, University of Minnesota, 1976.

Edwards, David, W. "Orthodoxy During the Reign of Tsar Nicholas I: A Study in Church-State Relations." Ph.D. dissertation, Kansas State University, 1967.

Ehrenberg, Hans, and Bubnoff, N., eds. *Oestliches Christentum: Dokumente.* 2 vols. Munich: C.H. Beck, 1925.

Fedotov, Georgii P., ed. *A Treasury of Russian Spirituality.* New York: Sheed and Ward, 1948.

———. *The Russian Religious Mind.* 2 vols. Cambridge: Harvard University Press, 1966.

Filaret, (Dmitrii Grigor'evich Gumilevskii). *Geschichte der Kirche Russlands.* Frankfurt an Main, 1872.

Florovsky, Georges. *Collected Works,* 4 vols. Belmont, Mass.: Nordland Publishing Company, 1974-75.

———. "Three Masters: The Quest for Religion in Nineteenth Century Russian Literature." *Comparative Literature Studies,* III, 1966, 119-37.

———. "Vladimir Solov'ev and Dante: The Problem of Christian Empire." In *For Roman Jakobson.* The Hague, 1956.

Frank, S. *God With Us.* London, 1946.

Frank, Victor [ed.] . *Russisches Christentum.* Paderborn, 1889.

Freeze, Gregory L. "The Russian Parish Clergy: Vladimir Province in the Eighteenth Century." Ph.D. dissertation, Columbia University, 1972.

———. "Social Mobility and the Russian Parish Clergy in the Eighteenth Century." *Slavic Review,* XXXIII, no. 4, 641-62.

French, Reginald. *The Slav Orthodox Churches.* London: S.P.C.K., 1923.

Frere, Walter Howard. *Some Links in the Chain of Russian Church History.* London: Faith Press, 1918.

Gagarin, Jean. *De l'enseignement de la théologie dans l'église russe.* Paris, 1856.

———. *The Russian Clergy.* Translated by C. Du Gard Makepeace. London: Burns and Oates, 1872.

———. *Tendances catholique dans la société russe.* Paris, 1860.

Germanotta, Dante. "The Moral Ordering of Society in Sergius Bulgakov." Ph.D. dissertation, Boston University, 1968.

Gogol, N. *The Divine Liturgy.* London, 1960.

Gordillo, M. "Russie (Pensée religieuse)." In *Dictionnaire de théologie catholique,* XIV, pt. 1, cols. 207-371.

Gorodetzky, N. *The Humiliated Christ in Modern Russian Thought.* London, 1938.

——. "Missionary Expansion of the Russian Orthodox Church." In *International Review of Missions*, XXXI, 400-411.

——. *Saint Tikhon Zadonsky*. London, 1951.

Graham, Stephen. *The Way of Martha and the Way of Mary*. New York: Macmillan, 1915.

Gratieux, A. A.S. *Khomiakov et le mouvement slavophile*. 2 vols. Paris, 1939.

Grigorieff, D.F. "Dostoevsky's Elder Zossima and the Real Life of Father Amvrosy." *St. Vladimir's Seminary Quarterly*, XI, 1967, 22-34.

Grunwald, C. *Saints of Russia*. Translated by Roger Cape. New York: Macmillan, 1960.

Hackel, S. *One of Great Price: The life of Mother Maria Skobtsova*. London, 1965.

——. "Questions of Church and State in 'Holy Russia': Some Attitudes of the Romanov Period." *Eastern Churches Review*, III, Spring 1970, 3-17.

Hardy, E.R., Jr. "Russian Orthodox Church at Home and Abroad." *Christendom*, XI, 2, 153-64.

Härtel, H.J. *Byzantinisches Erbe und Orthodoxie bei Feofan Prokopovič*. Würzburg, 1970.

Heard, Albert F. *The Russian Church and Russian Dissent, Comprising Orthodoxy, Dissent, and Erratic Sects*. New York: Harper, 1887.

d'Herbigny, Michel. *Vladimir Soloviev: A Russian Newman (1853-1900)*. Translated by A.M. Buchanan, London, 1918.

Horologion, A Primer for Elementary Village Schools. Translated and Published by the Most Holy Governing Synod of Russia. London: J. Davy, 1897.

Inge, W. "Russian Theology." *Hibbert Journal*, LI, 107-12.

John of Kronstadt [John Ilyich Sergiev]. *My Life in Christ*. Translated by E.E. Goulaeff. London, 1897.

Karpovich, M. "Church and State in Russia." *Russian Review*, III, no. 2, 10-20.

Kidd, Beresford. *The Churches of Eastern Christendom from A.D. 451 to the Present Time*. London: Faith Press, 1927.

Kline, George. "Darwinism and the Russian Orthodox Church." In *Continuity and Change in Russian and Soviet Thought*, edited by Ernest J. Simmons, 307-28. Cambridge: Harvard University Press, 1955.

——. *Religious and Antireligious Thought in Russia*. Chicago: University of Chicago Press, 1968.

——. "Religious Motifs in Russian Philosophy," *Studies on the Soviet Union*, IX, no. 2 (1969), 84-96.

Kniazeff, A. *L'Institut Saint-Serge*. Paris, 1974.

Koch, Hans. *Die russische Orthodoxie im Petrinischen Zeitalter*. Breslau: Priebatsch's Buchh., 1929.

Kondakov, N. *The Russian Ikon*. Oxford, 1927.

Kowalyk, G. *Ecclesiologia Theophanis Prokopovycz: influxus protestantismi*. Rome, 1947.

Laicub. "Church Reform in Russia: Witte versus Pobedonostseff." *Contemporary Review* (London), LXXVII, 1905, 712-26.

Lossky, V. *In the Image and Likeness of God*. Edited by John Erikson and Thomas Bird. Crestwood, N.Y.: St. Vladimir's Seminary Press, 1974.

———. *The Mystical Theology of the Eastern Church*. London, 1957.

———. "Le Starets Ambroise." *Contacts*, XL, 1962, 219-36.

———. "Le Startsy d'Optino." *Contacts*, XXXIII, 1961, 163-76.

———. "Le Starets Macaire." *Contacts*, XXXVII, 1962, 9-19.

———. "Le Starets Leonide." *Contacts*, XXXIV, 1961, 99-107.

———. "The Successors of Vladimir Solovyev." *Slavonic Review*, III, 1924.

Lowrie, Donald A. *The Light of Russia: An Introduction to the Russian Church*. Prague: YMCA Press, 1923.

———. *Saint Sergius in Paris: The Orthodox Theological Institute*. London: S.P.C.K., 1954.

Lutteroth, Henri [Nikolai Ivanovich Turgenev]. *La Russie et les Jésuites de 1772 à 1820 d'après de documents la plupart inédits*. Paris, 1845.

Macarius. *Letters of Direction 1834-1860*. Edited by I. de Beausobre. London, 1944.

Malvy, Antoine. "La réforme de l'église russe." *Études p.d. pères de la compagnie de Jésus* (Paris), CVII, 1906, 100-182, 306-29.

Manning, Clarence. "Khomyakov and the Orthodox Church." *Review of Religion*, VI, 169-78.

Marshall, Richard H. Čexov and the Russian Orthodox Clergy." *Slavic and East European Journal*, VII, no. 4, 375-91.

Masaryk, T.G. *The Spirit of Russia*. 3 vols. London, 1919, 1965.

Mercenier, E.F. Paris, and Bainbridge, G., eds., *La prière des églises de rite byzantin*. 3 vols. Chevetogne, 1947-53.

Meyendorff, John. "History of Eastern Orthodoxy." *Encyclopaedia Britannica*, 15th ed., 1974.

———. *The Orthodox Church: Its Past and Its Role in the World Today*, 2d rev. ed., New York: Pantheon Books, 1969.

Miliukov, Paul. *Religion and the Church*, Outlines of Russian Culture, I, edited by Michael Karpovich; translated by V. Ughet and E. Davis. New York: A.S. Barnes, 1942.

Milovidov, V.F. *Staroobriadchestvo v proshlom i nastoiashchem*. Moscow, 1969.

Mouravieff, A.N. *A History of the Church of Russia*. Translated by R.W. Blackmore. London: J.H. Parker, 1842.

Muller, Alexander. V., ed. and trans. "Historical Antecedents of the Petrine Ecclesiastical Reform." Ph.D. dissertation, University of Washington, 1973.

———. *The Spiritual Regulation of Peter the Great*. Seattle: University of Washington Press, 1972.

Munzer, Egbert. *Solovyev: Prophet of Russian-Western Unity*. London, 1956.

Nelson, Dale L. "Konstantin Leontiev and the Orthodox East." Ph.D. dissertation, University of Minnesota, 1975.

Newman, John Henry Cardinal. *A Visit to the Russian Church*. London, 1882.

Nichols, Robert L. "Metropolitan Filaret of Moscow and the Awakening of Orthodoxy." Ph.D. dissertation, University of Washington, 1972.

Okenfuss, Max J. "Jesuit Origins of Petrine Education." In *The Eighteenth Century in Russia*, edited by J.G. Garrard. Oxford: Oxford University Press, 1973.

Oljančyn, D. *Hryhorij Skoworoda, 1722-1794, der ukrainische Philosoph des XVIII. Jahrhunderts und seine geistigkulturelle Umwelt*. Berlin, 1929.

The Orthodox Liturgy, Being the Divine Liturgy of S. John Chrysostom and S. Basil the Great, According to the Use of the Church of Russia. London: S.P.C.K. for the Fellowship of SS. Alban and Sergius, 1964.

The Orthodox Prayer Book. Wilkes-Barre, Pa.: Svit, 1934.

Ostapov, A. "Rosiki ekklesia." in *Thriskevtiki ke Ithiki Engiklopédia,* X, 976-1086. Athens, 1966.

Ostkirchliche Studien. Würzburg: Augustinus-Verlag, I-, 1952-.

Ouspensky, L., *Essai sur la théologie de l'icone dans l'église orthodoxe.* Paris, 1960.

———, and Lossky, V. *The Meaning of Icons.* Olten, 1952.

Owen, J. *Bible Researches and Travels in Russia.* London, 1826.

Palmer, W. *Notes of a Visit to the Russian Church in the Years 1840, 1841.* Edited by John Henry Cardinal Newman. London, 1882.

Palmieri, F.A. "The Ecclesiastical Training of the Russian Clergy." *American Catholic Quarterly Review,* XLIII, 1918, 529-43.

———. "L'educazione morale del clero russo: I, seminari." *Bessarione* (Rome), VI, no. 3, 1908, 26-39.

———. *Nomenclator litterarius theologiae orthodoxae Russicae ac Graecae recentioris.* 3 vols. Velehrad, Moravia, 1911.

Parsons, Reuben. "Some Heterodoxies and Inconsistencies of Russian Orthodoxy." *American Catholic Quarterly Review* (Philadelphia), XXV, 1900, 675-96.

Paterson, J. *The Book for Every Land: Reminiscences of Labour and Adventure in the Work for Bible Circulation in the North of Europe and in Russia.* Edited by W.L. Alexander. London, 1858.

"Pensées russes sur l'église." *Orientalia christiana* (Rome), VI, 1926.

Petrov, V. *Rossiiskaia dukhovnaia missiia v Kitae.* Washington, D.C.: Kamkin, 1968.

Pfleger, Karl. *Wrestlers with Christ.* New York, 1936.

Pierling, P., S. J. *La Russie et le Saint-Siège.* Paris, 1896.

———. *La Sorbonne et la Russie. 1717-1747.* Paris: E. Leroux, 1882.

———. "Un disegno di reunione della chiesa russa." *Civiltà cattolica* (Rome). LXI, no. 2, 1911, 286-308.

Pinkerton, Robert. *Russia: or, Miscellaneous observations on the past and present state of that country.* London: Seeley and Sons, 1833.

Platon, Archbishop [Porfirii Fiodorovich Rozhdestvenskii]. *On the Question of the Union of the Churches.* Philadelphia, 1911.

Poltoratzky, Nikolai, P. *Russian Religious-Philosophical Thought of the 20th Century.* Pittsburgh: University of Pittsburgh Press, 1972.

Popivchak, Ronald P. "Peter Mohila, Metropolitan of Kiev (1632-1647)." Ph.D. dissertation, Catholic University, 1975.

Reyburn, Hugh. *The Story of the Russian Church.* London: A. Melrose, 1924.

Reynolds, Rothay. "The Russian Church and the Revolution." *Contemporary Review,* CXIII, 1918, 397-405.

Rigdon, Vernon B. "Alexei Stepanovich Khomiakov: Advocate for Orthodoxy." Ph.D. dissertation, Yale University, 1968.

Riley, A. *Birkbeck and the Russian Church.* London, 1917.

Rochcau, Vsevolod. "Innocent Veniaminov and the Russian Mission to Alaska: 1820-1840." *St. Vladimir's Seminary Quarterly*, XV, 1971, 105-20.

Romanoff, H. *Sketches of the Rites of the Greco-Russian Church*. London, 1869.

Rouëtde Journal, M.J. *La compagnie de Jésus en Russie: Un collège de Jésuites à Saint-Pétersbourg, 1800-1816*. Paris, 1922.

———. *Nonciatures de Russie: d'après les documents authentiques, v. V, Intérim de benvenuti, 1799-1803* [Studi e testi no. 194]. Vatican City, 1957.

Rouse, R. and Neill, S.C. *A History of the Ecumenical Movement*. London, 1954.

Runciman, Steven. *The Great Church in Captivity*. Cambridge: Cambridge University Press, 1968.

———. *The Orthodox Churches and the Secular State*. Auckland: Auckland University Press, 1971.

Sabaneff, Leonid. "Pavel Florensky – Priest, Scientist, Mystic." *Russian Review*, XX, no. 4, 312-25.

———. "Religious and Mystical Trends in Russia at the Turn of the Century." *Russian Review*, XXIV, no. 4, 354-68.

Sawatsky, Walter W. "Prince Alexander N. Golitsyn (1773-1844): Tsarist Minister of Piety." Ph.D. dissertation, University of Minnesota, 1976.

Scheibert, P., "Die Petersburger religiös-philosophischen Zusammenkünfte von 1902 und 1903." *Jahrbücher für Geschichte Osteuropas*, n.s. XII, 1964, 513-60.

Scherer, Stephen. "The Life and Thought of Russia's First Theologian, Gregory Savvič Skovoroda, 1722-1794." Ph.D. dissertation, Ohio State University, 1969.

Schmemann, Alexander. *The Historical Road of Eastern Orthodoxy*. Translated by L.W. Kesich. New York: Holt, Rinehart, and Winston, 1963.

———, ed. *Ultimate Questions: An Anthology of Modern Russian Religious Thought*. New York, 1965.

Seraphim, Metropolitan. *Die Ostkirche*. Stuttgart, 1950.

Šerech, J. "On Teofan Prokopovic as Writer and Preacher in his Kiev Period." *Harvard Slavic Studies*, II, 1954, 211-23; reprinted 1971.

———. "Stefan Iavorski and the Conflict of Ideologies in the Age of Peter the Great." *Slavonic and East European Review*, XXX, December 1951, 40-62.

Sergieff, John. *My Life in Christ*. 1897.

Service Book of the Holy Orthodox-Catholic Apostolic (Greco-Russian) Church. Compiled and edited by Isabel Florence Hapgood. Boston: Houghton Mifflin, 1906.

Sheshko, Peter L. "The Russian Orthodox Church Council of Moscow of 1917-1918." Ph.D. dissertation, University of Ottawa, 1972.

Simon, Gerhard. "Church, State and Society." In *Russia Enters the Twentieth Century 1894-1917*, edited by Erwin Oberlander, *et al.* New York: Schocken Books, 1971, 199-235.

Simon, G. *K.P. Pobedonoscev und die Kirchenpolitik des Heiligen Sinod 1880 bis 1905*. Göttingen, 1969.

Smirnoff, E. *Russian Orthodox Missions*. London, 1903.

Smolitsch, I. *Geschichte der russischen Kirche 1700-1917*. I, Leiden, 1964.

———. *Moines de la Sainte Russie*. Paris, 1967.

———. *Russisches Mönchtum: Entstehung, Entwicklung und Wesen, 988-1917.* Würzburg: Augustinus-Verlag, 1953.

Sofrony. *The Undistorted Image: Staretz Siloun (1866-1938).* London, 1952.

Soloviev, V. *God, Man, and the Church: The Spiritual Foundations of Life.* London, 1937.

———. *The Justification of the Good.* London, 1918.

———. *The Meaning of Love.* London, 1945.

———. *La Russie et l'église universelle.* Paris, 1889.

———. *A Solovyov Anthology.* Edited by S.L. Frank; translated by Natalie Duddington. New York, 1950.

———. *War, Progress, and the End of History.* London, 1915.

Spectorsky, Eugene. "Dukhovnoe nasledie XIX veka." In *Transactions of the Association of Russian-American Scholars in the USA,* V. Edited by Constantine Belousow, *et al.* New York, 1971.

Spiridon, Archimandrite. *Mes missions en Siberie.* Paris, 1950.

Stanley, Arthur P. *Lectures on the History of the Eastern Church.* London: J.M. Dent, 1907.

Stavrou, Theofanis G. *Russian Interests in Palestine 1882-1914: A Study of Religious and Educational Enterprise.* Thessaloniki: Institute for Balkan Studies, 1963.

Stourdza, Alexandre. *Considerations sur la doctrine et l'Esprit de l'église orthodoxe.* Stuttgart, 1816.

Stremooukhoff, D. *Vladimir Soloviev et son oeuvre messianique.* Strasbourg, 1935.

Struve, Nikita A. "Orthodox Missions, Past and Present." *St. Vladimir's Seminary Quarterly,* VII, no. 1, 31-42.

Stupperich, Robert. *Staatsgedanke und Religionspolitik Peters des Grossen.* Königsberg, Berlin: Ost-Europaverlag, 1936.

———. "Feofan Prokopovič in Rom." *Zeitschrift für osteuropäische Geschichte,* V, 1931, 327-39.

———. "F. Prokopovičs theologische Bestrebungen." *Kyrios,* IV, 1936, 350-62.

———. "Feofan Prokopovič und Johann Franz Buddeus." *Zeitschrift für osteuropäische Geschichte,* IX [=n.s., V], 1935, 341-62.

———. "F. Prokopovič und seine akademische Wirksamkeit in Kiev." *Zeitschrift für slavische Philologie,* XVII, 1941, 96-99.

Sydorenko, A. "The Kievan Academy in the 17th Century," Ph.D. dissertation, University of Illinois at Urbana-Champaign, 1974.

Talbot Rice, T. *The Russian Ikon.* London, 1947.

Teodorovich, Nadezhda. "Monasteries of the Russian Orthodox Church." *Bulletin of the Institute for the Study of the USSR,* XIII, no. 9, September 1966, 3-12.

Tolstoy, Dmitry. *Le catholicisme romain en Russie.* 2 vols. Paris, 1863-64.

Treadgold, Donald W. "The Peasant and Religion." In *The Peasant in Nineteenth Century Russian History,* edited by Wayne S. Vucinich. Stanford: Stanford University Press, 1968.

Troitsky, S.V., and Minns, G.H., "Russian Church." *Hastings' Encyclopedia of Religion and Ethics,* X. New York, 1919.

Trubetskoi, Eugene N. *Icons: Theology in Color.* Translated by Gertrud Vakar. Crestwood, N.Y.: St. Vladimir's Seminary Press, 1973.

Turkevich, Leonid. *Essays of Orthodox Theology.* New York, 1918.

Valliere, Paul R. "M.M. Tareev: A Study in Russian Ethics and Mysticism." Ph.D. dissertation, Columbia University, 1974.

Vreis, Wilhelm De. *Der christliche Osten in Geschichte und Gegenwart.* Würzburg: Augustinus-Verlag, 1951.

Ware, Timothy. *The Orthodox Church.* Baltimore: Penguin Books, 1963.

The Way of a Pilgrim. Translated by R.M. French. London, 1954.

Weisensel, Peter, "Avraam Sergeivich Norov: Nineteenth-Century Russian Traveler, Bureaucrat and Educator," Ph.D. dissertation, University of Minnesota, 1973.

Winter, Eduard. *Halle als Ausgangspunkt der deutschen Russlandkunde im 18. Jahrhundert.* Berlin, 1935.

———. "Die Jesuiten in Russland (1772 bis 1820): Ein Beitrag zur Auseinandersetzung zwischen Aufklärung und Restauration." In *Forschen und Wirken: Festschrift zur 150-Jahr-Feier der Humboldt-Universität zu Berlin, 1810-1960,* III. Berlin, 1960, 167-91.

———. *Russland und das Papsttum.* 2 vols. Berlin: Akademie-Verlag, 1960-61.

Zacek, Judith Cohen. "The Lancastrian School Movement in Russia." *Slavonic and East European Review,* XLV, July 1967, 343-67.

———. "The Russian Bible Society, 1812-1826." Ph.D. dissertation, Columbia University, 1964; Ann Arbor, Mich.: University Microfilms, 1967.

———. "The Russian Bible Society and the Russian Orthodox Church." *Church History,* XXXV, no. 4, December 1966, 3-29.

Zalenski, P. Stanislas. *Les Jésuites de la Russie-blanche.* Paris, 1886.

Zenkovsky, V.V. *A History of Russian Philosophy.* Translated by George L. Kline. 2 vols. New York, 1953.

Zernov, Nicholas. *Eastern Christendom: A Study of the Origin and Development of the Eastern Orthodox Church.* New York: G.P. Putnam, 1961.

———. "Peter the Great and the Establishment of the Russian Church." *Church Quarterly Review,* CXXV, no. 250, January-March 1938, 265-93.

———. "The Reform of the Church and the Pre-Revolutionary Russian Episcopate," *St. Vladimir's Seminary Quarterly,* VI, no. 3, 1962, 128-38.

———. *The Russian Religious Renaissance of the Twentieth Century.* Darton, Eng.: Longman and Todd, 1963.

———. *The Russians and Their Church.* London: S.P.C.K., 1945.

———. *Three Russian Prophets (Khomiakov, Dostoevsky, and V. Soloviev).* London, 1944.

LIST OF CONTRIBUTORS

List of Contributors

James Cracraft is Associate Professor of History at the University of Illinois at Chicago Circle. His publications include *The Church Reform of Peter the Great* (1971) and two special studies of Prokopovich. The first, in J. G. Garrard, ed., *The Eighteenth Century in Russia* (1973), is a general survey of Prokopovich's career; the second is a complete bibliography of Prokopovich's works, in *Oxford Slavonic Papers* (n.s., VIII, 1975, 1-36 with plate). Professor Cracraft is currently writing a comprehensive study of culture and politics in Petrine Russia.

David W. Edwards, a native of Illinois, was born in 1939. After studying at Oklahoma State University and the University of Colorado, he received his Ph.D. in 1967 from Kansas State University. At present he teaches Russian History at the University of Arkansas. His principal area of research has been church-state relations in Russia during the first half of the nineteenth century.

Gregory L. Freeze is Associate Professor of History at Brandeis University and has recently published *The Russian Levites: Parish Clergy in the Eighteenth Century* (1977).

Edward Kasinec, Research Bibliographer and Librarian for the Ukrainian Studies program at Harvard University, is the author of more than twenty studies in the field of library and information science. He has lectured on these subjects at numerous North American and British institutions of higher learning. Mr. Kasinec has received several awards for his work.

The Reverend John Meyendorff, Professor of Church History and Patristics at St. Vladimir's Orthodox Theological Seminary and Professor of Byzantine History at Fordham University, is the author of several books. These include *A Study of Gregory Palamas, Christ in Eastern Thought, Orthodoxy and Catholicity,* and *Byzantine Theology.* In 1977 he was elected Corresponding Fellow of the British Academy and in 1978 became Acting Director of Studies, Dumbarton Oaks Center for Byzantine Studies, Harvard University.

Alexander V. Muller, Associate Professor of History at California State University, Northridge, specializes in early Russian history. He has edited and translated *The Spiritual Regulation of Peter the Great.* Another book, *The Character of Old Russia,* an edited translation from S. M. Solov'ev's *History of Russia,* is scheduled to appear soon.

Robert L. Nichols, Associate Professor of History at Saint Olaf College, is currently writing a biography *Metropolitan Filaret (Drozdov) and the Awakening of Orthodoxy.*

Theofanis G. Stavrou, Professor of History at the University of Minnesota, concentrates his research on Russia and Orthodoxy in the context of Slavic-Near Eastern cultural relations. His publications include *Russian Interests in Palestine 1882-1914, A Study of Religious and Educational Enterprise* (1963), *Russia under the Last Tsar* (ed., 1969), *The Great Revival, The Russian Church under German Occupation* (with Wassilij Alexeev, 1976), and several articles on Russian religious thinkers. He has just completed, with Peter Weisensel, an annotated bibliography *Russian Travelers to the Orthodox East from the Twelfth to the Twentieth Century,* which will appear soon.

Marc M. Szeftel, Professor of History Emeritus at the University of Washington, has recently published two books: *Russian Institutions and Culture up to Peter the Great* (1975) and *The Russian Constitution of April 23, 1906* (1977). He is also the author of several other books and numerous shorter studies.

Donald W. Treadgold is currently chairman of the Department of History at the University of Washington and president of the American Association for the Advancement of Slavic Studies; for eleven years he was editor of the *Slavic Review*. He has published several books, including *Twentieth Century Russia* (4th ed., 1976) and *The West in Russia and China* (2 vols., 1973), and articles.

Paul Valliere grew up in Massachusetts and graduated from Williams College in 1965. He received a doctorate in religion from Columbia University in 1974. Currently he is an assistant professor of religion in Columbia University, where he is also Chairman of Columbia College Humanities and an associate member of the Russian Institute.

INDEX

Index

Academy of Sciences, 37, 73; Division of Russian Language and Literature, 73
Act of Succession (1797), 130
Administration of church: canon law, 175, 186; centralized, 174; control of, 143; decentralized, 174, 175, 198
Adrian, Patriarch, 142
Agafangel (Solov'ev), Archbishop, 209
Akhmatova, Anna, 8, 39
Aksakov, N. P., 190, 191
Alekseevskii Monastery, 221
Aleksei of Zossima, 38
Aleutian Islands, 26, 177, 180
Alexander I, 74, 79, 80, 82, 85, 220; and church reform, 114; "pietist conversion" of, 83
Alexander II, 24, 28, 72, 91, 103, 112, 113, 114, 115, 116, 123; as member of Synod, 168n
Alexander III, 25, 28, 211
Alexander Nevskii Monastery, 146, 220
Alexander Nevskii Seminary, 68, 81

All-Russian National Council. See Sobor
Alston, Patrick, 66
American autocephalous church, 177
American Historical Association, 42n
American scholarship on Orthodoxy, 42n
Amur region, 208
Amvrosii, Bishop of Nizhnii Novgorod, 162-63
Anastasii, Bishop of Iamburg, 28
Anatolii, Bishop of Chistopol, 28
Ancillon, Jean Pierre Frédéric, 81
Anna Ivanovna, Empress of Russia, 25
Annenkov, P. V., 122
Anticlericalism of overprocurators, 24
Anti-intellectualism and church, 11, 21
Anti-Semitism: and Christianity, 34; and Orthodoxy, 8, 34, 36, 40, 42n; and parish clergy, 35; and political reaction, 34
Antonii (Khrapovitskii), Archbishop, 38, 133, 176, 179, 180-81, 209

Antonii (Vadkovskii), Metropolitan of
    St. Petersburg, 38, 172, 173, 179,
    185
Apostolic canon, 30, 175
Apostolic Council of Jerusalem, 195
Aquinas, St. Thomas, 48
Archaeographic Commission, 72, 119n
Archangel province, 114
Archbishop of Armed Forces
    (proposed), 164
Archdioceses, 26
Archival commissions (eparchial), 221
Archive of Ancient Acts (TsGADA),
    222
Archives of Holy Synod, 220
Arifmetika (Magnitskii), 54
Aristotle, 54, 55, 56, 77
Arseniev, Vasilii, 38
Arsenii (Stadnitskii), 38
Askochenskii, V. I., 210
Augurskii, Mikhail, 4
Augustine, St., 75
Austria, 213
Avvakum, Archpriest, 4

Bacon, Francis, 57
Bakhtiarov, A. A., 206, 227
Bakunin, M., 86
Balkans, 128
Bantysh-Kamenskii, N., 66
Baptism, 32
Baronius, Caesar, 75
Baroque culture, 51, 54
Barshev, Iakov, 87n
Barshev, Sergei, 87n
Barsov, T. V., 214
Basileus, 130, 170
Batiushkov, P. N., 91, 117
Bayer, G. Z., 46, 49, 50, 51, 55, 61n
Bazhanov, V. B., 103, 108, 113, 122n
Beliaev, I. D., 73, 87n, 88n
Belliustin, I. S., 11, 12, 91, 104, 111,
    118n, 119n; career, 93, 94, 95, 96,
    104, 107, 108, 109, 113, 114, 115;
    church reform, 99, 100; and church
    schools, 100; and clerical service,

93, 100; as conservative, 92, 97;
    diocesan reform, 101, 103; and em-
    peror, 115; and gentry, 93; and his-
    torical research, 98; and imperial
    family, 107; and "learned priests,"
    96; and monasticism, 95, 97, 103,
    104-5, 112; and official mistrust,
    114, 115; and Old Belief, 114;
    and parish priests, 92; and parish
    reform, 101, 112; and Pogodin,
    97-98, 99, 108, 109, 112; as radi-
    cal, 92, 112, 114, 115; and scholar-
    ship, 194; and serfdom, 93, 99;
    and schools for girls, 113; as
    Slavophile, 97; and "spiritual
    magnetism," 98; as "tool" of state,
    115. See also Description of the
    Rural Clergy
Belliustin, Nikolai, 107, 117n
Belliustin, Stefan Ioannovich, 118n
Belorussia, 36, 176
Berdiaev, Nicholas, 39, 214
Berdnikov, Ilia, 195, 196, 197, 198,
    201n
Berlin, 227
Bethany (monastery), 38
Betskoi, I. I., 76
Bezhetsk, 118n
Bible Society, 206, 209
Bible, Russian translation of, 14, 156
Bingham, J., 83
Biographical Dictionary (Biograficheskii
    slovar', of Moscow University), 69
Birkbeck collection, 213
Bishops: and anti-Semitism, 34-35;
    attitude of, 28; "auxiliary," 176;
    and church administration, 157;
    congresses of, 25; distinguished
    from archbishops, 189; and Duma,
    36; election of, 180; equality of,
    189; knowledge of diocese, 166;
    overwork of, 7, 29-30; reports of,
    165; and schools, 41n; selection of,
    23; separation from flock, 7, 26,
    29, 30; vocation of, 188. See also
    Hierarchy

Black Hundreds, 34, 35

Blanc, Simone, 213

Bodianskii, O. M., 73

Bodleian Library (Oxford), 213

Bogdanovskii, Evstafii, 71, 87

Bogoiavlenskii Monastery, 221

Bogorodskii, S. O., 87n

Böhme, Jacob, 75

Boltin, I. V., 24

Bookprinting, Russian, 66, 219

Borelli, G. A., 55

Bossuet, J. B., 3

Bowen, James, 65, 86

Boyle, Robert, 55

Brahe, Tycho, 55

Brotherhood Monastery (Kiev), 45, 46

Brotherhood movement, 45, 59, 62

Brotherhood of Lwow, 59

Buchan, William, 70

Buddeus, J. F., 83

Buddhism, 35

Bulgakov, Sergei, 39, 214

Bulgarian church, 197

Bunakov-Fundamenskii, Ilia, 40

Butkevich, Fr., 37

Caesaropapism, 127, 129, 130

Canon: apostolic canon 30, 15; as basis of church, 15; "canonical territorialism," 131; and discipline, 189, 190; and freedom, 188, 189, 190, 191; and independence, 199; norms, 175; return to, 186

"Canon and Freedom" (Aksakov), 190

Canonizations, 131, 208

Cathedral of the Assumption (Moscow), 220

Cathedral of the Dormition (Moscow), 128

Catherine II, 24, 67, 69, 75, 76, 78, 85, 86, 137

Catholicism, 32, 35; and Orthodoxy, 105, 109

Catholicos of Georgia, 176, 182n

Catullus, 50

Caucasus, 35, 176

Censorship, 23, 95, 103, 110, 112, 121n; St. Petersburg Committee on, 109, 112

Central Administration of Monasteries, 144

Central Asia, 35

Chaadaev, Peter, 9

Chebyshev, P. P., 24

Cherkasskii, V. A., 99

Chernigov, 209

Chernigovskii Monastery, 221

Chernyshevskii, N., 92

Chicherin, Adjutant General, 160

Chief Military Chaplain of Army and Navy Forces, 164, 207

Chrismation (miropamazanie), 28, 32

Christianity: and revolution, 37; and science, 55; and socialism, 37

"Christianity and Science in the Nineteenth Century" (Belliustin), 94

Chrysostom, St. John, 75

Church: autonomy of, 30, 172, 188; bureaucratization of, 131, 140n; discipline, 174; independence of, 184; and intelligentsia, 192; local administration, 103; as ministry, 156, 157, 170; as "nation," 193; as popular assembly, 193; and scholarship, 37-38; as "spiritual collegium," 131; as state institution, 13, 14, 37, 90. See also Reform of church

Church and state, 12, 16; Byzantine-Muscovite legacy, 12, 127, 128, 129, 137, 170; "illegal" dependency of church, 173; in reign of Alexander I, 115

Church of England, 130

Church-School Department, 161

Churikov, Ivan, 7

Chuvash, 28

Cicero, 50, 75

Clergy: attitude to state, 171; as caste, 27, 67, 90, 91, 92, 178, 179; as citizens, 179; and city duma, 179; as civil servants, 165; cultic role,

178, 179; dependence of 161, 165;
and Duma, 36, 37; and education,
27-28, 66; loyalty to throne, 137;
and politics, 37, 180; "privileged"
position of, 171; "question" of,
91; and reform, 171; salary, 102,
137; social responsibilities, 180;
special commission on (1862),
103; as state tool, 136; as witness
of Christ's message, 179. See also
Education of Clergy; Parish priest
Code of Laws (1833), 156, 167
College of Economy of the Synodal
Administration, 23, 25
College of Justice, 150
College of St. Athanasius, 9, 49, 50
"Collegial principle," 131
"Combined ministry" of cults and
education, 24
Commission for the Description of the
Archives of the Holy Synod, 220
Commission on Ecclesiastical Schools,
80, 160-61, 168n
Committee of Ministers, 133, 158,
172, 185, 218
Conception Monastery, 223
Conference on Ecclesiastical Affairs,
173
Confession: Catholic, 49; disclosure
of, 137
Confessionalism, 197, 198
Congress of Russian Jurists (1875),
73
Consistory, 25; diocesan, 157;
Lutheran, 23; Moscow, 221; reform
of, 157
Constitution (1906): and church, 12,
131, 133, 138; and legal status of
church, 130, 133, 140n
Control Department of Ecclesiastical
Affairs, 159
Conversions in Polish provinces, 36
Copernicus, 55
Coronation, religious element in, 129,
137
Council. See Sobor

Courts, ecclesiastical, 103, 174
Crimean War, 98
Culture and Orthodoxy, 28, 31
Curtiss, John S., 3, 35, 42n

Danilov Monastery, 222
Dashkova, Princess, 73
Das Leben Jesu (Strauss), 94
Davydov, I. I., 85
Deism, 10, 24
Delianov, I. D., 99
Democratic intelligentsia, 66
Demosthenes, 50
Denisov, L. I., 217
Department of Orthodox Church, 170
Descartes, René, 57
Description of the Rural Clergy (Opi-
sanie sel'skogo dukhovenstva)
(Belliustin), 11, 91, 104, 105, 106,
107, 109, 112, 123n; foreign
debate of, 110-11, 112; radical
critique of, 123n
Diaconate for women, 32, 39, 42n
Diarchy, 12, 128
Diocese, 26; administration of, 90;
courts, 157; gazettes (vedomosti),
208, 209; Moscow, 23; reform of,
101, 103, 136, 145; structure of,
26, 30; subdivision of, 189
Directory of the Christ the Savior
Cathedral, 223
Discipline in church, 187
Divine right monarchy, 12
Division of Russian Language and
Literature. See Academy of
Sciences
Divorce laws, 158
Dmitrii (Muretov), Archbishop, 209
Dobroliubov, N., 110, 112
Dogma, 154; emphasis on Spirit, 199
Donskoi Monastery, 223
Dorosh, John, 212
Dositheus, Patriarch of Jerusalem,
48
Dostoevsky, F. M., 11, 86
Dukhovnaia beseda, 38

Dukhovnyi Sobor of Trinity-St. Sergius Monastery, 222
Duma, 8, 13, 133, 180; and church budget, 13, 134, 136; and church schools, 134, 138, 179; election of clergy to, 135, 179; and national synod, 139
—First: and clergy, 135
—Second: and clergy, 135
—Third, 134, 138; and clergy, 135, 140n
—Fourth: and clergy, 136

Eastern Slavs, 44
Ecclesiastical academies, 6, 15, 28, 29, 57, 181
Ecclesiastical College, 23, 142, 145
Ecclesiastical provinces, 174, 175, 176
Ecclesiastical Regulation (1720), 22, 26, 56, 76, 131, 145, 165, 166, 214; article 8, 145
Ecclesiastical stewards (zakashchiki), 145
Ecclesiastical superintendents (blagochinnye), 145
Ecclesiastical Synod, 23
Economic College, 221
Economic Committee of the Holy Synod, 160, 161
Eckhartshausen, 83
Ecumenical councils, 186; fathers of, 193
Edinovercheskii Monastery, 221
Edinoverie, 210
Education of clergy, 6, 7, 22, 28, 65, 66, 74; as barrier to laity, 9; and career, 93-94; compared to nobles, 10, 11, 76-77, 79; reform of, 27, 72; theological character, 174; and tradition, 77, 83, 86; and westernization, 78, 79-84. See also Schools
Ekaterina, Abbess of Lesna, 39, 42n
Elagin, Nikolai, 111
Elena Pavlovna, Grand Duchess, 108
Elizabeth, Empress of Russia, 23, 24, 25, 70, 75

Elizaveta Fedorovna, Grand Duchess, 38
Emancipation, 33
Emancipation Proclamation, 33
Émile, 76
Encyclopedists, 88n
Entsiklopediia zakonovedeniia (Nevolin), 72
Ethics, subject at Kiev academy, 56
Evgenii (Bolkhovitinov), 81, 218; proposal for academic conference, 80
Evlogii (Georgievskii), Metropolitan of Western Europe, 136, 180
Exarch of Georgia, 82, 132, 176, 177, 182n

Feofilakt (Rusanov), Bishop, 81, 82, 83
Fesler, Ignatius, 81, 82, 83, 84
Filaret (Amfiteatrov), Metropolitan of Kiev, 14, 132, 160
Filaret (Drozdov), Metropolitan of Moscow, 10, 11, 14, 34, 40, 42n, 70, 79, 94-95, 105, 109, 111, 132, 159, 207; and education, 79, 82, 85; and emancipation, 33, 42n; and episcopal authority, 163; and monasticism, 79; and Nicholas I, 162, 163, 164; and Petrine reform of church, 159, 171-72; rector, 83; recovery of Orthodoxy, 11, 33, 84; school reform, 86; and science. 95
Filaret (Gumilevskii), 165, 218
Filosofov, D. V., 29
Finances: of church, 23, 30; accounting, 159
First World War, 138
Fiscals: ecclesiastical, 145; secular, 13; of Senate, 144
Flavian (Gorodetskii), Metropolitan of Kiev, 38, 175-76, 216
Fletcher, Giles, 73
Florentine Union. See Union of Florence
Florinskii, M. T., 42n

Florovsky, Georges, 47, 64n, 78
Foreign confessions, 222
Frank, S. L., 40
Freemasonry, 10, 78, 214
Fundamental Laws, 131, 156; article
    7, 133; article 10, 140; article 62,
    129; article 63, 129, 133; article
    64, 129, 130; article 65, 133;
    article 86, 133, 134; article 87,
    134; article 107, 133
    —(1906), 129, 134; article 4, 137

Galich, A. I., 85, 86
Gamaleia, 214
Gapon, Fr., 42n
Gavriil (Petrov), Metropolitan, 73
Gavrilov, A. V., 218
General procurator of Senate, 147
"Geometria." See Prokopovich, Feofan
Georgia, 26, 182n; separatism in, 176
Germany, 213
Gethsemane Hermitage, 221
Giliarov-Platonov, N. P., 212
Glubokovskii, N. N., 216
Golitsyn, A. N., 24, 82, 214
Golubinskii, Fedor, 84
Gorizontov, I., 217
Gorskii, A. V., 165, 219
Great Reforms, 90, 91, 103, 115
Greek church, 197; and Russian
    Orthodoxy, 9
Gribowski, W., 130, 131
Grigorii (Postnikov), Metropolitan of
    St. Petersburg, 38, 94, 96, 104,
    105, 106, 109, 120, 209, 210
Grigorovich, N. I., 220
GUA (Glavnoe Upravlenie Arkhikov),
    222
Gumilevskii, A. V., 210

Hans , Nicholas, 66
Haven, Peder von, 56, 64n
"Helleno-Greek" Academy, 26, 41n,
    75
Helsinki University Library, 212
Heresy: Synod combating, 23; and
    Orthodoxy, 136-37

Hermogen Hermitage, 221
Herzen, Alexander, 33, 86, 111, 121
Hierarchy: and intelligentsia, 172;
    and overprocurator, 172; and
    reform, 115, 116, 171, 174; social
    background of, 179; and Synod,
    177. See also Bishops
Historical-statistical committees, 221
History of Russian Civil Law (Istoriia
    rossiiskikh grazhdanskikh zakonov)
    (Nevolin), 72
Horace, 50, 77

Iaroslavl, 209
Iaroslavl Juridical Lyceum (lycée
    Demidov), 72
Iaroslavl Seminary, 87n
Iasynskii, Varlaam, 47, 49
Iavorskii, Stefan: 47, 48, 49, 54, 57,
    59, 61, 62n. See also Rock of
    Faith
Idealism, 10, 39, 84
Illiustratsiia, 110
Imperial Historical Society, 216
"In Coena Domini," 49
Indekeu, Fr. Charles, 227
Inheritance, 23
Innokentii, Bishop of Tambov, 34
Innokentii (Borisov), Archbishop of
    Kherson, 27
Innokentii (Veniaminov), Metropolitan
    of Moscow, 102
Inquisitors, 13, 143, 145; duties of,
    148; contrasted with overprocura-
    tor, 148; requirements for, 149-50;
    restrictions on, 149
Intellectuals: and Orthodoxy, 7, 8, 21,
    22, 29, 39, 40, 74; separation from
    Russian tradition, 21, 22, 76
Ioasaf (Krokovskii). See Krokovskii,
    Ioasaf
Iosif, Archimandrite, 33
Iosifo-Volokalamskii Monastery, 222
Ireland, 31
Isidore, Metropolitan, 105
Islam, 35
Italy, 31, 49, 51

Iur'ev Monastery, 222
Iurodstvo, 208
Ivanovskii Monastery, 221
Iz glubiny (1921), 39
Iz pod glyb, 39

Jacobi, F. H., 84
Jesuits, 48, 49, 52, 56, 105, 214;
colleges of, 47; of Poland, 53, 54,
59; and rhetoric, 54; scholasticism,
50; and schools, 26
Jesus, 36
Jews, 39-40, 43n
John of Kronstadt, 7
Johnson, Samuel, 86
Johnson, W. H. E., 66
Joseph II, Emperor of Austria, 67
*Journey from St. Petersburg to
Moscow* (Radishchev), 77, 91
Judaism, 34, 40
Judicial reform of 1864, 132
Jung-Stilling, H., 83
Juvenal, 50

Kadets, 9; and clergy, 36
Kalachov, N. V., 99, 107
Kaliazin, 92, 93, 99. 108, 115, 116,
122
Kamer-kontora, 23
Kant, Immanuel, 82, 84
Kantemir, Antioch, 62n
Kashin, 96
Katholikos, 196
Katkov, M., 86
Kazan, 176, 181
Kazan Ecclesiastical Academy, 195,
209, 214, 217
Kazan Seminary, 217
Kazanskii Monastery, 221
Kazanskii, P., 140n
Kharbin, 227
Kh'arkov Seminary, 210
Kh'arkov University, 69
Kharlamov, I. G., 209
Kherson diocese, 209
Kholmgory diocese, 150
Khomiakov, A. S., 193

Khotkovskii Monastery, 221
Khristianskoe chtenie, 38
Khvorostinin, Makarii, 146
Kiev, 45, 47, 176, 181, 208, 209;
seminary, 85
Kiev Academy, 9, 10, 44, 45, 46, 47,
51, 52, 55, 56, 61, 62n, 67, 105,
217
Kiev University, 87n
Kinoveia Monastery, 221
Kireevskii brothers, 86
Kliuchevskii, V. O., 69, 144
Kochanowski, Jan, 52
Kolomna, 79
Kolosov (librarian), 217
Kondrashev, S. I., 28
Konstantin Nikolaevich, Grand Duke,
108-9
Korobanov Monastery, 96
Korsunskii, I. N., 217
Kotlin, 146
Kovalevskii, E., 135
Kozlovskii, A. S., 24
Krajcar, Fr., Jan, 213, 227
Krokovskii, Ioasaf, 47, 49
Krylov, Nikita, 72
Kudriavtsev, 27, 28
Kufaev, 206
Kursk Seminary, 69

Lambin brothers, 215
Latin: in schools, 6, 9, 27, 78, 100;
"Latin learning," 48, 57, 80
Lavrentii, Bishop of Tula, 174
Law: and Orthodox church, 10, 11
70, 71-72, 85, 87n, 132, 156, 157,
167, 218; Soviet law, 179
Learned societies, 68, 73
Learned professions, 10, 11, 85, 88n
Lebedev, A. A., 216
Leibnitz, G. W., 57
Lenin Library, 213
Lenin, V. I., 6
Leningrad Theological Academy, 213
Leonid, Suffragan Bishop of Moscow,
40
Leshkov, V. N., 72-73, 87n

Leskov, N., 207
Levitskii, Dmitri, 66
Liberalism: and constitutional reform, 133; and church, 90, 91, 92, 98; among clergy, 11, 116, 132
Library of Congress, 212
Lieb Library (Basle), 213
Liturgy, 23, 31, 32, 174; impact of, 31; reform of, 32; and Russian language, 31
Liubopytnyi, P., 218
Living Church, 37, 179
Livy, 50
Lomonosov, M. V., 54, 66, 75
Lopukhin, A. P., 216
"Lovers of Wisdom," 84, 85
Luk'ianov, (Overprocurator), 134
L'vov, A. N., 220
Lwow, 47, 59

Magdalena, Abbess, 39
Magnitskii, M., 54
Main Archival Administration. See GUA
Makarii (Bulgakov), Metropolitan of Moscow, 37-38, 132, 210, 214
Makarii (Khvorostinin), Hieromonk, 146, 147
Mandelshtam, Osip, 8, 39
Mansurov, Pavel, 38
Mansurov, Sergei, 38
Marriage, 23, 50, 135, 158, 174; and imperial family, 222
Martial, 50
"Marvelous decade" (1830s), 84
Marxism, 39, 40
Matossian, Mary, 7
Maximov, Vladimir, 3
Mazepa, Hetman, 60
Medicine, 10, 11, 70, 71, 73, 85, 87n, 100, 112
Medico-Chirurgical Academy: Moscow, 70; St. Petersburg, 70, 87n
Melanges de littérature et de philosophie (Ancillon), 81
Mel'gunov, S., 42n
Melissino, I. I., 24

Melnikov-Pecherskii, P. I., 207
"Memorandum of the Thirty-two." See Thirty-two Priests of St. Petersburg
"Memorandum on the Contemporary Situation of the Russian Church" (Witte), 194
Merezhkovskii, D., 7, 192, 198
Meshchanstvo, 45
Meshcherskii, P. S., 155, 156, 158, 160, 166
Metafizika v drevnei Gretsii (S. Trubetskoi), 37
Metricheskaia kniga, 165, 166
Metropolitan, 189; councils, 189; metropolitanates, 26; of Caucasus, 176; of St. Petersburg, 177
Mezhov, V. I., 215
Ministerial schools, 141n
Ministry of Agriculture and State Property, 221
Ministry of Culture, 222
Ministry of Education, 69, 99, 114, 138
Ministry of Foreign Affairs, 222
Ministry of Interior, 91, 222
Ministry of War, 72
Minor, The (Nedorosl'), 77
Miracles, Synod verification of reports concerning, 23
Miron (inquisitor), 150
Missionary Survey (Missionerskoe obozrenie) 14, 187
Missions, 189; congress of, 25
Missouri Synodal Lutherans, 33
Młodzianowski, Thomas, 53, 59
Moderate Right, 36, 37
Modernity, effects on Orthodoxy, 16, 186, 194, 197
Modernization, 186; of church, 142; in Russia, 199
Mogilev Seminary, 87n
Monasterial Prikaz, 23
Monastery of the Caves (Kiev), 44, 60, 206, 210
Moroshkin, M., 214
Moscow, 146, 147, 176, 181

Moscow Ecclesiastical Academy, 38, 62n, 84, 209, 213, 217, 222; "student colloquium," 84
Moscow Eparchial Library, 222
Moscow Regional Archives (TsGAMO), 222
Moscow seminary, 222-23
Moscow Synodal Office. *See* Synod
Moscow synodal typography, 218
Moscow University, 38, 68, 69, 73, 80; gymnasium, 68
Moskovskie vedomosti, 98
Moskvitianin, 97, 98
Mozhaisk Luzhets Monastery, 223
Murav'ev, A. N., 90, 109, 111, 117n
Murom, 207
Muscovy, 127, 128, 170
Music and Russian liturgy, 31, 32
Mysli svetskogo cheloveka (Murav'ev), 109, 110

Nadezhdin, N. I., 86
Napoleon I, 80, 83
Narodnichestvo, 74, 180
National Council. *See Sobor*
Nationalism, 176
Nationalists, 36, 37
National synod, Duma pressure for, 136
Naturphilosophie, 71
Nazis, 34
Nechaev, S. D., 24, 155, 156, 160, 161, 162, 163, 164, 166
Nedelia, 91
Nevolin, K. A., 72
Nevostruev (priest), 219
New York Public Library, Slavonic Division, 227
Nicea, council of: canons 4 and 5, 173; second council of, 129
Nicene Creed, 75
Nicholas I, 5, 11, 13, 21, 24, 73, 98, 104, 113, 154, 155, 156, 158, 159, 162, 165, 166, 167; and over-procurator, 154, 155; personality of, 154
Nicholas II, 24, 28, 39, 131, 138,

173, 185, 211
Nikanor, Archbishop of Kherson, 27
Nikitenko, A. V., 105
Nikitskii Monastery, 221
Nikol'skii Edinovercheskii Monastery, 221
Nikolskii, N. V., 28
Nizhnii Novgorod, 163
North America. 26, 38, 177, 180
Novgorod diocese, 118n
Novikov, N. I., 54, 78, 88n, 208, 214
Novodevichy Institute, 76
Novodevichy Monastery, 221
Novoe vremia, 37
Novospaskii Monastery, 222
Novyi grad, 40

Obshchestvo, 22
October Manifesto, 133
Octobrists, 29, 36, 37; and clergy, 136
Odoevskii, Prince, 86, 108
Okenfuss, Max J., 66
Old Believers, 28, 29, 35, 102, 150, 194, 209, 214, 215, 216, 218, 222; Rabinovskii sect, 28
Old Regime, 16, 44, 181, 224
"On the Polemics about the Book 'Description of the Rural Clergy'", 110
On the Reconciliation of the Russian and Catholic Churches (Gargarin), 105
One day school census (1911), 141n
Opisanie sel'skogo dukhovenstva. *See Description of the Rural Clergy*
Optina Pustyn (monastery), 38
Oranienbaum, 108
Orlov-Davydova, Countess. *See* Magdalena, Abbess
"Orthodox church in exile," 180-81
Orthodox-Ukrainian Brotherhood movement. *See* Brotherhood movement
Orthodoxy: beliefs of, 170; and Catholicism, 94; community identity of, 184, 185; and early church, 175; and high culture, 9;

historiography of, 3, 4, 9, 171; as
"privileged" religion, 136, 157,
172; and Protestant influence, 83;
relativization of, 194, 197; and
thought, 171; and West, 84; and
western provinces, 121n ˙
Ostapov, A. D., 213
Otechestvennye zapiski, 110
Overfiscals of Senate, 143
Overprocurator, 218; and bishops,
162, 171; development of office,
12, 24; and diocesan consistories,
133; financial power of, 161; as
head of church, 133; and inquisitors, 148; as minister, 133, 158,
160, 161, 166; "right of report,"
132; and schools, 161; and
Synod, 25

Pafnutev-Borovskii Monastery, 222
Pafnutii, Hierodeacon, 146, 148
Paisii, Bishop of Turkestan, 177
Palestine, 34
Palienko, N., 140n
Paraclete Monastery, 221
Paris, Orthodox community in, 180
Parish: councils in, 25; elders of, 102;
legal status, 172, 174; pre-Petrine,
194; reform of, 91, 101, 136;
schools, 138, 179
Parish priest: drunkeness of, 30; duties
of, 27; and education, 30; and
flock, 30; and hierarchy, 11; ignorance of, 6, 37; and politics, 36;
poverty of, 30; as state official,
30, 36. See also Clergy
Pasternak, Boris, 8, 39
Pastoral failure of church, 29
Patriarch: All-Russian, 189; and
bishops, 178, 188; election of, 178,
185; powers of, 178; residence of,
178; responsibility of, 177
Patriarchate, 12, 15, 34, 38; abolition
of, 142; of Antioch, 197; of Constantinople, 177; restoration of,
25, 142, 174, 179, 185, 187, 199;
since 1943, 199

Paul, St., 75, 82, 137
Paul I, 85, 130
Pavel (Prusskii), Archimandrite, 210
Pavlov, M. G., 85, 86, 214
Peasantry and Orthodoxy, 7, 21
Pedagogical Institute (formerly
Teachers Seminary; later Central
Pedagogical Institute), 69, 85
Penza, 163
Penza ecclesiastical school, 69
Penza Seminary, 69
Perevinskaia Seminary, 223
Pericles, 193
Periodicals, ecclesiastical, 176, 182n,
208, 210
Persecution of Bolsheviks, 199
Peter I, 5, 6, 9, 13, 15, 22, 23, 24, 25,
44, 45, 56, 58, 60, 66, 76, 127,
142, 150, 151, 170, 175, 177; and
church reform, 127, 128, 150, 156,
165, 171, 179, 222; and moderni-
zation, 186; and raison d'état, 13,
152
Peter III, 75
"Philosophical Letter" (Chaadaev), 9
Philosophy, Orthodox, 84
Pietism, 10, 24, 75; "pietist revolu-
tion," 82
Pilgrimages, 208
Pilgrims, 45
Pitim, Metropolitan of Petrograd,
132
Platon, Bishop of Kiev, 34
Platon (Levshin), Metropolitan, 10, 74-
79; catechetical lectures, 88n;
definition of church, 88n; and
Orthodoxy, 77-78; and Rosicru-
cianism, 88n
Pluralism, religious, 194
Pobedonostsev, Konstantin, 14, 24, 25,
32, 138, 173, 185; views of episco-
pate, 173
Pochaev Monastery, 210
Podol (or podil), 45
Poetics, Polish, 50-51, 52
Pogodin, M. P., 97, 98, 103, 104, 108,
109, 110, 117n, 122n

Pokrovskii Cathedral, 223
Pokrovskii Monastery, 221
Poland, Kingdom of, 36, 48, 60
Politics and clergy, 8, 15, 36, 37
Poltava, Battle of, 60
Pontifical Oriental Institute, 213
Popov, K. N., 213
Popov, V. M., 213
Popovitskii, A. I., 210
Porfirii (Uspenskii), 214, 218
Prague, 227
Pravoslavnyi sobesednik, 28, 38
Preaching: Synod supervision of, 23;
    Polish eloquence, 53, 54, 59
Preconciliar meetings: of 1906, 26,
    173, 185, 195; of 1912, 26
Problemy idealizma (1902), 39
"Professional Institute" (Dorpat
    University), 71
Professional schools, 68, 70
Progressists, 36, 37
Progressive Bloc, 136
Prokopovich, Feofan, Archbishop of
    Pskov, 9, 10, 22, 24, 44-64; on
    absolutism, 61; and aristocracy, 45;
    and Catholicism, 48-49, 50, 59, 60,
    63n; and church fathers, 50, 56,
    57, 59; as churchman, 46; and
    classical antiquity, 51; early years,
    61; as educator, 46, 51; and foreign
    travel, 51; freedom of inquiry, 10,
    56; "Geometria," 54; as *homo
    politicus*, 58, 60, 61; and Kiev
    Academy, 46, 47, 51; later writings,
    49; on learning, 50-51; and logic,
    54, and mathematics, 54; and
    metaphysics, 56; and modern
    authors, 57; and monasticism, 50;
    and Muscovite traditionalists, 57;
    and Old Believers, 57; as orator,
    46; and patriotism, 45, 58-59, 61;
    and Peter I, 58, 60, 61; and philo-
    sophy, 49-50, 54, 55, 56; on
    poetics, 50-51; and Protestantism,
    57, 58, 64; and rhetoric, 52-53,
    54, 59, 61; and "Russia," 59; and
    scholasticism, 55; on science and

Scripture, 55; and Scripture, 56,
    57; St. Petersburg period, 58; and
    Stefan Iavorskii, 47, 54; and theol-
    ogy, 47, 48, 49, 50, 55, 56, 57, 58;
    and Ukrainian nationalism, 56, 60.
    See also Vladimir
Prokopovich, Feofan (uncle), 46
Property of church, 24, 137, 174
Prostakov (publisher), 206
Protasov, N. A., 13, 14, 109, 132, 133,
    155, 156, 160, 164, 165, 166; and
    Catholicism, 156; and hierarchy,
    155, 163, 164; and Nicholas I,
    163; report on ecclesiastical admini-
    stration (1836), 160; and school
    reform, 100
Protestantism, 35, 196; anticerimonial-
    ism of, 31; church administration
    and, 12; scholasticism of, 6, 22; and
    system of *summus episcopus*,
    127, 130, 131, 139n
Protoinquisitors, 145, 146
Prugavin, A. S., 215
Publishing houses, 206
Pushkin, A. S., 21

Quenstedt, J. A., 83
Quintilian, 50

Radishchev, A., 77, 80, 91
Raeff, Marc, 76
Ranke, Leopold von, 72
Rasputin, 135, 138, 139
Reform of church, 25, and bishops,
    14; canonical basis for, 184; of
    consistories, 25; decentralization,
    15, 16; diversity of opinions, 183;
    ecclesiological presuppositions for,
    180; and events of 1905-6, 14, 22;
    and Great Reforms, 6, 11, 12, 14;
    and Peter I, 5, 6, 9, 13, 22, 23; and
    relation to state, 183; and social
    thought, 180; special commission
    on (1861-62), 91
Religio-Philosophical Assemblies of
    1901-3, 29, 74, 192, 201n
Renaissance, 52, 56

Replies (Otzyvy), 14, 51, 171, 173, 175, 176, 177, 178, 179, 180, 181
Repnina, Princess Varvara Nikolaevna, 38
Research and Orthodoxy, 17, 39, 40, 91, 212
Revolution (1917) and Orthodoxy, 5, 7, 8, 12, 13, 15, 21, 26, 32, 40, 127, 136, 138, 209; (1905), 183
Riga Ecclesiastical Academy, 210
Rock of Faith (Kamen' very) (Iavorskii), 57, 75
Rome, 9, 48, 49, 50
Rosicrucians, 88n
Rosseau, J. J., 75-76
Rossi (architect), 157
Rostislavov, D. I., 91, 122n, 212
Rozanov, V. V., 30, 192, 207
Rozhdestvenskii Monastery, 221
Rudnev, Mikhail, 71, 87n
Rufus, Quintus Curtus, 75
Russian Academy, 73
Russian Church Abroad, 38
Russian Student Christian Movement, 32
Russia's Educational Heritage (Johnson), 66
Russkii zagranichnyi sbornik, 104, 105, 121n
Russkoe dukhovenstvo, 110, 112

Sabler, V. K., 133, 134, 136
Sacraments, 7, 22, 31
Saints, 21, 23
Sakharov, F. K., 215
Sallust, 50
Saltykov-Shchedrin Library, 213
Samarin, Iu. S., 99
Savigny, Friedrich Carl von, 72, 87
Savva-Storozhevskii Monastery, 222
Schelling, F. W., 84, 85
Schism, 22, 23, 157, 189
Scholasticism, 55, 56, 57, 83, 85; Catholic, 9
Schools, 7, 10, 11, 23, 26, 27, 66, 67, 68, 85, 141n; and agriculture, 100; congress of parish teachers, 25;

and philosophy, 81-82, 84; reform of, 81; and western education, 85. *See also* Education of clergy; Seminaries
Sectarians, 29, 35, 183, 214, 215, 216, 218, 222; "warmth" of, 30
Secularization, 142, 186, 194; of church lands (*See* Property of church); of public life, 128
Semenov-Rudnev, Dmitrii (Damaskin), 61n
Seminaries: commission on, 102; conditions in, 90; and intelligentsia, 77
Senate, 13, 23, 87, 143, 144, 149, 155, 159
Sentimentalism, 10, 75
Serafim (Glagolevskii), Metropolitan of St. Petersburg, 155-56
Serafim, St. of Sarov, 21, 208
Sergei, Archimandrite, 112
Sergii (Stragorodskii), Archbishop of Finland and *locum tenens*, 178, 180, 200
Service. *See* Liturgy
Seven Days of Creation (Maximov), 3
Sevsk (seminary), 85
Shakhovskoi, I. P., 24
Sheremetev, S. D., 216
Siberia, 176
Simeon, Bishop of Ekaterinoslav, 35
Simonov Monastery, 223
Singing, church, 31, 32
Skorbiashchenskii Monastery, 221
Skvortsov, V. M., 14, 187, 188, 189
"Slav Brothers" of Balkans, 128
Slavic Bibliographic and Documentation Center, 213
Slavo-Latin Academy. *See* "Helleno-Greek" Academy
Slavonic language, 31, 75
Slavophiles, 74, 84, 85, 92, 99
Smirnov, N. P., 216
Smolnyi Institute, 76, 109
Sobor, 13, 14, 16, 25, 26, 29, 31, 32, 38, 172, 173, 178, 183, 185, 187, 199, 200; All-Russian Council, 189;

as bicameral parliament, 178; and
bishops, 187; as commune, 186;
composition of, 173, 176, 187,
195, 200; and democracy, 176,
196, 197; liberal-historic view of,
16, 187; and modernity, 186; petition for, 185; politics of, 184;
problem of, 184; social background
of, 185; as social symbol, 185, 186;
spiritualizing ideal, 16, 187; and
theological populism, 192, 193;
theology of, 185
Sobornost', 16, 172, 175, 177, 178,
186, 188, 189; bishops as embodiment of, 188; as catholicity, 197;
as charismatic community, 198;
communal aspects of, 194, 195,
196; and Duma, 136; and Holy
Spirit, 195; inadequacy of, 180;
as mass consciousness, 193; as
moral force, 198; as Orthodoxy,
186; as religious confessionalism,
197; social aspects of, 191; as social
reality, 192
Sobornyi (Catholicity), 186
Society for Aid to Needy Writers, 122n
Society of Friends of Learning, 80
Society of History and Russian Anti-
quities, 73, 80, 88n
Sokolov, I., 177
Sokolov, V., 7, 29, 30, 31
Solovetskii Monastery ("Solovki"),
107, 150, 220
Solov'ev, A. N., 218
Solov'ev, S. M., 69
Solov'ev, V. S., 7, 11, 30, 40, 74, 86,
214; and anti-Semitism, 40
Solzhenitsyn, Alexander, 8, 39, 40, 41
Sortavala, 227
Spain, 31
Spaso-Andron'evskii Monastery, 223
Spaso-Evfimovskii Monastery, 220
Spasskii Monastery, 222
Speranskii, M. M., 66, 72, 80, 81, 82,
83, 87n
Spinoza, 57
Sremski Karlovci (Yugoslavia), 181

Sretenskii Monastery, 221
St. Nicholas Monastery (Greek), 223
St. Petersburg, 105, 146, 147, 173,
181, 221
St. Petersburg Ecclesiastical Academy,
81, 87n, 91, 105, 196, 200n, 209
St. Petersburg University, 69, 85
Strastnoi Monastery, 221
St. Sergius Orthodox Theological
Academy (Paris), 212
St. Vladimir, University of (Kiev),
72
Stalin, J. V., 3
Stankevich, N., 86
Staritsa, 92, 118n
Startsy, 38
State Archives (Gosudarstvennyi
Arkhiv) 222
State Council, 116, 133, 135, 158,
172, 179
Statute on Ecclesiastical Consistories
(Ustav dukhovnoi konsistorii)
(1841), 140n, 157, 158, 167
Stefan, Bishop of Mogilev, 176
Stefan (Iavorskii). See Iavorskii, Stefan
Stelletskii, 214
Stolypin, P., 133
Strauss, David F., 94
Stroev, Iu. M., 217
Struve, P., 39
Stundists, 29, 36
Subbotin, N. I., 210
Suetonius, 50
Sumarokov, A. P., 54
Superintendents, election of, 103
Superstition, Synod extirpation of, 23
Suvorin, A. S., 206, 216
Suvorov, N., 140n
Svetlov, Paul, 216
Svirelyn (publisher), 206
Sweden, 60
Swedish Lutheran church, 131
"Symphonia," 170
Synod, 12, 25, 30, 69, 96, 106, 107,
112, 113, 121n, 122n, 131, 132,
133, 134, 139, 142, 145, 146, 148,
149, 150, 151, 154, 155, 157, 159,

160, 161, 163, 164, 167n, 171, 172, 173, 175, 184, 185, 187, 212, 217, 218, 220; appointments to, 164; buildings of, 159-60, 168n; crisis of 1842, 14; as ecclesiastical collegium, 133; educational council, 210; and hierarchy's power, 163; history of, 158; as ministry, 166; Moscow office of, 158; and political unrest, 24; president of, 25; reorganizations of, 23-24; responsibilities of, 22-23; structure of, 214; uncanonical character of, 189
Synodal Chancellery of Economic Administration, 23
Synodal (Patriarchal) Library, 219
Syrku, P., 218
Sytin, I. D., 206

Tacitus, 50, 77
Tambov, 209
Tarsis, V., 8, 39
Tasso, 52
Teachers Seminary (1783), 68, 69
Temperance, 208
Ternavtsev, V. A., 29, 192, 201n
Thaumaturgy, 207, 208
Theological academies. *See* Ecclesiastical academies
Theology and theologians, 7-8, 22, 32, 34, 36, 37, 38, 85; beginnings of Orthodox, 84; diversity of, 156; in eighteenth century, 78; error, 32; practical, 38
Thirty-two Priests of St. Petersburg, 173, 188, 189, 190
Tiflis, 176
Tíkhon (Bellavin), Patriarch of Moscow, 38, 177, 178, 180, 199; reform proposals, 177, 180
Tikhonov, Aleksandr, 150
Tilsit, 80
Time of Troubles, 128
Titus Livius, 77
Tiutchev, F. I., 42n
Toleration, church's, 4-5, 6, 8, 32, 35, 172, 184-85, 186, 191

Tolstoi, A. P., 103, 107, 111, 122n
Tolstoi, D. A., 24, 214
Tolstoi, Iu. V., 217
Tolstoy, Leo (Tolstoi, L. N.), 33, 74, 207, 214
Tradition, of Orthodoxy, 17, 24, 48, 177, 184, 197
Trinity Seminary, 70, 79, 83, 223
Trinity-St. Sergius Monastery, 206, 210, 213, 219, 221, 222
Troitskii, S., 42n, 217
Trubetskaia (née Lopukhina), Princess, 38
Trubetskoi, Evgenii, 38
Trubetskoi, N. I., 103, 104
Trubetskoi, Sergei, 37, 38, 214
Tsar: as "Christian Ruler," 157; as "Head of Church," 130, 167; as "Highest Judge," 131, 145; as "Highest Earthly Ruler," 131
Tsarskoe Selo lyceé, 87n
Tserkovno-Arkheologicheskii Kabinet, 213
Turgenev, Ivan, 33
Tuzov, I. L., 206
Tver, 105; seminary, 118n
Tver diocese, 92, 103, 104
Tverskie gubernskie vedomosti, 94
Typographies of Synod, 206, 207

Ukraine, 35, 36, 48, 176
Ulianinskii, D. V., 216
Uniat College at Polotsk, 24
Uniats, 8, 35-36, 49, 59, 105
Union of Florence, 193
Union of October 17. *See* Octobrists
Union of the Archangel Michael, 34, 42n
Union of the Russian People, 8, 34, 35
Urusov, S. N., 99, 108, 122n
Utkin, Ia., 209
Uvarov, S., 210

Valuev, P. A., 91, 116
Varentsov, 214
Varlaam (Iasynskii). *See* Iasynskii, Varlaam

Varnava of Bethany, 38
Vasilino, 92, 93
Vekhi (1909), 39, 214
Venevitinov, 86
Verkhovskoi, P. V., 214
Vellanskii, Daniil (Kavunnik, D. M.),
    71, 86
Victoria, Queen, 38
Vilnius, 47, 208
Virgil, 50, 77
Vital statistics, collecting of, 165
Vladimir (Prokopovich), 52, 58, 59,
    61, 64n
Vladimir, Archbishop of Kazan, 166,
    169n
Vladimir, Metropolitan of Petrograd,
    132
Vladimir, Prince, 59
Voronezh Seminary, 85
Voznesenskii Monastery, 222
Vsesviatskii Monastery, 221
Vysokopetrovskii Monastery, 222

Ware, Timothy, 64n
Warren, Earl, 33
Warsaw, 227
Warsaw, Archbishop of, 162

West and Orthodoxy, 21, 105
Western Education (Bowen), 65
Widowed priests and deacons,
    113
Witte, S. Iu., 173, 194

Yearbook (Vremmenik) of lycée
    Demidov, 72
Yudin, G. V., 216

Zagorsk, 38, 213
Zahn, Johann, 10, 55
Zaikonospasskii Monastery, 222
Zander, L. A., 31
Zavadovskii, P. V., 67, 69
Zdravomyslov, K. I., 220
Zemstvo, 73; and clergy, 172, 179;
    congress of, 172; and schools, 138
Zenkovskii, V. V., 214
Zernov, N., 42n
*Zhurnal ministerstva narodnogo
    prosveshcheniia*, 99
Zlatoustovskii Nikolai Ugreshnyi
    Monastery, 222
Znamenskii, V. P., 87n, 222
Zossima (monastery), 38
Zverinskii, M. V., 217